Adjusting to Life in the USA

Adjusting to Life in the USA

A Complete Guide to Culture, Belonging, and Essential Life Skills for Newcomers, Long-Time Residents, and Their Supporters

Selma Toporan

Aspire USA Coaching, LLC

Copyright Page

Table of Contents

Copyright Page iv
About This Book.. xx
   Welcome! xx
Disclaimer xxv
Preface xxvi
SECTION 1: EVERYDAY COMMUNICATION AND SOCIAL
NORMS xxviii
Chapter 1: Translation Services and Helpful Tools..................... 1
   Helpful Translation and Language Tools 1
   Translation Tools for Computer, Tablet, Smartphone, and
   Websites 1
      How to Use Google Translate 2
      Using Chrome's Translation Tool to Translate Websites into
      Your Language 2
      Microsoft Translator – Free Translation............................... 2
   Interpretation via Phone... 3
   Case Study: The Importance of Using a Medical Interpreter 3
   Read-Aloud Features on Devices 4
      How to Enable Read-Aloud.. 4
   AI Tool: Chat GPT 5
      How to Use ChatGPT.. 5
Chapter 2: Communicating in Everyday Situations..................... 8
   Being Polite and Introducing Yourself..................................... 8
      Useful Phrases 8
   Asking for Help 9
   Ordering Food at a Restaurant 9
   Shopping and Buying Things..10
      Useful Phrases 10
   Going to the Doctor 10
      Making an Appointment 10
      If You Need a Translator... 10
   Taking Public Transportation 11
      Common Types of Public Transport..................................... 11

Paying a Fare 11

Case Study: Too Formal for Everyday Interaction 12
   Formal vs. Informal Speech Example 12

Language Learning Tools 13
Emergency Contacts Sheet 13
Chapter 3: Understanding Non-Verbal Communication 16
Smiling and Eye Contact in the U.S. 16
   When Do Americans Smile? 16

Eye Contact in the U.S. 17
Cultural Differences in Smiling and Eye Contact 18
How to Practice Non-Verbal Communication in the U.S. 18
Case Study: Learning to Smile and Make Eye Contact at Work
.... 19
Chapter 4: Understanding Cultural Differences – Collectivist vs.
Individualistic Values 22
   Comparing Collectivist and Individualistic Cultures 23
   Why Does This Matter? 25

Case Study: Cultural Confusion 25
SECTION 2: SOCIAL AND PERSONAL RELATIONSHIPS 28
Chapter 5: Building Personal Relationships in the U.S.: Family and
Friends 29
   Understanding Personal Relationships in the U.S. 29
   Family Relationships in the U.S. 30
   Parenting Styles in the U.S. 30
      Family Time and Meals 32

Friendships in the U.S. 33
Pets 33
Personal Boundaries and Safety 34
Case Study: Balancing Family Expectations and Independence
in an Immigrant Household 34
Chapter 6: Hosting Guests and RSVP – A Guide for Social Events
for Newcomers 39
   Part 1: Hosting a Party 39
      Choosing a Date, Time, and Location 39

      Deciding on the Type of Event 39

Sending Invitations... 39

Asking for RSVPs 40

Planning Food and Drinks.. 40

Setting Up Your Space.. 40

Being a Friendly Host.. 40

Part 2: How to RSVP and Attend a Party 41
Reading the Invitation Carefully 41

How to RSVP 41

Small Talk.. 41

Case Study: "Five o'clock" Really Means Five o'clock 42
Chapter 7: Understanding Romantic Relationships in the U.S.....45
Casual Dating Versus Serious Dating.....................................45
Dating and Immigrant Families 46
Different Expectations Between Cultures 46

The Pros and Cons of Dating...46
Modern Dating and Changing Expectations............................47
How to Show Respect when Dating..48
What Happens If a Relationship Ends? 49
Online Dating Safety Tips..49
Case Study: Differences in Acculturation and Its Impact on
Dating..50
The Immigrant Advantage: More Stability in Immigrant Families
....51

Chapter 8: Handling Conflicts and Disagreements 54
Communicating Through Conflict...54
Apologizing Effectively 55

Conflict in Immigrant Families...55
Mutual Support in Relationships 56
Taking Care of Yourself..56
Learning from Conflict 56
Case Study: Taking Things Too Literally 56
SECTION 3: FINANCIAL LITERACY AND WORK CULTURE 60

Chapter 9: Understanding Money and Financial Rules in the U.S.
.... 61
Types of Money in the U.S. 61
Banking in the U.S. 62
Opening a Bank Account 62
High-Yield Savings Accounts: A Better Way to Save 62
Paying Taxes 63
Earning Money and Jobs.. 64
Case Study: Miguel's Surprise 64
Credit in the U.S... 65
How to Build Credit (Simple Steps).................................. 65
Budgeting and Living Expenses 65
Maria's Budget 66
Saving for Retirement 68
Case Study: Indira's Story.. 68
Retirement Saving Tips... 70
Making Smarter Purchases 71
Chapter 10: Renting and Buying a Home – Understanding Leases,
Apartments, and Homeownership....................................... 73
Understanding Leases and Renting a Home 73
Moving Into an Apartment 74
Setting Up Utilities 74
Renter's Insurance 75
Steps to Buying a House.. 75
Case Study: Helping My Parents Buy a House 76
Chapter 11: Job Interview Procedure and Skills for Newcomers. 79
Step 1: How to Apply for a Job... 79
Find Job Openings 79
Create a Resume 79
Write a Cover Letter 81
Submit Your Application 82
Step 2: Preparing for the Interview 83
Research the Company... 83

Practice Common Questions.. 83

Dress Professionally 84

Plan Your Trip.. 84

Online Interviews 85

Step 3: During the Interview 85

Answer Questions Clearly.. 86

Ask the Interviewer Questions... 86

Thank the Interviewer 86

Step 4: After the Interview 87

Follow Up if Needed... 87

Learn from Rejections... 88

Step 5: Onboarding – Starting Your New Job 89

Complete Paperwork 89

Orientation 89

Learn Workplace Rules... 90

Improve Workplace Communication................................. 90

Strategies for Career Advancement in Business....................90

Chapter 12: Understanding Work Behavior and Culture.............95

Workplace Behavior: Professionalism and Respect................95

Be Professional.. 95

Be Punctual (On Time).. 96

Be Polite and Respectful... 96

Communicate Clearly.. 96

Understanding Work Culture in the U.S. 96

Teamwork Is Important 96

Respect Workplace Hierarchy and Culture........................ 96

Flexibility at Work... 97

Handling Workplace Challenges...98

Case Study: Be Professional at Work..................................98

Avoid Gossip.. 99

Job Evaluations and Career Growth 99

Asking for a Raise 99

Social Norms and Expectations at Work 99

Dress Code (What to Wear) 100

Respect Personal Space 100

Work-Life Balance 100

Workplace Norms in Different Countries 100

Constructive Criticism and How It's Given 101

Not Everyone Is a Friend for Life 101

Chapter 13: Understanding Work Ethic and the Economic System in the U.S. 103

What is Work Ethic? 103

Hard Work Matters 104

Being Responsible 104

Punctuality (Being on Time) 104

Motivation and Goals 104

The Economic System in the U.S. (Capitalism) 105

Free Market Economy 105

Private Property 105

Earning Money (Jobs and Careers) 105

Competition 105

Why Work Ethic is Important in the U.S.? 105

Case Study: Work Your Wage, but Remember Your Worth .. 106

Setting Boundaries to Avoid Burnout 107

SECTION 4: SCHOOL LIFE AND YOUTH CULTURE 109

Chapter 14: Understanding the School Environment in the U.S. for Newcomer Students and Parents 110

A Personal Story: My First Snow Day Surprise 110

The Structure of the U.S. Education System 111

School Schedule and Daily Routine 112

School Subjects and Grading System 112

Understanding Grading System in the U.S. 113

School Behavior and Expectations 113
    School Safety Drills 115

Understanding the Role of School Staff in the U.S. 116
Making Friends and Social Life 117
School Calendar 118
Case Study: Omid's Journey to Graduation 121
Chapter 15: Parent Participation in U.S. Schools 124
    Case Study: Turning Struggles into Success Through Family
Support 124
Parent Involvement Helps Children Perform Better 125
Ways to Be Involved: Attend These School Events 126
    Volunteer at School 126

    Talking to Teachers and School Staff 127

    Reading School Newsletters 127

    Using Online Portals 127

Helping Your Child at Home 127
    Reading Together 128

    Setting Expectations 128

Understanding School Rules and Programs 128
    School Calendar 128

    School Rules 128

    Special Programs 128

Adjusting to School Culture in the U.S. 129
    Be Open to New Ideas 129

    Language Support 129

    Making Connections 129

    Helping Schools in Other Ways 129

Chapter 16: How to Behave at a Dance: A Guide for High School
and Middle School Students 131
    Types of Dances 132

Before the Dance 132

During Dance 133

Being Polite and Respectful.. 134

Asking Someone to Dance 134

At the End of the Dance 135

If There is a Problem.. 135

Chapter 17: After-School Activities – A Guide for Newcomer Students and Parents 136

What Are After-School Activities?..................................... 136

Examples of After-School Activities 136

Overcoming Challenges and Trying New Activities 137

Why Are After-School Activities Important?........................ 138

How to Choose the Right Activity 139

How Parents Can Support Their Children in After-School Activities.. 139

Chapter 18: Post-High School Plans – A Guide for Students and Parents.. 142

Going to College or University.. 142

High School GPA.. 142

Standardized Test Scores 143

Extracurricular Activities 143

Personal Statement or Essay 144

Letters of Recommendation.. 144

Application Deadlines 144

What is College or University? 144

Types of Degrees... 145

Why Go to College? 145

Scholarships and Financial Aid 146

Types of Scholarships 146

Where to Find Scholarships?.. 147

Jobs That Pay for College 147

How to Qualify for Employer Tuition Assistance 148

Vocational or Trade School 148
Entering the Workforce (Full-Time Job) 148
How AI is Changing the Future of Work.............................149
Chapter 19: Gender Roles and Expectations at School and Work:
A Simple Guide for Students and Parents 152
    Personal Story: Learning About Gender Roles............... 152

Gender Roles at School..153
Gender Roles at Work 153
Understanding the Gender Pay Gap...................................154
Staying Home and Career Impact.......................................154
    Fixing the Pay Gap 155

Respecting Gender Differences..156
SECTION 5: DAILY LIFE AND PRACTICAL SKILLS 158
Chapter 20: Keeping Yourself and Your Environment Clean.....159
Personal Hygiene: Taking Care of Yourself 159
Keeping School and Workspaces Clean.............................160
    Cleaning Up Shared Spaces... 161

Keeping the Home Clean..161
    Cleaning Chart Example 162

Building Responsibility and Respect Through Daily Cleaning
Habits 162
    Cleanliness is Important.. 163

Case Study: "You Live Here, You Work Here".....................163
Chapter 21: Shopping in the United States: A Guide for
Newcomers..166
How to Shop in a Store...166
    Customer Service 166

    Self-Checkout 167

    Common Shopping Manners... 167

    Paying for Items 168

    Returns and Exchanges... 168

Consumer Culture and Materialism 168
Smart Shopping Tips 169
Understanding Weight and Measurement in the U.S. 170

Weight Measurements.. 170

Volume Measurement 170

Length Measurements... 171

Understanding Temperature Measurements..................... 171

Chapter 22: Doctor's Office Visits 173
Making an Appointment and Being On Time 173
Who You Will Meet at the Doctor's Office?........................... 174
Asking for an Interpreter 175

Doctor's Office vs. Urgent Care vs. Emergency Room (ER).. 175
What to Expect at Each Place 176

Case Study: A Family's Tough Choice 176
Advance Medical Directives: Planning for the Unexpected.... 177
Using Health Portals to Manage Your Care 177

Understanding Health Insurance in the United States 178
If You Do Not Have Insurance... 178
Annual Enrollment: What You Need to Know 179
Medicare Enrollment for Older Adults................................. 179
Why Is Important to Review Your Insurance Each Year? 180
Emergency Rooms Use by Uninsured Patients: Not for Long
Term Care 180

What Happens If You Need Cancer Treatment Without
Insurance? 181

Plan Ahead for Your Health and Your Future 181
Chapter 23: Managing Stress and Building Wellness – A Guide to
a Healthy Mind and Body... 184
Types of Stress 184
Acute Stress (Short-Term Stress)................................... 184

Chronic Stress (Long-Term Stress) 184

Coping with Stress in the Moment................................... 185
The 90-Second Emotion Rule.. 185

Deep Breathing Meditation Strategy 186

Managing Negative Emotions with the RAIN Strategy 186

Physical Techniques to Help You Feel Safe...................... 187

Case Study: Mira's Journey to the 5-4-3-2-1 Grounding Strategy
....188

Daily Ways to Prevent Stress 189

The Five Areas of Wellness...189

Mental and Emotional Wellness 189

Social Wellness.. 190

Physical Wellness 190

Spiritual Wellness 190

Building Self-Esteem and Problem-Solving Skills 190

How to Build Self-Esteem 191

Solving Problems Also Builds Your Self Esteem 191

SECTION 6: SOCIAL EXPECTATIONS AND CULTURAL
ADAPTATION...195

Chapter 24: Religious Practices in a Diverse Society...............196

Religious Practices 196

Religious Traditions 197

Respecting Religious Differences 198

Examples of Respecting Religious Differences 198

Case Study: Religious Respect in Everyday Life 199

Respecting Religion Matters..199

Chapter 25: Personal Space and Social Customs in the U.S.: A
Guide for Newcomers 202

Personal Space 202

Saying "Excuse Me" 202

Greetings and Handshakes 203

Using "Please" and "Thank You" 203

Waiting Your Turn (Taking Turns)...204

Case Study: Cultural Differences in Communication.............204

Respecting Privacy..206

Dressing for Different Occasions 206

Tipping in Restaurants...206

Using Phones and Technology 207

Chapter 26: Common Social Mistakes Newcomers Make and How to Avoid Them 208
Not Making Eye Contact.. 208
Standing Too Close or Too Far 208
Speaking Too Loudly or Too Quietly 209
Not Saying Please and Thank You... 209
Being Too Direct or Too Indirect.. 209
Forgetting to Smile or Greet People 209
Not Understanding Small Talk.. 210
Offering Too Much Food 210
Being Too Honest in a Harsh Way 210
Being Late... 211
Not Tipping at Restaurants... 211
Smiling Too Much in Serious Situations 211
Taking Words Too Literally.. 212
Chapter 27: Understanding American Values 214
Freedom and Individual Rights.. 214
Equality 214
Hard Work and Success.. 215
Respect for Others 215
Independence and Self-Reliance 215
Family and Community 216
Fairness and Justice 216
Diversity and Inclusion 216
Innovation and Progress 217
Responsibility and Accountability 217
Case Study: Lessons Learned from "A Different Mirror" 218
SECTION 7: ADVANCED SOCIAL UNDERSTANDING 221
Chapter 28: Understanding Political Systems in the U.S........... 222
Conservatism 222
Liberalism 223
Political Parties and Their Ideologies 223
  1. Republican Party (GOP) – Aligned with Conservatism...223
  2. Democratic Party – Aligned with Liberalism 224
How Can You Participate in Civic Life When You Become a Citizen?.. 225

Staying Safe and Informed as a Green Card Holder..............226
Chapter 29: Understanding Prejudice, Racism, Stereotypes,
Microaggressions, and Bias in Immigrant Experiences 228
  What is Prejudice?...228
  What is Racism?...229
  What Are Stereotypes?...229
  What is Bias? 230
  Microaggressions: Small Words, Big Impact..........................230
  Intersectionality: When Multiple Identities Overlap................231
  How Prejudice, Racism, Stereotypes, and Bias Affect Us......232
  How to Address Prejudice, Racism, Stereotypes, and Bias ...232
    What Can Schools and Workplaces Do? 233

    How Parents Can Help.. 234

  Case Study: Unequal Discipline and Cultural Perceptions.....234
Chapter 30: Regulating Emotions...238
  Emotional Regulation 238
  Importance of Emotional Regulation 238
  Strategies for Controlling Your Emotions 239
    1. Take Deep Breaths 239

    2. Pause and Think (Meta-moment)................................. 240

    3. Talk About Your Feelings 240

    4. Use Positive Self-Talk 241

  Emotions in the U.S...242
    Personal Story: It Helps to Share Your Experiences 242

    Life Coaching Can Help Immigrants................................. 243

  Get Better at Managing Emotions...245
  Case Study: Cultural Differences in Parenting and Dating.....245
    Decision-Making Chart: Dating Rules and Safety.............. 246

  Use Logical Strategies to Make Good Decisions 249
Chapter 31: How to Have Constructive Conversations.............251
  Steps for Having a Constructive Conversation......................251
    1. Listen Carefully 251

    2. Stay Calm and Respectful... 252

3. Use "I" Statements 252

4. Ask Questions 252

5. Find Common Ground 253

6. Know When to Take a Break 253

Case Study: Using Appropriate Communication Strategies in a Cross-Cultural Friendship.. 254

SECTION 8: CITIZENSHIP AND LONG-TERM INTEGRATION 257

Chapter 32: Becoming a U.S. Citizen 258
Who Can Apply for U.S. Citizenship?............................... 258
Step-by-Step Guide to Becoming a U.S. Citizen 258
Step 1: Check If You Qualify.. 258

Step 2: Fill Out Form N-400... 259

Step 3: Biometrics Appointment..................................... 259

Step 4: Interview with a USCIS Officer 259

Step 5: Take the Citizenship Test 259

Step 6: USCIS Decision.. 260

Step 7: Take the Oath of Allegiance 260

How Long Does It Take?... 260
Do You Need a Lawyer? 261
What Happens After You Become a Citizen? 261
Case Study: Overcoming Fear of Legal Paperwork.............. 262
Chapter 33: Advice for Newcomers to America 264
Embrace the Journey of a New Life 264
Connect with Others.. 264
Learn English: It is a Step-by-Step Process 265
Navigate Emotional Process 266
Learn American Culture and Social Norms 267
Take Advantage of Opportunities 267
Welcome to Your New Adventure: You Belong Here............. 268
References 270
List of Tables 284
GLOSSARY... 285

Glossary of Terms..286
APPENDICES...292
Appendix A: Newcomer Skills Checklist 293
Appendix B: Resources for Newcomers to the United States 296
Appendix C: Important Documents Checklist for Life in the U.S.
....302
Appendix D: Legal and Privacy Disclaimer.............................304
Detailed Index..305
About the Author..308
Connect With Me 310

About This Book

Welcome!

Moving to a new country is an exciting and challenging experience. This book is designed for newcomers to the United States who want to learn about American customs, values, and social norms. The goal of this book is to make daily life and interactions easier and more manageable by providing clear explanations and practical examples that can be used right away.

Many immigrants and refugees do not have the opportunity to learn about American culture before arriving in the United States. As a result, they experience culture shock, the feeling of confusion when faced with new customs, behaviors, and expectations. Understanding these cultural differences can help reduce stress and improve confidence when navigating everyday situations. This book was created to support those who are adjusting to life in the U.S. by offering simple, clear, and useful information.

What You Will Find in This Book

This book covers various topics to help you adapt to different aspects of American life. Each section focuses on important themes, such as communication, relationships, work culture, financial literacy, school life, and daily routines. The chapters are designed to stand alone, so you can read them in any order and focus on the topics that matter most to you.

The book is divided into eight sections:

Section 1: Everyday Communication and Social Norms
Understanding translation tools, basic conversation skills, and how to interpret non-verbal communication like eye contact and smiling.

Section 2: Social and Personal Relationships
Building friendships, handling family relationships, hosting events, dating, and managing conflicts.

Section 3: Financial Literacy and Work Culture
Learning how to manage money, rent or buy a home, prepare for job interviews, and understand workplace behavior.

Section 4: School Life and Youth Culture
Helping parents and students navigate the American school system, extracurricular activities, and career planning.

Section 5: Daily Life and Practical Skills
Essential daily routines, shopping tips, visiting a doctor, and maintaining mental and physical wellness.

Section 6: Social Expectations and Cultural Adaptation
Learning about religious diversity, personal space, and common social mistakes.

Section 7: Advanced Social Understanding
Exploring politics, stereotypes, emotions, and constructive conversations.

Section 8: Citizenship and Long-Term Integration
Understanding the steps to becoming a U.S. citizen and embracing opportunities for long-term success.

A Personal Approach to Learning

I have included real-life situations gathered over my twenty-nine years in the U.S. Some are drawn from my own experiences, others from people I know, and some are based on situations I have heard about through my work in the community. Names and identifying details have been changed to protect privacy, and certain events have been adjusted or partially fictionalized for clarity and illustrative purposes. In some cases, composite characters or events have been created. These examples reflect common challenges and lessons that can help you avoid unnecessary difficulties.

Many immigrants are expected to learn English, but they are rarely taught how to follow American customs. Often, these customs are only noticed when mistakes are made. This book explains those unspoken rules so that you learn them and feel more comfortable and confident in your own life.

The language in this book is designed to be simple to read and translate. I wrote this book with my own family in mind, thinking about the guidance I wish we had when we first arrived in the U.S. If you prefer reading in your native language, I recommend using the digital version and using a translation tool to translate it. Chapter 1 also includes resources for free translation tools that can help you understand unfamiliar words or phrases.

Cultural Adaptation Without Losing Your Identity

It is important to remember that you do not have to give up your own customs and traditions to live in the U.S. These aspects of your culture are part of your identity and can be a source of strength and pride. However, learning about American values and behaviors can help you adjust more easily and feel more at home in your new environment.

Who Is This Book For

This book is for anyone who wants to:

- Adjust to life in the U.S. and learn about daily social norms.
- Understand American culture and avoid common misunderstandings.
- Build confidence in social and workplace interactions.
- Feel more comfortable in a new environment while maintaining their cultural identity.
- Help others adjust to their new life in the U.S.

Whether you are a new or established immigrant, refugee, international student, visitor, or an ally, this book will serve as a helpful guide to understanding life in the U.S.

How to Use This Book

Read chapters in any order. Each topic stands alone, allowing you to focus on what is most relevant to you. Refer to real-life examples to learn from the experiences of others. Additionally, keep this book as a resource for reference on workplace norms, social interactions, and practical advice.

Free Workbook and Access to ESL Lessons

A free workbook is now available for download at aspireusacoaching.com for those who want to explore the material more deeply and apply what they have learned. Educators and tutors using this book can also request complimentary ESL lesson plans by emailing aspireusacoaching@gmail.com with proof of purchase. These resources are intended to support English language learners in both group and individual settings; however, they may be updated or discontinued in the future.

Helpful Tools and Acknowledgments

Writing this book took time, research, and careful editing to make sure it is clear and easy to understand for English Language Learners (ELLs). I used AI tools, including ChatGPT by OpenAI, to help gather ideas, check my writing, and make difficult words and ideas easier to understand. These tools helped me explain things more clearly and make the book better for readers who are still learning English.

Even though I used these tools, the material included in the book has been carefully revised by me to reflect accurate information, personal insights, and cultural relevance. The final content is the result of thoughtful editing and personalization to meet the specific needs of my audience.

I also want to say that AI tools can be very helpful for people who are new to the U.S. They can make learning and finding information easier. In Chapter 1, you can find free translation tools to help with understanding and learning English.

Final Words

I created this book to turn my own experiences into something positive. I hope it helps you feel more prepared, confident, and comfortable as you begin your journey in the U.S.

If this book has been helpful, I would love to hear about your experience! If you have questions, feedback, or want to share your journey, please feel free to reach out.

Thank you for reading. I hope this book makes your transition smoother and more enjoyable

Disclaimer

This book is written solely by me, Selma Toporan, and published by my business, Aspire USA Coaching, LLC. It is not affiliated with, endorsed by, or representative of any other organization, employer, or entity with which I am or have been associated.

The content in this book is based on my personal experiences, observations, and insights, as well as situations shared with me by others. Names and identifying details have been changed to protect privacy, and certain events have been adjusted or partially fictionalized for clarity and illustrative purposes.

This book is intended for informational and educational purposes only. It does not constitute legal, medical, financial, or professional advice. Readers should seek appropriate professional guidance when necessary.

Preface

This book is not about politics. It's about real people who are navigating big changes and finding their way in a new country. I share these stories and tips from my own experience as an immigrant, not to judge anyone, but to encourage hope, understanding, and confidence in those walking a similar path. My goal is to offer practical guidance and emotional support to anyone seeking to build a better life in the United States, without losing who they are in the process. This is a journey of growth, not division, and I invite you to walk it with an open heart.

When I first arrived in the U.S., I carried more than just my clothes. I brought with me memories of war, the weight of being a refugee, and the fear of starting over in a place where I barely spoke the language. I was overwhelmed, but I was also determined.

Over time, I learned how to navigate schools, workplaces, parenting styles, and social expectations. I made mistakes, had moments of doubt, and questioned if I would ever feel like I truly belonged. But I also found kindness, opportunities, and resilience I didn't know I had.

Adjusting to Life in the USA: A Complete Guide to Culture, Belonging, and Essential Life Skills for Newcomers, Long-Time Residents, and Their Supporters is a practical guide for immigrants, refugees, and international students seeking to navigate life in the United States. Through real-life situations and actionable advice, this book offers guidance on overcoming common challenges, such as language barriers, cultural differences, and finding a sense of belonging. Whether you have just arrived or have been here for years, this book will empower you to adapt without losing your identity, build confidence in your new life, and thrive in your community.

You won't find complicated theories or lectures here. This is just real talk: practical insights, encouragement, and tools to help you adjust, thrive, and feel empowered in your new home.

You don't have to give up your roots to grow new ones. You don't have to change who you are to succeed. This book is here to remind you that you already have what it takes. You just need a little guidance and support along the way. Let's begin this journey together.

SECTION 1: EVERYDAY COMMUNICATION AND SOCIAL NORMS

Chapter 1: Translation Services and Helpful Tools

If you are new to the United States and still learning English, you might find it hard to understand books, articles, or conversations. Luckily, there are many free translation tools that can help. These tools can translate words, signs, and sentences. They can also help you with writing, checking your text for clarity, spelling and grammar, finding information in your language, and translating entire documents (Google, 2024).

These tools are not perfect and do not replace a real person helping you translate, but they can help you understand what people are saying. With these tools on your smartphone, you do not need to carry a dictionary with you.

Helpful Translation and Language Tools

There are many language tools we can use, and the most helpful I found will be described here. They fall into three categories: translation, accessibility, and Artificial Intelligence (AI). Translation Tools change text or speech into another language (Google, 2024). Read-Aloud Features can read English text out loud at a speed that is easier to understand (Apple, 2023). They can also help you learn to pronounce words correctly by letting you hear how they are spoken in English. AI Tools, such as ChatGPT, check spelling and grammar before you send an email or assignment and help you write and learn about many topics in different languages (OpenAI, 2024). These tools make it easier to learn English and adjust to life in the U.S. However, the instructions may change, so check each website for updates.

Translation Tools for Computer, Tablet, Smartphone, and Websites

Google Translate is a free app for translation that can be downloaded or used on its website.

How to Use Google Translate

1. Download Google Translate from the App Store or Google Play to your device. Or, if you are using the Google website go to translate.google.com.
2. Open the app or website and choose your native language and English. If you are translating to English, list English second. If you are translating to your native language, list it second.
3. To translate text, type or paste it into the app. If you want to translate from English to your native language, select English first, then your native language.
4. Use the microphone to speak words and have them translated.
5. Use the camera feature to scan and translate text from books or signs (Google, 2024).

Using Chrome's Translation Tool to Translate Websites into Your Language

1. Open Chrome: Start the Chrome browser on your computer or tablet.
2. Go to a Website: Visit a website that is not in English. Chrome will notice it's in a different language.
3. See the Translation Bar: A bar will automatically appear at the top of the page asking if you want to translate the page.
4. Click Translate: Click the "Translate" button on the bar to change the website's text to English.
5. Change Language (If Needed): If you need the website in a language other than English, click the three dots on the translation bar. Then, you can pick a different language.

Microsoft Translator – Free Translation

1. Download Microsoft Translator from the App Store or Google Play, or access it directly on its website by visiting https://www.bing.com/translator.
2. Select your native language and English to translate from your language to English. To translate back to your native language, select English as the source language and your native language as the target language.

3. Type or paste text to see a translation.
4. Tap the microphone to speak and hear the translation in either language.
5. Use Conversation Mode to have a real-time bilingual conversation.
6. Use the camera to scan and translate signs, menus, or documents.
7. Download language packs for offline translation (Microsoft, 2024).

Interpretation via Phone

Many hospitals, government offices, and businesses offer free interpretation services for their clients over the phone (LanguageLine Solutions, 2024). To access this service, simply ask, "Can I use an interpreter?" at a hospital or office. The staff will then contact LanguageLine Solutions, or another provider, and an interpreter will assist you in real time. It is best to use a professional interpreter, rather than a friend or a family member, when discussing important health issues.

Case Study: The Importance of Using a Medical Interpreter

In 1980, a man named Willie was taken to a hospital in Florida. His family told the hospital staff that he was "intoxicado," a Spanish word that can mean feeling sick from something you ate or drank. However, the staff thought "intoxicado" meant he was drunk or had used drugs. They were wrong, and it was too late when they found out. Because of this mistake, they didn't realize Willie had a serious problem in his brain. He had a bleed in his brain, which caused permanent damage and left him unable to move (paralyzed). This story shows why hospitals need to use professional interpreters to avoid such big mistakes (Institute for Healthcare Advancement, 2020).

I have been helping my family and friends by interpreting since I was fourteen years old. When we first came here, hospitals did not have many professional interpreters. Even though I tried my best, I didn't know many medical terms and sometimes heard things that were not appropriate for children. I know I was not the only person who has felt the pressure and obligation of having to interpret for my family. While sometimes this is needed and very useful, Willie's case teaches us that mistakes can happen if the interpreter is not trained well. It's best to use a professional interpreter when discussing important health information. For simpler tasks like making appointments, it's okay to use family or friends who speak English.

Read-Aloud Features on Devices

Device accessibility features can help with pronunciation, reading comprehension, and learning new words (Apple, 2023). The Read-Aloud feature allows you to hear English words displayed on device screen. Often, you may understand the main information better if it is spoken aloud rather than being available only in written form.

How to Enable Read-Aloud
On iPhone

1. Go to Settings, then find and click on Accessibility.
2. Tap Spoken Content.
3. Turn on Speak Selection to hear text read aloud when highlighted.
4. Turn on Speak Screen to have the entire screen read aloud (Apple, 2023).

On Android

1. Go to Settings, find and click on Accessibility.
2. Tap Select to Speak and turn it on.
3. Highlight text and tap the Speak button to hear it read aloud (Google, 2024).

On Windows

1. Press the Windows Key + Ctrl + Enter to start Narrator.
2. Highlight text and click the Read Aloud option in Microsoft Edge or Word (Microsoft, 2024).

On Mac

1. Go to System Preferences, then click on Accessibility.
2. Select Spoken Content and turn on Speak Selection.
3. Highlight text and press Option + Esc to hear it read aloud (Apple, 2023).

AI Tool: Chat GPT

AI tools like ChatGPT can help immigrants catch up and stay competitive in school, work, and everyday life. They assist with writing, grammar, speaking, summarizing, and learning new topics, even in different languages (OpenAI, 2024). These tools not only build vocabulary but also provide helpful feedback on grammar, pronunciation, and writing, allowing you to practice English more effectively. Best of all, they are available 24/7 and never get tired. Each AI tool has its own unique features and may offer limited free access, while paid versions provide more advanced functions that will likely continue to improve over time. Take the time to explore and get comfortable with these tools. They can make your life easier and support your learning and communication goals.

How to Use ChatGPT

1. Go to https://chat.openai.com and log in.
2. Type a question or request, such as "Check my grammar".
3. Review and edit the response. AI-generated text is useful, but always check for errors.
4. Use it for learning and practice, such as summarizing articles or explaining difficult words (OpenAI, 2024).

Key Takeaways

- Google Translate is a tool that helps translate text, voice, and conversations.
- Microsoft Translator is another tool that translates text, voice, images, and conversations, even offline.
- Over-the-phone interpretation providers offer services to assist at hospitals and offices, which are then provided free of charge to clients.
- Read-Aloud Features help with learning and pronunciation.

- AI tools (ChatGPT) help with writing, speaking, grammar, and overall learning. They also support learning in different languages and offer translation features.
- These tools help you understand English and adjust to life in the U.S.

Activity

Use Google Translate, Microsoft Translator, or ChatGPT to translate a page from this book into your native language.

If you are using the paperback version, take a clear picture of the page and upload it to your translation app.

If you are using the Kindle or digital version, you can:

- Highlight the text and choose the translation option (if available), or
- Copy and paste the text into a translation tool.

If your language is not supported, and you are using a digital version, try using the read-aloud feature on your device to listen to the content in English.

Reflection Questions

1. How comfortable are you using technology to communicate?
2. Which of the tools we discussed do you think would help you the most when you need language support?

References

Apple. (2023). *Using spoken content on iPhone and iPad*. Retrieved from March 7th, 2025, https://support.apple.com

Google. (2024). *Google Translate Help Center*. Retrieved March 7th, 2025 from https://support.google.com/translate

Google. (2024). *Use Select to Speak on Android*. Retrieved March 7th, 2025 from https://support.google.com

Institute for Healthcare Advancement. (2020, October 22). *Language, Culture, and Medical Tragedy: The Case of Willie Ramirez*. Health Affairs. https://www.healthaffairs.

org/content/forefront/language-culture-and-medical-tragedy-case-willie-ramirez

LanguageLine Solutions. (2024). *Language Interpretation Services*. Retrieved from https://www.languageline.com

Microsoft. (2024). *Microsoft Translator Help Center*. Retrieved March 7th, 2025, from https://translator.microsoft.com

Microsoft. (2024). *Use Read Aloud on Windows*. Retrieved March 7th, 2025, from https://support.microsoft.com

OpenAI. (2024). *ChatGPT User Guide*. Retrieved March 7th, 2025, from https://openai.com/chatgpt

Chapter 2: Communicating in Everyday Situations

Moving to a new country can be difficult and overwhelming. Talking to people may feel challenging and can make you nervous, but knowing common, simple phrases that you can rely on can be very useful (Cambridge Dictionary, 2024). Knowing how to ask for help wherever you go can reduce uncertainty.

Then, you can use the translation tools from Chapter 1 not only to prepare for conversations but also to translate dialogue in the moment. This chapter will teach you useful phrases that are helpful for daily life. It also includes English learning tools that you can use to practice English daily. Mastering English will enhance your experience and opportunities in the United States. Keep practicing daily, and you will see results.

Being Polite and Introducing Yourself

When you meet someone for the first time, it is polite to introduce yourself (ESL Library, 2024). Being polite means showing good manners and respect. This can be done by smiling, using kind words, and behaving in a way that makes others feel comfortable.

Useful Phrases

"Hello, my name is (your name). Nice to meet you!"

"Hi, I am new here. What is your name?"

"It is nice to meet you. Where are you from?"

Responding to an Introduction
"Nice to meet you too!" is a polite way to respond to instructions.

"I am from (your country). How about you?"

Asking for Help

If you need help in a store, on the street, or in a public place, use these polite phrases (U.S. Department of Education, 2024):

"Excuse me, can you help me?" This can be used to get someone's attention politely.

"Could you please help me with...(directions, price)"

"Can you tell me where (place) is?"

"I do not understand. Can you say it again, please?"

If You Do Not Speak English Well
"I am still learning English. Can you speak slowly?"

"Can you write it down for me?"

Ordering Food at a Restaurant

When you go to a restaurant, knowing how to order food is important (Cambridge Dictionary, 2024).

Useful Phrases
"I would like (food, drink) please."

"Can I see the menu?"

"Do you have vegetarian options?"

"Can I get the check, please?"

"Can I get a (food item)?"

If You Do Not Understand the Menu
"What do you recommend?"

"What is in this dish?"

Shopping and Buying Things

If you go shopping, you may need to ask for prices or sizes (ESL Library, 2024).

Useful Phrases

"How much does this cost?"

"Do you have this in a different (size, color)?"

"Can I pay with a credit card?"

When you finish shopping, the cashier might say, "Have a nice day!" You can respond:

"Thank you! You too!"

Going to the Doctor

If you need to see a doctor, these phrases can help (U.S. Department of Education, 2024):

Making an Appointment

"I have an appointment at (time)."

"I do not feel well."

"I have pain in my (body part)."

"Can you explain this medicine to me?"

If You Need a Translator

"Do you have an interpreter?"

"Can someone help me in my language?"

Taking Public Transportation

Public transportation is a low-cost way to travel, and it includes buses, trains, subways, trolleys, and ferries (Cambridge Dictionary, 2024). Private transportation, such as taxis or Uber, is more expensive.

Common Types of Public Transport

Buses: Stop at marked signs. Check schedules online or ask the driver for help.

Trains: Travel long distances and cost more than buses.

Subways: Underground trains that come often. Buy a ticket or transit card before entering.

Trolleys: Operate on city streets.

Paying a Fare

You pay a fare (the ticket price) to ride public transportation. Some cities accept cash, but most use transit cards. If you travel often, buy a pass to save money. Always check the schedule before you leave.

Asking for Information

"Which bus goes to (place)?"

"How much is a ticket?"

"Where is the nearest train station?"

"What time does the bus arrive?"

If You Do Not Understand an Announcement

"Can you repeat that, please?"

"Where do I get off for (place)?"

Case Study: Too Formal for Everyday Interaction

When I first came to the U.S., I was buying a few items at a convenience store. Bread, of course, was on my list, and I remember buying two loaves since we were a family of five. The bread was different from what I was used to eating. It was sweeter and much thinner, but once I started toasting it, I learned to enjoy it and even made warm sandwiches for an easy lunch.

At the checkout, I greeted the cashier with, "Good afternoon." She responded, "Good afternoon." Then, I asked, "How are you?" She answered, "Good." However, she did not ask me how I was, so I did not continue the conversation.

After scanning my items, she asked, "Do you need a bag?" I replied, "Yes, please, that would be great. Thank you." She then looked at me, smiled, and said, "You must not be from here. No one speaks like that."

Lesson Learned: Informal Speech is Common

The level of formality in speech varies depending on location and cultural expectations. In some regions, such as parts of the Southern U.S., friendly and polite conversation with strangers is more common. However, in the Northeastern U.S., where people tend to be in a hurry, small talk at a convenience store is less expected. People tend to use more informal speech in everyday conversation.

As a new English learner, I expected people to follow the same conversational patterns I had practiced in class. However, I realized that everyday speech in the U.S. is often more casual than what is taught in formal lessons.

Formal vs. Informal Speech Example

Formal: "Good afternoon. How are you today?"

Informal: "Hey! How's it going?"

Formal: "Yes, please, that would be great."

Informal: "Yeah, sure, thanks!"

Understanding when and where to use formal or informal speech can help in daily interactions and make conversations feel more natural.

Language Learning Tools

Learning English well will greatly enhance your experience and open up more opportunities to you in the United States. Whether you are just starting or simply looking to improve your English, these tools are excellent resources. Try to practice English every day.

- Duolingo is an easy-to-use app that supports learners from beginner to advanced levels, allowing you to practice English at your own pace (Duolingo, n.d). Available at: https://www.duolingo.com
- BBC Learning English offers many free resources, including videos, quizzes, and grammar guides (BBC Learning English, n.d). Available at: http://www.bbc.co.uk/learningenglish
- The HelloTalk allows you to practice English with native speakers through text, voice messages, and phone calls (HelloTalk, n.d.). *This app is recommended for adults only.* Available at: https://www.hellotalk.com
- ChatGPT is an AI tool that can help with writing, speaking, grammar, and language learning. It can also provide content and support in many different languages, and give you feedback on your speaking. (OpenAI, 2024). Available at: https://chat.openai.com/

Emergency Contacts Sheet

It's important to have quick access to emergency contacts. This sheet includes important phone numbers and addresses that you should fill out and keep handy for quick reference in any emergency.

Included Contacts:

- Emergency Services (911): Immediate assistance for police, fire, and medical emergencies.
- Poison Control Center (1-800-222-1222): Assistance with the ingestion of poisonous substances. They will connect you to a local line that is familiar with local chemicals and treatment.
- Local Police Station (find number): Non-emergency assistance and local concerns.
- Nearest Hospital (find number and address): Address and phone number for the closest emergency medical care.
- Immigrant Support (find your local groups and their contact information): Help with urgent immigration issues.

Make copies of this information and keep them in your home, car, and workplace to ensure you are prepared for any situation.

Key Takeaways

- Practice simple phrases every day to improve your English (ESL Library, 2024).
- Be polite and ask for help if you do not understand something (U.S. Department of Education, 2024).
- Use body language, gestures, and translation tools if you need help communicating (Cambridge Dictionary, 2024).
- Do not be afraid to make mistakes; learning a language takes time and consistent effort.
- Keep a list of important phone numbers handy because you never know when you may need them.

Reflection Questions

1. How comfortable are you communicating with people in English?
2. What information from the chapter can you use in your daily interactions?

References

BBC Learning English. (n.d.). *Learn English online.* Retrieved from http://www.bbc.co.uk/learningenglish

Cambridge Dictionary.(2024). *Basic English phrases for communication* Retrieved from https://dictionary.cambridge.org

Duolingo. (n.d.). *Learn a language for free.* Retrieved from https://www.duolingo.com

ESL Library. (2024). *Speaking English in daily life.* Retrieved from https://esllibrary.com

HelloTalk. (n.d.). *Learn languages by chatting with native speakers.* Retrieved from https://www.hellotalk.com

OpenAI. (2024). *ChatGPT response to a prompt about AI tools* (Mar 14 version) [Large language model]. https://chat.openai.com/

U.S. Department of Education. (2024). *Language learning for newcomers.* Retrieved from https://www.ed.gov

Chapter 3: Understanding Non-Verbal Communication

People communicate in many ways, not just with words. Non-verbal communication includes things like smiling, looking at each other, moving your hands (gestures), and the way you stand. These actions help us understand what others mean, but they can be different in each culture.

In this chapter, we will learn about two important types of non-verbal communication in the U.S.: smiling and eye contact.

Smiling and Eye Contact in the U.S.

In many places, people smile for different reasons. In the United States, it's common for people to smile a lot, even at people they don't know (Hall, 1966). However, just because someone smiles at you doesn't always mean they want to talk or that they are very happy. Sometimes, a smile is just a polite gesture (Brown & Levinson, 1987). Often, in America, a smile is just a friendly way to say hello or be polite without using words. It's a way to be nice to others when you see them.

When Do Americans Smile?

Americans often smile in many everyday situations. Here are some examples when you might see people in the U.S. smiling:

- Saying Hello: It is common to smile when greeting someone. People smile at their neighbors or cashiers as a friendly way to say hello (Andersen et al., 2002). It is nice to smile when greeting someone or saying goodbye.
- Thanking Someone: When someone helps you or gives you something, you might smile to show thanks. This is a way to show that you appreciate what they have done (Givens, 2005).
- Working in Customer Service: If you go to a store or a restaurant, you might see workers like cashiers and waiters

smiling. They smile to look friendly and make you feel welcome (Tidd & Lockard, 1978).

- Making Small Talk: During light, casual conversations, people often smile. This makes the chat more pleasant and helps everyone feel more comfortable. (Gudykunst & Ting-Toomey, 1988). Start and end conversations with a smile. Smile to show you are listening, understanding, or agreeing, but do not smile the entire time. Let your smile match the situation so it feels natural.

In all these cases, smiles are used to be friendly and polite. This shows that smiling is not always about showing deep personal feelings, but rather about being kind and respectful to others.

Eye Contact in the U.S.

Eye contact is an important part of communication. In the U.S., looking into someone's eyes shows you are paying attention and being respectful (Argyle & Dean, 1965). However, different rules apply depending on the situation. Polite eye contact is a short look into someone's eyes, which shows that you are listening. However, looking at someone for too long, or staring, can make the other person feel uncomfortable (Kendon, 1967). On the other hand, if you avoid eye contact too much, people may think you are nervous or hiding something (Burgoon et al., 1989).

In the U.S., eye contact shows confidence, respect, and interest during a conversation. However, it is important to find a balance. Looking at someone briefly is polite, but staring too long or avoiding eye contact too much can send the wrong message.

A helpful tip is the 50/70 rule: look at the other person about 50% of the time when you are talking and 70% when you are listening. Try to look at the person for about 4 to 5 seconds at a time, then glance away briefly before looking back. Always begin a conversation by looking at the person, and end the conversation the same way. This shows that you are friendly and paying attention.

Cultural Differences in Smiling and Eye Contact

Different cultures have different rules for smiling and eye contact. In some countries, people do not smile at strangers, but in the U.S., this is normal (Triandis, 1995). In some cultures, smiling too much may seem strange. For example, the British actor Daniel Craig, who plays James Bond, does not smile much in public because, in his culture, smiling at strangers is not common (Triandis, 1995). In business or formal meetings, smiling too much may not be appropriate (LaFrance & Mayo, 1976). Also, people in small towns smile at strangers more often than people in big cities (Henley, 1977).

Eye contact is also different in each culture. In some places, looking down or avoiding eye contact is a sign of respect, but in the U.S., it can seem like you are not interested (LaFrance & Mayo, 1976). If you come from a culture where people do not smile at strangers or use less eye contact, American habits may feel unusual at first.

How to Practice Non-Verbal Communication in the U.S.

Using nonverbal communication correctly is important because it communicates fitting in and interacting appropriately. If you are new to the U.S., you can practice using smiling and eye contact in small ways:

- Smile slightly when making eye contact with someone. This shows friendliness.
- Look at someone's eyes for a few seconds when talking, but do not stare. This shows that you are listening.
- Observe others and see how Americans use smiles and eye contact in different situations.
- Follow what others do if you are unsure how to act. Learning by watching can help you feel more confident.

Helpful Tip: You can practice by watching TV or movies. Pay attention to how Americans smile and use eye contact during conversations.

Case Study: Learning to Smile and Make Eye Contact at Work

When my family and I first came to the U.S., we were not used to smiling at strangers. In our home country, people were polite, but they did not smile as much in everyday interactions, especially with people they didn't know. However, in the U.S., I quickly learned that smiling was not just a social habit; it was often an expectation, especially in the workplace.

My sister and I worked at Walmart, and in the mornings, I liked to start my day slowly. I focused on my tasks, not thinking much about my facial expressions. But my manager would always remind me, "Don't forget to smile!" At first, I found this strange. I was doing my job well, so why did it matter if I smiled? In my culture, a neutral facial expression was normal, but in the U.S., a smile was expected, especially in customer service.

Over time, I realized that in American workplaces, you are not only paid to do your job; you are also expected to interact with others in a certain way. This includes being friendly, making eye contact, and engaging with customers. Smiling makes you seem approachable, and eye contact shows confidence and attentiveness. Even if I didn't feel like smiling early in the morning, I learned that it was part of professional behavior in the U.S., so I needed to adapt to this expectation.

Lesson Learned: The Importance of Smiling and Eye Contact in the U.S.

Smiling and eye contact are an important part of communication in American culture. In customer service jobs, smiling shows that you are friendly and willing to help. Even outside of work, making eye contact when speaking to someone is a sign of confidence and respect. Below are a few situations where you should consider smiling and making eye contact.

In the workplace: Employees are expected to smile and greet customers, even if they are busy. A neutral expression may be seen as unfriendly.

In conversations: Americans often make direct eye contact when speaking. Avoiding eye contact might make someone think you are nervous or not paying attention.

In different cultures: Some cultures do not use smiling or direct eye contact in the same way. In some places, too much eye contact can even seem rude as in questioning someone's authority. Make sure to learn the cultural expectations of your new environment so you can integrate and fit in.

For example, when I visit Bosnia, I have to remind myself not to smile as much, and I train myself to get used to people openly staring at me, especially in smaller cities. Learning these small social expectations, or social norms, has helped me adjust to my new environment and feel more comfortable at work and in different situations.

Key Takeaways

- Smiling is a common way to show friendliness and politeness in the U.S.
- A smile does not always mean someone wants to talk.
- Eye contact is expected when interacting with someone, but staring too long can be rude.
- Learning these habits can help you make a good first impression and feel comfortable in the U.S.

Activity

Practice making polite eye contact and smiling in different situations.
1. When saying hello to someone in a store or school.
2. When listening to someone talk.
3. When talking with a friend.

Write down your experience. Did it feel natural? How did the other person react?

Reflection Questions

1. What do smiling and making eye contact usually mean in the United States?

2. How does your home culture compare to the U.S. in terms of smiling, eye contact, and nonverbal communication?

References

Andersen, P. A., Gannon, J. L., & Tan, J. (2002). *Nonverbal communication: Forms and functions.* Wadsworth.

Argyle, M., & Dean, J. (1965). *Eye-contact, distance, and affiliation.* Sociometry, 28(3), 289-304.

Brown, P., & Levinson, S. C. (1987). *Politeness: Some universals in language usage.* Cambridge University Press.

Burgoon, J. K., Buller, D. B., & Woodall, W. G. (1989). *Nonverbal communication: The unspoken dialogue.* Harper & Row.

Givens, D. B. (2005). *Love signals: A practical field guide to the body language of courtship.* St. Martin's Press.

Gudykunst, W. B., & Ting-Toomey, S. (1988). *Culture and interpersonal communication.* SAGE Publications.

Hall, E. T. (1966). *The hidden dimension.* Doubleday.

Henley, N. M. (1977). *Body politics: Power, sex, and nonverbal communication.* Prentice Hall.

Kendon, A. (1967). *Some functions of gaze-direction in social interaction.* Acta Psychologica, 26, 22-63.

Kreuz, R. J., & Roberts, R. M. (2017). *Becoming fluent: How cognitive science can help adults learn a foreign language.* MIT Press.

LaFrance, M., & Mayo, C. (1976). *The social and personality functions of nonverbal behavior.* Springer Science & Business Media.

Tidd, K. L., & Lockard, J. S. (1978). *Effects of smiling and body position on interpersonal attraction.* Journal of Personality and Social Psychology, 36(12), 1531-1539.

Triandis, H. C. (1995). *Individualism & collectivism.* Westview Press.

Chapter 4: Understanding Cultural Differences – Collectivist vs. Individualistic Values

When you move to a new country, it is important to understand the values and customs of the people around you and learn the culture of the country you are living in. Culture is the way a group of people lives, thinks, and interacts. It includes language, traditions, beliefs, food, and ways of communicating. Every country, and even different groups within a country, have their own culture.

Values are the ideas and beliefs that are important to people. Values help people decide what is right or wrong and guide how they live their lives. For example, in some cultures, respect for elders is a strong value, while in others, independence is very important. Every culture has different values about family, work, and communication (Hofstede, 2001). One of the biggest cultural differences is how people see themselves in relation to their community.

In the United States, people often focus on their own goals and being independent. This is called individualism (Triandis, 1995). People believe in making their own choices and being responsible for their own success. In many other countries, people focus more on family and community. This is called collectivism. People work together and support each other in their daily lives. Neither individualism nor collectivism is better than the other; they are simply different ways of thinking which can be used as a starting point when learning about a new culture.

Understanding these differences can help you adjust, avoid misunderstandings, and appreciate both cultures (Ting-Toomey, 1999). These views help guide you in understanding what people in a particular culture consider important and provide a useful foundation when learning about new cultural expectations.

Comparing Collectivist and Individualistic Cultures

The table below shows the main differences between these cultural values. I will not explain each category in detail, so please read each category carefully and study how each culture views what is valued. As you read, reflect on these differences to consider your own views.

Category	Collectivist Cultures (Group-Focused)	Individualistic Cultures (Self-Focused)
Family	Large families that often live together	Small families, usually just parents and children
Elders	Respected and cared for at home	Often live independently or in retirement homes (Kagitcibasi, 2007)
Marriage	Family may help choose a spouse	People choose their own partners based on love
Celebrations	Big, community-based events	Smaller, personal gatherings
Communication	Indirect, polite, and tries to avoid conflict (Ting-Toomey, 1999)	Direct, honest, and open discussions
Decision-Making	The group makes decisions together	Individuals make their own choices

Community Role	Helping each other is very important	Focus on personal success but may volunteer (Fiske, 1992)
Independence	Rely on family and group support	Value independence and solving problems alone (Matsumoto, 2000)
Education	Seen as a way to help family and community	Seen as a personal achievement for success
Work Values	Teamwork is very important	Individual success is encouraged
Solving Problems	Problems are handled within the group to avoid conflict	Problems are discussed directly to find fair solutions
Time Focus	Focus on the past (tradition) and present (relationships)	Focus on the future, progress, success, and planning (Hofstede, 2001)
Common Locations	Found in Asia, Africa, Latin America, and Eastern/ Southern Europe	Found in the U.S., Canada, Australia, and Northern/ Western Europe

Note: Not everyone from a specific country follows these values exactly! These are general patterns that help explain cultural differences.

Why Does This Matter?

People from different cultures think, act, and communicate differently. Learning about these patterns can help you understand others better (Triandis, 1995). Also, knowing about general cultural values of the group you are visiting or interacting with can help you adapt more easily, feel more comfortable, and avoid confusion in a new environment.

But, you do not have to change who you are! You can keep your traditions and appreciate your own culture while learning new ways to succeed in a different culture.

Activity

1. Look at the chart again and circle the values that match your own experiences.
2. Compare the values you circled to the U.S. values. What patterns do you notice?
3. Think about the individualistic values that you may not personally follow. How can learning about these values help you communicate more effectively and better understand Americans?

Case Study: Cultural Confusion

Amira traveled to Bosnia and Herzegovina to take care of her elderly mother. When she returned to work in the U.S., her coworkers asked about her trip.

John: "How was your vacation?"
Kate: "Did you do anything fun?"
Amira: "I took care of my mother."
John: "Oh... so you didn't get to relax?"
Amira: "Not really, I mostly helped my mom and cleaned."
Kate: "That's too bad!"

Amira felt frustrated. Her coworkers did not understand why taking care of family was more important to her than relaxing.

Discussion Activity

1. Why were Amira and her coworkers confused?
2. How do individualistic and collectivist cultures explain their different views?
3. Have you ever had a cultural misunderstanding? What happened?

What Caused the Confusion?

Different Views on Vacation: In the U.S., vacations are usually for relaxing and having fun. Amira's coworkers expected her to go sightseeing or do outdoor activities. In many collectivist cultures, people use their vacation time for family responsibilities (Triandis, 1995).

Different Perspectives on Elder Care: In the U.S., many elderly parents live in retirement homes and are expected to plan for their own retirement (future-focused). In Bosnia and many other cultures, family members care for elders at home (Kagitcibasi, 2007). Amira believed it was her duty to care for her mother, which was more important than having a fun vacation. "What would other people think of her?" was something she considered when making decisions. In some collectivist cultures, families may feel shame if they let someone else take care of their elders (Matsumoto, 2000). Understanding differences between collectivistic and individualistic views helps us communicate better and avoid misunderstandings (Ting-Toomey, 1999).

Key Takeaways

- Individualistic cultures value independence, personal goals, and direct communication. They often focus on the future (Hofstede, 2001).
- Collectivist cultures prioritize family, teamwork, and community. They often focus on the present and traditions.
- Cultural values shape how people see the world. Neither way of thinking is "right" or "wrong" (Hofstede, 2001).
- Blending both sets of values can help you adjust to a new culture while keeping your own identity.
- It's normal to feel different or confused at first! Over time, you will learn to balance both cultures while staying true to yourself.

Reflection Questions

1. In individualistic cultures, people communicate directly. In collectivist cultures, people prefer polite communication and avoiding conflict. How can these differences cause misunderstandings in friendships or at work? Can you give an example?
2. The first table in this chapter shows that different cultures think about time in different ways. Collectivist cultures focus on the past and present, while individualistic cultures focus on the future. How can this difference affect how people set goals or plan for the future?

References

Fiske, A. P. (1992). *The four elementary forms of sociality: Framework for a unified theory of social relations.* Psychological Review, 99(4), 689-723.

Hofstede, G. (2001). *Culture's consequences: Comparing values, behaviors, institutions, and organizations across nations.* Sage Publications.

Kagitcibasi, C. (2007). *Family, self, and human development across cultures.* Erlbaum Associates.

Matsumoto, D. (2000). *Culture and psychology: People around the world.* Wadsworth.

Ting-Toomey, S. (1999). *Communicating across cultures.* The Guilford Press.

Triandis, H. C. (1995). *Individualism & collectivism.* Westview Press.

SECTION 2: SOCIAL AND PERSONAL RELATIONSHIPS

Chapter 5: Building Personal Relationships in the U.S.: Family and Friends

Building relationships in the United States may be different from what you are used to experiencing in your own culture. In American culture, relationships, whether with family, friends, or romantic partners, often focus on personal space, individual choice, and equality (Anderson & Patel, 2021).

This chapter provides an overview of family and friendship and explains how middle-class American customs shape these relationships today. I focus on middle-class values because teachers, managers, and many people newcomers meet often follow these mainstream values. Understanding these cultural differences will help newcomers build strong relationships in the U.S.

Understanding Personal Relationships in the U.S.

Three key values shape how personal relationships are viewed in the U.S.: personal space, individual choice, and equality.

Personal space is highly valued, and people often expect others to respect their privacy and physical boundaries. For example, when talking to someone, it is common to leave some space between you and the other person. Standing too close or touching someone you do not know well may make them uncomfortable.

Individual choice is another important value. In the U.S., people usually make their own decisions about education, career, friendships, and even relationships. Parents encourage their children to express their opinions and make choices that reflect their personal preferences.

Equality is also a key factor in relationships. Everyone's opinion and feelings are valued, regardless of age or social status. In many American families, children and parents discuss decisions together, and children are often encouraged to share their thoughts openly (Anderson & Patel, 2021).

Family Relationships in the U.S.

Families in the U.S. come in many forms, including nuclear families, single-parent families, blended families, and extended families. The most common type is the nuclear family, which consists of parents and their children. However, many families are also single-parent families, where one parent raises the children, or separated couples take turns raising children on different days. There are also blended families, where parents remarry and bring children from previous marriages into one household. Some families also include extended family members such as grandparents, aunts, uncles, or cousins, who may live together or nearby (Bruno, 2018).

Respect and independence are both important in American families. Parents care for their children, but they also encourage them to be independent. Teenagers are often expected to make their own choices about school, extracurricular activities, and future careers. Many young adults move out of their parents' homes at age 18 or after high school, although some stay for college or work (Duncan, 2018).

Parenting Styles in the U.S.

Parenting styles vary across cultures. Some key differences between collectivist and individualist cultures are summarized in the table below. Parents in the U.S. focus on teaching their children to become independent adults by interacting with them in ways that encourage decision-making and responsibility. From a young age, children are encouraged to make their own decisions and take responsibility for their actions. Activities such as sports, music, and clubs help children develop important skills, make friends, and learn how to manage their time and responsibilities. However, many parents worry about overscheduling their children, believing that too many structured activities can leave little time for free play. Balancing structured activities with free time is considered an important part of parenting responsibilities in the U.S.

American parents typically prefer positive discipline over punishment. This view is especially common in middle-class American culture and is reflected in the media, schools, and the business world. While some subgroups may differ and practice more authoritarian or discipline-based parenting style, middle-class parents typically teach children through guidance and by modeling good behavior. Emotional management and problem-solving are seen as important responsibilities that parents must pass on to their children. This includes managing their own emotions, pausing before reacting, and helping children understand their mistakes and learn from them, rather than simply punishing them. When children experience meltdowns, parents often understand this as a sign of emotional overload and encourage them to develop healthy coping strategies. Rather than reacting harshly, parents may apologize if they overreact, explain what they wish they had done differently, and commit to doing better next time. This way, children learn that even adults are still learning and growing.

Many American parents also believe that setting household routines, such as consistent bedtimes and age-appropriate chores, helps children feel secure. These routines create a sense of predictability and consistency, which can reduce stress and resistance. Discipline in American parenting is not just about punishment; it's about teaching problem-solving, empathy, and emotional control to help children grow into responsible adults. Overall, parents see their role as preparing their children for the future by teaching them the skills they need to succeed in life.

Parenting Styles Across Cultures

Parenting Style	Individualistic Cultures (United States, Canada, Australia, Northern/Western Europe)	Collectivist Cultures (Asia, Africa, Latin America)
Focus	Independence – Children make	Group needs – Family decides

	choices (Triandis, 1995)	together (Kagitcibasi, 2007)
Decision-Making	Children choose their college and career (Hofstede, 2001)	Parents often guide major decisions (Kagitcibasi, 2007
Privacy	Children have personal space and their own rooms	Family life is more shared
Obedience	Parents allow children to question rules	Respect and obedience to elders are expected (Matsumoto, 2000)

Family Time and Meals

Dinner is often the biggest meal of the day and a time for families to connect. In the U.S., dinner is typically between 5:30 PM and 7:30 PM, though this varies depending on family schedules. Because of busy lifestyles, many families rely on fast food or takeout for convenience (Clark, 2019). Food portions in the U.S. are larger than in many other countries, and drinks often come with ice (Jones, 2020).

Meal customs also differ across cultures. In the U.S., children may be allowed to choose their own meals, while in other cultures, parents decide what the family eats (Gonzalez, 2019). In some households, family members eat together, while in others, people eat separately based on their schedules.

Meal Structures and Cultural Differences

Meal Culture	**United States**	**Other Cultures**
Meals	Multiple courses (appetizers, main dish, dessert)	Simpler meals (one main dish with sides)

Family Involvement	Family members sometimes eat separately	Everyone eats together
Food Choices	Wide variety, fast food and takeout are common	Home-cooked meals are preferred
Mealtime Conversation	Casual discussions about school, hobbies, daily life	Formal conversations or family matters

Friendships in the U.S.

Friendships in the U.S. often begin with casual conversations, or small talk. Peer friendships are important. Individuals may start a friendship by discussing something they have in common, such as a shared interest or experience. Shared activities, such as hobbies, sports, or group outings, also help friendships develop and build trust.

Being honest, reliable, and supportive strengthens friendships. This includes being a good listener, remembering details from past conversations, and offering encouragement. Developing a strong friendship takes time. One study found that casual friendships take about 50 hours to develop, while good friendships take around 90 hours, and close friendships require 200 or more hours of time together to form (Hall, 2018). All of us need supportive friendships, and it is important to nurture our friendships as we grow. Having close friends helps us stay emotionally healthy and balanced.

Pets

Many Americans treat pets like family members. Dogs and cats often live indoors and get regular veterinary care (Martin & Lee, 2022). Many pet owners walk their dogs regularly, and pet grooming is common. In some cases, pets even have special furniture, clothing, and celebrations, such as birthday parties. It is important to always ask permission before petting someone's pet.

Personal Boundaries and Safety

Personal space is an important part of American culture. People expect some physical distance when talking or walking and usually avoid unnecessary touching unless they know someone well. In public places, people typically walk in a straight line and try to avoid bumping into others.

Respect for personal belongings is also important in American culture. It is considered impolite to touch someone's phone, bag, or other personal items without permission (Hall, 1966). You should always ask before holding someone's newborn, and it is best to never touch another person's child or scold them. People are expected to discipline their own children. In large cities, people do not usually talk to strangers, while in small towns, it is more common to greet others politely.

Parents often organize playdates for their children so they can spend time with friends. Young children in the United States are usually supervised more closely, especially in public or group settings. As they grow older, this level of supervision gradually decreases, allowing them to develop independence and responsibility. Teenagers usually manage their own schedules and friendships.

Physical punishment, such as hitting children, is strongly discouraged and may even have legal consequences (Oxford English Dictionary, 2023).

Case Study: Balancing Family Expectations and Independence in an Immigrant Household

Kevin, a 16-year-old high school student, moved from Vietnam to the U.S. when he was 10. His parents work long hours to provide for their family and expect Kevin to focus on school, help at home, and respect their cultural traditions. However, growing up in the U.S., Kevin wants more independence to join school activities and pursue his passion for art. This conflict comes from the differences between collectivist and individualist cultures.

Discussion Questions

1. How do different cultural values shape family expectations?
2. What challenges do teens face when growing up in a culture different from their parents' culture?
3. How can parents balance structure and independence when raising teenagers?

Cultural Conflict: Collectivism vs. Individualism

Kevin's parents come from a collectivist culture, where family, respect, and community are more important than personal desires. In Vietnam, decisions are often made based on what is best for the family, not just the individual. This is why they want Kevin to choose a high-paying career like medicine or engineering, to bring honor and stability to the family.

However, growing up in the U.S., Kevin is surrounded by individualist values, where people are encouraged to make their own choices and follow their personal interests. His friends' parents support their hobbies and allow them to make more independent decisions. Kevin feels caught between these two worlds. He wants to make his parents proud, but he also wants to follow his own path.

Challenges Kevin Faces

Let's take a closer look at some of the cultural and personal challenges Kevin is facing.

Different Expectations: Kevin's parents believe his time should be spent studying and helping at home, while Kevin wants to join school activities like his American friends.

Language Barriers and Responsibility: Since his parents do not speak English well, Kevin must translate for them in important situations. In collectivist cultures, it is normal for children to take on responsibilities for the family, but this can make Kevin feel overwhelmed.

Career Pressure: His parents see success in fields like medicine and engineering, while Kevin is drawn to art. In an individualist society, people are encouraged to follow their passions, but his parents worry about financial stability.

Identity Struggles: At school, Kevin wants to fit in with his American peers, but at home, his parents want him to hold on to Vietnamese traditions. This makes him feel like he is living in two different worlds.

Teen Brain Development and Parental Role
Kevin's parents worry that he is making bad choices, but they may not realize that teenagers' brains are still developing. The frontal lobe, which controls decision-making and impulse control, does not fully mature until age 25 (Casey et al., 2008). This means teens need guidance and structure, even if they want independence. They can make decisions based on momentary feelings and think about the consequences too late. Research shows that authoritative parenting, which combines clear rules with emotional support, helps teens make better choices while also feeling understood (Baumrind, 1991).

Finding a Compromise

Kevin's teacher helps him explain to his parents why extracurricular activities are important for college applications. At first, they resist, but eventually, they allow him to join one club. Over time, they also see his passion for art and allow him to take an art class alongside his required subjects.

Through compromise, Kevin's parents maintain their collectivist values of family responsibility while giving him some individualist freedom to explore his interests. This balance helps Kevin respect his heritage while also growing into his own person.

Lesson Learned: Communication and Flexibility are Important

Kevin's story is common among immigrant teens who struggle between collectivist family expectations and individualist cultural influences. By improving communication and understanding the science behind teenage development, families can find a balance where teens feel supported and parents feel respected. Being flexible and understanding the changes happening in each other's lives can be a good starting point.

Parents should remember that they brought their children to the U.S. to give them more opportunities. At the same time, children can learn to respect both cultures and choose which values to follow depending on the situation and their goals.

Key Takeaways

- Family life in the U.S. emphasizes independence and structured schedules.
- Friendships are based on shared interests, honesty, and personal space.
- Teenagers and young adults make their own choices about school, friends, and careers.
- Family meals are important but may be short due to busy schedules.
- Physical punishment is discouraged, and child safety is a priority.
- Understanding cultural differences can help you build stronger relationships in the U.S.

Reflection Questions

1. In the U.S., parents focus on independence, while in collectivist cultures, parents focus on family decisions. Based on the first table above, how might college or career decisions be different in each culture?
2. In the U.S., children often have their own rooms and personal space, while in collectivist cultures, family life is more shared. Why do you think privacy is valued more in individualistic cultures? How might this difference affect daily family life?

References

Anderson, K., & Patel, S. (2021). *The American social guidebook: Understanding family and friendships.* Culture Press.

Baumrind, D. (1991). The influence of parenting style on adolescent competence and substance use. *Journal of Early Adolescence, 11*(1), 56-95.

Bruno, M. (2018). *Cultural etiquette in the United States.* American Customs Society.

Casey, B. J., Jones, R. M., & Hare, T. A. (2008). The adolescent brain. *Annals of the New York Academy of Sciences, 1124*(1), 111-126.

Clark, J. (2019). *Party planning basics: Hosting with confidence.* Event Experts Publishing.

Duncan, L. (2018). *Parenting and independence in the U.S.: A guide for newcomers.* Parenting Matters.

Gonzalez, R. (2019). *Cultural Values and Food Habits.* Global Cultural Studies Journal, 12(3), 45-62.

Hall, E. T. (1966). *The Hidden Dimension: Personal Space in Different Cultures.* New York: Doubleday.

Hall, J. A. (2018). How many hours does it take to make a friend? *Journal of Social and Personal Relationships, 36*(4), 1278–1296. https://doi.org/10.1177/0265407518761225

Hofstede, G. (2001). *Culture's consequences: Comparing values, behaviors, institutions, and organizations across nations.* Sage Publications.

Jones, B. (2020). *Food Culture in the United States.* National Food and Society Research.

Kagitcibasi, C. (2007). *Family, self, and human development across cultures.* Erlbaum Associates.

Martin, D., & Lee, C. (2022). *Hosting Guests in American Society.* Cultural Practices Journal, 18(2), 78-95.

Matsumoto, D. (2000). *Culture and psychology: People around the world.* Wadsworth.

Oxford English Dictionary. (2023). *Definition of parenting and discipline norms.* Oxford University Press.

Triandis, H. C. (1995). *Individualism & collectivism.* Westview Press.

Chapter 6: Hosting Guests and RSVP – A Guide for Social Events for Newcomers

Social events are an important part of American culture. Whether it is a birthday party, holiday gathering, or casual get-together, understanding the customs around hosting and RSVPing (responding to invitations) will help you feel comfortable and included (Bruno, 2018). This chapter explains how to plan, host, and attend social events in the United States.

Part 1: Hosting a Party

If you want to invite people to your home or a venue for a gathering, follow these steps to plan a successful event.

Choosing a Date, Time, and Location

Most gatherings take place on weekends or in the evenings when people are free (Bruno, 2018). The location depends on the type of event and can be held at home, a restaurant, a park, or a community center. Parties usually last between two to four hours, unless it is a wedding or large event. Guests typically expect to leave at the time stated on the invitation. If your event is outdoors, it is a good idea to have a backup plan in case of bad weather.

Deciding on the Type of Event

The type of event will help set expectations for guests. A casual hangout may include snacks and music, while a potluck allows guests to bring food to share (Anderson & Patel, 2021). A dinner party involves serving a full meal, whereas a birthday or holiday party often includes decorations and planned activities. It is important to make the type of event clear on the invitation, so guests know what to expect (Williams, 2017).

Sending Invitations

The way you invite guests depends on the size and formality of the event. Formal events like weddings or large celebrations require invitations four to eight weeks in advance (Martin & Lee, 2022). Casual events such as dinners or birthday parties usually need one to two weeks' notice, while small gatherings can be planned just a few days in advance.

Ways to invite guests vary. Printed invitations are common for weddings and large events, while text messages or phone calls are used for casual meetups. Emails or digital invitations work well for medium-sized gatherings, and social media can be used for larger groups.

Asking for RSVPs

RSVP comes from a French phrase meaning "Please respond" (Oxford English Dictionary, 2023). If you ask guests to RSVP, they should confirm whether they are coming so you can plan for food, seating, and other arrangements. It is also helpful to send a reminder a few days before the event to confirm who will attend. This can help prevent wasting money on extra food or unnecessary space (Clark, 2019).

Planning Food and Drinks

The type of food served typically depends on the event. A casual party may include chips, dips, and finger foods (Jones, 2020). A dinner party requires a full meal, while a potluck involves guests bringing dishes. Drinks should include water, soft drinks, and alcoholic beverages if appropriate (Gonzalez, 2019). It is important to consider dietary restrictions. Some guests may avoid certain foods due to religion, allergies, or personal preferences (Williams, 2017). Knowing that ahead of time can help you plan and make sure everyone feels included.

Setting Up Your Space

Before guests arrive, clean the main areas where they will gather and arrange seating and tables for food and drinks. If it is a special event, decorations can enhance the atmosphere. Playing soft music in the background helps create a welcoming environment (Bruno, 2018).

Being a Friendly Host

A good host makes sure guests feel welcome. Greet guests warmly at the door and introduce people to each other if they do not know one another. Keep conversations flowing and check that everyone is comfortable.

Entertainment such as games, music, or activities can help guests have fun. Hosting does not mean you have to do everything alone. You can ask a friend or family member to help with setting up and running the event to make things easier (Martin & Lee, 2022).

Part 2: How to RSVP and Attend a Party

If someone invites you to a party, knowing how to RSVP and behave as a guest will help you make a good impression.

Reading the Invitation Carefully

Before responding to an invitation, check for important details:
- Date and time – Make sure you do not have another commitment before agreeing to attend.
- Location – Find out how far the event is from you.
- Dress code – Find out if it is formal, casual, or themed so you can know what to wear.
- Food information – Check if food is provided or if you need to bring something to share.
- RSVP request – If the host asks for a response, make sure to reply by the deadline (Duncan, 2018). If the invitation says "RSVP by [date]", respond before that date.

How to RSVP

When responding to an invitation, be polite and clear.
- If you are attending, say: "Yes, I will attend. Thank you for the invitation."
- If you cannot attend, say: "Thank you for the invite, but I will not be able to make it."
- If you are unsure, say: "I will let you know by [date] if I can attend." It is best not to say yes if you are unsure. It is better to be honest than to cancel at the last minute (Taylor, 2021).

Small Talk

Small talk is important for building relationships at work, in friendships, and in social settings. It helps people feel comfortable and can lead to deeper conversations. Small talk is light, friendly, and usually focuses on everyday topics. It's best to keep the conversation positive and avoid personal or sensitive topics. Small talk is common in the workplaces, at social events, and even while waiting in line. For example, you might talk about the weather by saying, "It's such a nice day today!" or ask about hobbies with, "What do you like to do in your free time?" Try to ask a friendly question to keep the conversation going. Sports are also a popular topic, such as, "Did you watch the game last night?" Asking about weekend plans, like "Do you have any fun plans for the weekend?" is another great way to connect. During small talk, avoid topics like politics, religion, money, or controversial issues, as these can make people feel uncomfortable or lead to arguments.

Activity

Think about how you would reply if someone asked, "Hi, how was your weekend?" Try to come up with two different responses: one short and one with more detail. This kind of practice can help you feel more comfortable during casual conversations.

Case Study: "Five o'clock" Really Means Five o'clock

In my culture, socializing with people is a natural and expected part of life. Friends and family often drop by unannounced, and we gladly host them, prepare food, and enjoy time together. There is no expectation that visits need to be planned in advance, nor is there a set time for guests to leave. They may stay late, even if children have school the next day or parents have work early in the morning.

When we moved to the U.S., we quickly realized that this is not the case here. In American culture, when someone invites you over, you are expected to arrive at the specific time given. I felt a lot of pressure to get my family out of the house and into the car on time so we wouldn't be late. I knew that if we arrived late, I would have to explain why, whether it was because a family member took too long to get ready or because someone unexpectedly stopped by asking me to translate a document for them.

Over time, my family learned to adapt. However, we still maintain some of our customs. For example, we occasionally visit close family members without calling or texting first, as this is still common in our culture. But when it comes to people outside our family, we now understand that it is important to call or text beforehand to make sure it is okay to visit.

One thing we found funny is that when we make plans for events, like birthdays, we now ask, "American time or Bosnian time?" If it's American time, that means we have to be on time. If it's Bosnian time, we know that arriving at least 20 minutes late is normal. My dad still prefers Bosnian time, so he never feels rushed!

Lesson Learned: Balancing Cultural Expectations

Adapting to life in the U.S. means learning and following certain social expectations, especially in professional settings and social situations. Being on time is important, and people generally expect plans to be scheduled in advance. However, this does not mean we have to give up our cultural traditions entirely.

Within our family, we still follow some of the customs we grew up with, such as occasionally visiting without prior notice and using "Bosnian time" for certain gatherings. By understanding the differences between cultures, we can successfully adapt to new expectations while still holding on to the important aspects of our heritage.

Key Takeaways

- If you are hosting an event, plan ahead, invite guests early, and make them feel welcome.
- If you are asked to RSVP, respond on time and follow basic party etiquette.
- When attending an event, be respectful, arrive and leave on time, and don't forget to thank the host.
- Practice making small talk and prepare a few simple topics to talk about at get-togethers.
- By understanding social customs, you will feel more confident at social events and be better able to build strong, lasting friendships.

Reflection Questions

1. In some cultures, people speak politely and indirectly to avoid hurting others' feelings, while in other cultures, communication is more direct. How can these differences lead to misunderstandings in social situations?
2. How would you prepare for a dinner party?

References

Anderson, K., & Patel, S. (2021). *The American Social Guidebook: Hosting and Attending Events.* Culture Press.

Bruno, M. (2018). *Cultural Etiquette in the United States.* American Customs Society.

Clark, J. (2019). *Party Planning Basics: Hosting with Confidence.* Event Experts Publishing.

Duncan, L. (2018). *RSVP and Social Norms: Understanding Invitations.* Etiquette Matters.

Gonzalez, R. (2019). *Cultural Values and Food Habits.* Global Cultural Studies Journal, 12(3), 45-62.

Jones, B. (2020). *Food Culture in the United States.* National Food and Society Research.

Martin, D., & Lee, C. (2022). *Hosting Guests in American Society.* Cultural Practices Journal, 18(2), 78-95.

Oxford English Dictionary. (2023). *Definition of RSVP and Social Norms.* Oxford University Press.

Taylor, R. (2021). *Friendship in a Fast-Paced World.* Social Trends Press.

Williams, R. (2017). *Social Life and Networking in America.* Community Living Press.

Chapter 7: Understanding Romantic Relationships in the U.S.

In the United States, dating is a way for people to get to know each other before deciding if they want a serious relationship (Baumeister & Leary, 1995). Dating allows individuals to spend time together, talk, and learn about each other's interests, values, and personalities. In this chapter, we will look at how dating works in the U.S.

Casual Dating Versus Serious Dating

Casual dating means spending time together without a strong commitment. People may go on dates to have fun, enjoy each other's company, and explore their compatibility. Not all dating leads to marriage or long-term relationships (Johnson, 2021).

Serious dating happens when two people decide to be in a committed relationship. They may focus on building a future together, making important decisions as a couple, and discussing long-term goals.

At first, dating is often casual in the United States. People may go out for coffee, watch a movie, or attend an event together. Some dates turn into serious relationships, but many do not (National Institute of Mental Health, 2022).

Casual Dating

Many young people in the U.S. start dating during their teen years (Clark, 2019). Dating often includes group activities, such as going to the movies or eating at a restaurant, where young people can get to know each other in a relaxed setting. This is especially true for teens, as they may start with group outings and gradually move toward one-on-one dating time as they get older.

Casual dating means that people may go on dates with more than one person at a time if they are not in a serious relationship. This is common in American culture, as dating is seen as a way to explore compatibility before committing to one person (Johnson, 2021).

Dating and Immigrant Families

For immigrant families, dating can be a difficult or sensitive topic (Kagitcibasi, 2007). Some parents do not allow dating because of cultural or religious beliefs, while others may prefer that their children date someone from the same background. These differences in expectations can sometimes cause disagreements between parents and teens.

In some cases, teens may choose to hide their dating life from their parents to avoid conflict. However, open discussions between parents and teens can help create understanding. Some families set guidelines for dating, such as deciding where their teen is allowed to go or asking their child's date to meet the family before going out.

Different Expectations Between Cultures

Cultural differences shape the way families approach dating. In the U.S., parents often focus on preparing their children for the future by encouraging independence and decision-making (Triandis, 1995). Typically, avoiding the topic of dating does not prevent it from happening. Instead, setting healthy guidelines helps teens make responsible choices (Ting-Toomey, 1999). Some immigrant communities organize events and gatherings to help young people meet others from the same cultural background. These events allow young people to socialize in a way that aligns with their cultural traditions.

The Pros and Cons of Dating

Good Things About Dating

Dating can have many positive aspects. It allows people to make new friends and learn about different personalities (Baumeister & Leary, 1995). A healthy relationship can bring happiness and emotional support, helping individuals feel valued and understood.

Dating also provides an opportunity for self-discovery through learning more about oneself. By going on dates and getting to know different people, individuals can better understand what they are looking for in a future partner (National Institute of Mental Health, 2022).

Challenges of Dating

Dating also comes with challenges. Rejection is a common experience. Sometimes, one person has stronger feelings that the other, which can be hurtful (Clark, 2019). Meeting new people can be stressful, and it is normal to feel nervous. However, this is a natural part of the learning process.

Dating can be expensive, as activities like going to restaurants, movies, or amusement parks cost money. But dating does not always have to cost a lot. Simple activities like going for a walk in the park or getting ice cream can be fun and affordable alternatives (Johnson, 2021). It is important to respect a person's choices. If someone does not want to go on a date, their decision should always be respected (Johnson, 2021).

Modern Dating and Changing Expectations

Today's dating expectations are shifting. People are now looking for more qualities in a partner than ever before. Physical attraction is still important, but people also care about other things in a relationship. Many individuals seek emotional connection, shared values, good communication skills, respect, and long-term compatibility. Some also look for financial stability, a sense of humor, kindness, or support for their personal goals. Online dating has also changed the way people meet. With just a few swipes or clicks, it's possible to view many profiles in a short time.

This has created a "scroll culture," where it's easy to keep searching for more options. Because of this, many people experience FOMO, the fear of missing out. They may worry that if they stop looking, they could miss the chance to meet someone even better. This can make it harder to appreciate the people they do meet, as they are always wondering if someone else might be a better match.

How to Show Respect when Dating

There are certain social expectations when it comes to dating in the U.S. Being on time is important. If you are running late, it is polite to send a message letting the other person know. Expressing gratitude is also valued; saying "thank you" after a date shows appreciation.

Listening carefully is another important part of dating etiquette. Giving the other person your full attention and showing interest in what they say creates a positive and respectful experience (Ting-Toomey, 1999). Also, be sure to share about yourself and see if your values are compatible. When values are compatible, it makes it easier to find similarities, especially if both people are looking for the same goals in dating, such as a serious commitment.

Respect and Consent

Respecting personal boundaries is essential in dating. If someone does not want to hold hands, hug, or kiss, that choice must be respected. Consent is a key part of healthy relationships, and it is always important to ask before touching someone in any way (Johnson, 2021).

A clear rule in dating is that "no" means "no." If someone says they are not interested, they should never be pressured or made to feel uncomfortable (Clark, 2019). When dating, it is also important to know what you do not want in a partner. For example, if you value honesty and find that the person you are dating is not honest, you need to think about whether this is okay with you. If it's not, then they are not the right partner for you.

It's better to find out early if someone has a habit or behavior you cannot accept. These are called "dealbreakers" or "red flags." A dealbreaker is something that makes you decide not to continue the relationship. For example, if you do not smoke, you may not want to date someone who does. That way, you can save time and not get too close to someone who isn't a good match for you.

Also, something you do might be a dealbreaker for someone else. If they tell you what bothers them and you don't want to change that behavior, it's better for both of you to find out early so you can move on. Talking to someone on the phone or through video before meeting in person can help you see if they may be a good match for you.

What Happens If a Relationship Ends?

Not all relationships last forever, and breakups are a normal part of life (National Institute of Mental Health, 2022). Some people choose to remain friends after ending a relationship, while others prefer to take time apart.

Feeling sad after a breakup is normal, but emotions improve with time. Spending time with family, friends, or engaging in hobbies can help people heal. While breakups can be painful, they also provide an opportunity to learn and grow. Through these experiences, individuals gain a better understanding of what they want in a future partner (Clark, 2019).

Online Dating Safety Tips

Online dating is common, but it is important to stay safe (Johnson, 2021).

1. Never share private information, like your address, school, or phone number, with someone you just met.
2. Meet in a public place for the first few dates.
3. Tell a friend or family member where you are going.
4. Do not send personal pictures to people you do not know well.
5. Trust your feelings. If something seems wrong, leave the situation.
6. Get to know someone before going on a date by talking on the phone and having a virtual conversation.
7. Being careful and smart online keeps you safe.

Case Study: Differences in Acculturation and Its Impact on Dating

When we first came to the U.S., we attended Bosnian parties and gatherings. These events were a time for our community to come together, enjoy Bosnian music, share traditional food, and stay out late, making the most of our time together. Bosnian youth also participated, and everyone dressed up, often wearing stylish outfits and makeup. I still smile when I look back at pictures from those days, seeing how much makeup we used to wear!

One of the benefits of these cultural gatherings was that people from the same background had the opportunity to meet and, if interested, start dating. Of course, today, social media allows people to connect more easily, but there are still occasional events, such as informal concerts, where Bosnians gather and meet in person.

Through these experiences, I learned that just because people come from the same culture, their level of acculturation, or how much they adapt to American culture, can vary. People do not change at the same rate, which can lead to conflicting expectations in relationships. I tended to adapt more quickly out of pure necessity, while others, especially those who mainly socialized within the Bosnian community, adjusted more slowly and held on to more traditional beliefs.

One area where this difference became clear was gender roles. I always knew that even though I was a woman, I planned on having a career. However, I also felt that if both partners worked, house chores should be shared more equally. At the same time, I noticed that men in the U.S. seemed to help more at home. We saw this firsthand during our first week with our host family. My mom was shocked to see that Joe, the husband, helped his wife with everything, from cooking dinner to taking care of the children.

Lesson Learned: Adapting Happens at Different Paces

Acculturation is a personal process, and not everyone adapts to a new culture at the same pace. Some people adjust quickly due to necessity, while others hold onto traditional beliefs, especially if they are surrounded by others from their home culture. This can impact relationships, as differing expectations about gender roles, responsibilities, and lifestyles can create misunderstandings.

Observing how American families function helped me develop my own expectations for the future I wanted. While I value my cultural background, I also learned to embrace aspects of American culture that align with my personal beliefs, such as sharing household responsibilities more equally in relationships.

The Immigrant Advantage: More Stability in Immigrant Families

Studies show that immigrant families in the U.S. have lower divorce rates than families born in the U.S. According to the Institute for Family Studies (2019), only 13 out of every 1,000 married immigrants between ages 18-64 get divorced, while 20 out of every 1,000 native-born Americans get divorced. Also, 72% of immigrant parents stay in their first marriage, compared to 60% of native-born parents (Institute for Family Studies, 2019).

There are many reasons why immigrant families may have fewer divorces. Some cultures value marriage and family commitment more, and many immigrants have strong community support that helps them during difficult times (Deseret News, 2021). However, not all immigrant families are the same. Divorce rates can be higher or lower depending on where immigrants come from, their education level, and their financial situation (ResearchGate, 2021).

Even though immigrant families are generally more likely to stay together, it is important to recognize that these statistics primarily apply to the first generation. This advantage does not necessarily extend to their children, who may experience different cultural, social, and economic influences that affect their marital stability. Every family is unique, and understanding the diverse factors behind marriage and divorce can help explain why some families stay together longer than others.

Key Takeaways

- Dating in the U.S. often starts casually, and relationships focus on respect and personal choice.
- In many immigrant communities, dating is often viewed as serious, and people may prefer to meet others from the same cultural background.
- Online dating can be risky, so it is important to be careful.
- Understanding cultural differences in dating and relationships helps prevent misunderstandings and build stronger connections.

Reflection Questions

1. In the U.S., dating usually starts casually, and people often talk openly about their feelings. How is this different from dating in your culture?
2. Respect and consent are important in dating. What are some ways to show respect and make sure both people feel comfortable on a date?

References

Baumeister, R. F., & Leary, M. R. (1995). The need to belong: Desire for interpersonal attachments as a fundamental human motivation. *Psychological Bulletin, 117*(3), 497-529.

Clark, M. (2019). *Emotional resilience: Handling breakups and moving forward.* Mindful Living Press.

Deseret News. (2021). *Are immigrant families more stable than native-born families?* Retrieved from https://www.deseret.com/indepth/2021/3/3/22309240/are-immigrant-families-more-stable-married-native-born-institute-family-studies-india-asia

Hofstede, G. (2001). *Culture's consequences: Comparing values, behaviors, institutions, and organizations across nations.* Sage Publications.

Institute for Family Studies. (2019). *Immigrant families are more stable.* Retrieved from https://ifstudies.org/blog/immigrant-families-are-more-stable

Johnson, R. (2021). *Building healthy relationships: Communication and respect in dating.* Relationship Studies Journal, 14(2), 19-35.

Kagitcibasi, C. (2007). *Family, self, and human development across cultures.* Lawrence Erlbaum Associates.

Matsumoto, D. (2000). *Culture and psychology: People around the world.* Wadsworth.

National Institute of Mental Health. (2022). *Social and emotional well-being in relationships.* Retrieved from www.nimh.nih.gov

ResearchGate. (2021). *Immigrant region of origin, divorce, and remarriage in the United States.* Retrieved from https://www.researchgate.net/publication/356022756_Immigrant_region_of_origin_divorce_and_remarriage_in_the_United_States

Ting-Toomey, S. (1999). *Communicating across cultures.* The Guilford Press.

Triandis, H. C. (1995). *Individualism & collectivism.* Westview Press.

Chapter 8: Handling Conflicts and Disagreements

Disagreements are a normal part of life. In the United States, it is common for people to experience disagreements in families, friendships, workplaces, and romantic relationships. Conflict is natural and can occur when people have different opinions, beliefs, or expectations. In some cultures, people try to avoid conflict, but in the U.S., many believe that discussing disagreements directly helps solve problems faster. This is not to say that everyone knows how to handle disagreements well. Everyone has mishandled a situation at least once. The key is to keep trying and growing. When handled well, conflict can strengthen relationships by building trust, improving understanding, and teaching better communication skills.

Communicating Through Conflict

The best way to handle a disagreement is through calm and respectful communication. Instead of yelling or ignoring the problem, try to:

- Listen to the other person's point of view without interrupting.
- Use "I" statements to express your feelings instead of blaming the other person.
- Work together to find a solution that is fair to both people.

For example, instead of saying, "You never return my things!" try saying, "I felt hurt when you forgot to return my book. Could you bring it back tomorrow?" A good "I" statement includes: A feeling word (such as hurt, frustrated, or disappointed), a description of the problem (such as forgetting to return a book), and a request for a solution (such as bringing the book back the next day).

Now, listen to their response. Maybe they were busy and forgot. It is always better to assume the person did not mean to hurt your feelings, as this prevents us from making negative assumptions about someone's intentions. Working together helps strengthen relationships.

Apologizing Effectively

If you make a mistake or hurt someone's feelings, a good apology can help fix the relationship. According to the Greater Good Science Center (2023), a good apology involves three steps:

1. Say you are sorry.
2. Acknowledge the mistake and explain how it affected the other person.
3. Offer a solution or promise to do better next time.

A bad apology might sound dismissive, like saying, "Sorry, whatever." A better apology would be, "I am sorry I forgot to return your book. I realize this caused you trouble with your teacher. Next time, I will return things on time." A good apology shows that you understand your mistake and care about making things right.

Conflict in Immigrant Families

For many immigrants, conflicts between parents and children can happen because of cultural differences. In some cultures, children must obey their parents without asking why. In the U.S., children are often encouraged to share their thoughts and make their own choices. These differences can cause misunderstandings, especially about dating, school choices, or future jobs.

Example of Cultural Conflict

Leah, a 16-year-old girl from Syria, wanted to attend a school dance, but her parents said no when she asked. In her parents' culture, dancing in public with boys was not acceptable, but for Leah, it was just a fun social event with friends. Instead of arguing, Leah used an "I" statement to explain her feelings: "I feel sad that I cannot go to the dance because my friends are all going, and I do not want to be the only one left out. Can we talk about it?"

Her parents listened and worked on a compromise. They agreed she could go if she went with a group of girls they already knew and was home by a certain time. She also promised not to dance with boys, which was not too difficult a compromise for her to make.

Mutual Support in Relationships

Healthy relationships should be balanced. This means helping each other with work, emotions, or responsibilities. It also involves giving as much as you receive in friendships and romantic relationships, while avoiding one-sided relationships where one person makes all the effort. A strong friendship or relationship is one where both people support and respect each other.

Taking Care of Yourself

Having a healthy relationship does not mean you should always be available for others. It is important to take care of yourself as well, and this is called self-care. Make time for self-care activities such as reading, listening to music, exercising, or spending time with family. It's also important to maintain different friendships and interests instead of focusing only on one person. Be flexible because, in the U.S., people often move for school or work, and friendships may change.

Learning from Conflict

Every relationship will have some disagreements. The important thing is how you handle them. In some cultures, people avoid conflict to keep peace, while in the U.S., people often express their opinions directly. No culture is right or wrong. Understanding different communication styles can help prevent misunderstandings. If a friendship or relationship does not work out, learn from the experience, move forward, and try again.

Case Study: Taking Things Too Literally

When Violet and her boyfriend had a huge fight, it was not immediately clear what caused it. She was busy planning a retirement party for her parents and was overwhelmed by how many things were going wrong. She felt that her boyfriend did not understand how important this event was to her. Her parents had worked hard their entire lives, and she wanted to honor them with a special celebration, something that is more common in the U.S. than in her home country.

Violet wanted everything to be perfect. She worried that if the food wasn't delicious, people might complain. She made a list of tasks for everyone to complete, but things were not getting done as quickly as needed. To make matters worse, the caterer got the order wrong. She asked her boyfriend to wait for the order to be fixed and bring the food to the party while she went ahead to finish decorating with a friend.

Her boyfriend, however, kept complaining and didn't seem very interested in helping. This frustrated Violet because she had always supported him when he needed help. Annoyed, she finally said, "I can't believe you're acting like this. I help you all the time! The one time I ask you for something, you make it so difficult!"

Her boyfriend angrily responded, "Well, you're being nasty."

Violet was shocked. "Nasty?! I'm being nasty?! That's how you talk to me?" She stormed out of the house, suddenly questioning whether this was the right relationship for her if this was how she was going to be treated.

Later, after they both had time to cool down, her boyfriend explained that to him, "nasty" simply meant "mean" or "rude." However, to Violet, the word had a very different meaning. She had only heard the word "nasty" in songs like *Nasty Girl*, where it implied something explicit or inappropriate. She had misunderstood his words, assuming he was insulting her in a much worse way than he had intended.

Lesson Learned: Words Can Have Different Meanings

This experience taught Violet an important lesson about language and communication. Words can carry different meanings depending on culture, personal experiences, and even the context in which they are used. For instance, the term "nasty" might be harmless in one setting but highly offensive in another. In relationships, especially multicultural ones, it's crucial to clarify misunderstandings instead of assuming the worst.

By learning to ask, "What do you mean by that?" or "What does that word mean to you?" rather than reacting immediately, people can avoid unnecessary conflict and strengthen their relationships. This approach can be compared to the idiom "to put the cart before the horse," which means taking actions in the wrong order; in communication, reacting before understanding is similarly backward and can lead to confusion and conflict.

Idioms are phrases or expressions whose meanings cannot be understood by simply analyzing the individual words. These words can easily lead to confusion as they need to be learned individually and often are puzzling to newcomers. They are metaphorical and culturally specific sayings that must be learned as they are used in conversation.

If you don't understand something, try asking someone or looking up the meaning of the word or phrase. If you are not completely sure what something means, or if you think someone may have insulted you, it's a good idea to ask the person if you misunderstood before reacting.

Key Takeaways

- Handling conflict is about calm communication and respectful disagreement.
- Using "I" statements helps solve problems without blaming the other person.
- A good apology includes saying sorry, acknowledging the mistake, and offering a solution.
- Healthy relationships require balance. Both people should put in effort.
- Cultural differences affect how people handle disagreements, especially in immigrant families.
- When you think you may have misunderstood someone's words or a phrase, ask what that phrase or word means to them so that you understand their intent.

Reflection Questions

1. How can using "I" statements help solve conflicts more effectively than blaming the other person? Write an example of an "I" statement that could be used in a disagreement with a friend.
2. What are the three key parts of an effective apology? Why do you think it is important to explain your mistake and offer a solution instead of just saying, "I'm sorry"?

References

Greater Good Science Center. 2023. *The Three Parts of an Effective Apology*. Retrieved from https://greatergood.berkeley.edu

SECTION 3: FINANCIAL LITERACY AND WORK CULTURE

Chapter 9: Understanding Money and Financial Rules in the U.S.

Many immigrants arrive in the United States believing the streets are "paved with gold" and that earning money will be easy. I have heard many unrealistic stories about people's plans to become wealthy after coming to the U.S. However, shortly after coming to the U.S., newcomers find the cost of living is high, and without financial knowledge, many struggle, working in less-than-ideal jobs that offer little room for financial mistakes. Learning how to manage money helps avoid common mistakes such as overspending, falling into debt, or failing to save for the future (Consumer Financial Protection Bureau [CFPB], 2023).

This chapter explains how to manage income, build savings, avoid debt, and plan for long-term financial security. Remember, in the U.S., people are expected to take responsibility for planning for their future.

Types of Money in the U.S.

Cash (Paper Money and Coins)

The U.S. dollar (USD) is the official currency in the U.S. Common forms of cash include coins, such as the penny (1 cent), nickel (5 cents), dime (10 cents), and quarter (25 cents), and paper money (bills) in denominations of $1, $5, $10, $20, $50, and $100.

Credit Cards, Debit Cards, and Digital Payments

Debit cards are linked to your bank account; you can only spend the money you have in your bank account. Credit cards allow you to borrow money, but you must repay it to avoid high-interest charges (CFPB, 2023). If you use credit cards, pay the balance off each month and do not charge more that you can pay so you do not build up debts.

Digital Payments: Apps like PayPal, Venmo, Apple Pay, and Cash App allow users to send and receive money electronically.

Banking in the U.S.

Opening a Bank Account

Opening a bank account is a recommended way to safely store money. Checking accounts are used for daily expenses such as rent, groceries, and bills, while savings accounts help store money for emergencies and earn interest (U.S. Department of Treasury, 2023). To open a bank account, you need a valid ID (such as a passport, state ID, or driver's license), proof of address (such as a bill or lease agreement), and a Social Security Number (SSN) or Individual Taxpayer Identification Number (ITIN).

Overdraft Fees

If you spend more money than you have in your checking account, the bank may allow the transaction but charge an overdraft fee, which can be as high as $35 per transaction (CFPB, 2023). Always check your balance to make sure you can cover anything that you are taking out to avoid these fees.

High-Yield Savings Accounts: A Better Way to Save

A high-yield savings account is a special type of savings account that helps your money grow faster than a regular savings account.

Why Use a High-Yield Savings Account?

A high-yield savings account offers several benefits:

- Earn More Money – The higher the interest rate, the more your money grows.
- Safe and Secure – Your money is protected and insured up to $250,000 per person per bank (FDIC, 2024).
- Great for Emergency Funds – Helps you save 3 to 6 months' worth of living expenses for unexpected events. This is the amount of money you would need to cover all your basic needs for up to six months. If you do not have enough saved to cover 3 to 6 months, building your emergency fund should be a priority.

How to Open a High-Yield Savings Account
1. Compare Banks – Online banks often offer higher interest rates than traditional banks.
2. Check for Fees – Find an account with no fees or minimum balance requirements.
3. Apply Online or In-Person – You will need identification (passport, driver's license, or state ID) and proof of address.
4. Deposit Money – Start with any amount and let your savings grow.

Below is a comparison of a regular saving account to a high yield saving account with 4% interest rate. By choosing a high-yield savings account, you can grow your money faster while keeping it safe and accessible for the future.

Account Type	Interest Rate	Money Saved	Interest Earned (1 Year)
Regular Savings	0.1%	$1,000	$1
High-Yield Savings	4.0%	$1,000	$40

Paying Taxes

Taxes fund schools, roads, and government services (Internal Revenue Service [IRS], 2023). In the U.S., there are different types of taxes. Income tax is taken directly from your paycheck. Federal tax is required by the U.S. government, while state tax is an additional tax that some states charge (IRS, 2023). If you overpay taxes, you may receive a tax refund when you file your tax forms.

Every adult who earns income must file taxes by April 15 each year (IRS, 2023). This is the law. You can hire a tax specialist or file taxes yourself.

What You Need to File Taxes?

To file taxes, you will need:

- Social Security Number (SSN) or Individual Taxpayer Identification Number (ITIN)
- W-2 Form (from your employer) or 1099 Form (if self-employed)
- Bank account information (for direct deposit refunds)
- Previous tax return (if applicable)
- Receipts for deductions (such as education expenses or medical costs)

Filing taxes correctly ensures you follow the law and, in some cases, receive money back through a tax refund.

Earning Money and Jobs

The minimum wage is the lowest hourly pay allowed by law, currently set at $7.25 per hour, though some states have higher wages (U.S. Department of Labor, 2023). In addition to wages, the U.S. has a strong tipping culture, especially in service industries. Waiters rely on tips because their base pay is often lower than the minimum wage, so it is customary to tip 15–20% of the bill (CFPB, 2023). Other workers, such as taxi drivers, hairdressers, hotel staff, and delivery workers, also depend on tips to supplement their income. Not tipping is considered rude and can upset workers who rely on tips to pay their bills. Understanding and following tipping practices is an important part of daily life in the U.S.

Case Study: Miguel's Surprise

Miguel moved to the U.S. from Colombia, hoping that earning money would be easy. Back home, he had a college degree and a good job, but when he arrived, he was surprised to learn that his qualifications were not accepted. Instead of finding a well-paying job, he had to work long hours at a low-paying job, struggling to pay for rent and daily expenses.

As he adjusted to his new life, Miguel realized that and finding ways to earn more money were important. He had to change his expectations and accept that success in the U.S. would take time, require learning new skills, and involve advancing to a higher-paying job. Even though it was hard, he learned that with patience and effort, he could build a better future.

Lesson Learned: Adjust Your Expectations

Many immigrants come to the U.S. with unrealistic expectations about making money. It is important to adapt quickly to your new reality, manage money wisely, and look for better opportunities to build a stable life in a new country. Remember to also be frugal and not change this habit due to the increased pressure to purchase more items. Material items do not make us happy; having people in our lives who accept and value us, experiencing new and positive things, and being grateful for what we have do.

Credit in the U.S.

Credit is borrowing money and paying it back later. Your ability to manage credit is measured by your credit score, a number between 300 and 850 that shows how good you are at repaying debt. A high credit score (700 or above) makes it easier to get loans for big purchases, such as a house (CFPB, 2023).

How to Build Credit (Simple Steps)
- Get a credit card – Use it for small purchases and pay the full amount every month.
- Pay bills on time – This includes rent, utilities, and phone bills.
- Avoid too much debt – Do not borrow more than you can afford to repay.
- Keep old accounts open – The longer your credit history, the better your score.

Budgeting and Living Expenses

A budget helps control spending and allows for saving toward future goals. A common method is the 50/30/20 rule, which provides a general guideline for dividing income into three categories: needs, wants, and savings. This rule serves as a good starting point for managing personal finances effectively. According to this method, 50% of income should go toward needs, such as rent, food, and bills. 30% can be used for wants, including entertainment and shopping. The remaining 20% should be set aside for savings and debt repayment. Following this guideline can help create financial stability and ensure long-term security.

Maria's Budget

Maria works full-time, earning $12 per hour for 40 hours per week. Her monthly gross income is $1,920, but after an estimated 17% tax deduction, her take-home pay is about $1,600. Despite her limited income, Maria wants to follow the 50/30/20 rule to save money each month, which she has not been doing successfully. By carefully budgeting her expenses, she hopes to balance her needs (50%), wants (30%), and savings or debt repayment (20%), helping her build financial stability over time.

Maria's Monthly Budget

Expenses	Amount ($)	Category
Rent	875	Needs
Utilities	120	Needs
Groceries	250	Needs
Transportation	50	Needs
Phone/Internet	80	Needs
Savings	35	Savings & Debt
Debt Payments	50	Savings & Debt

Entertainment	100	Wants
Clothing	40	Wants
Total	**1600**	

Maria's Budget Allocation

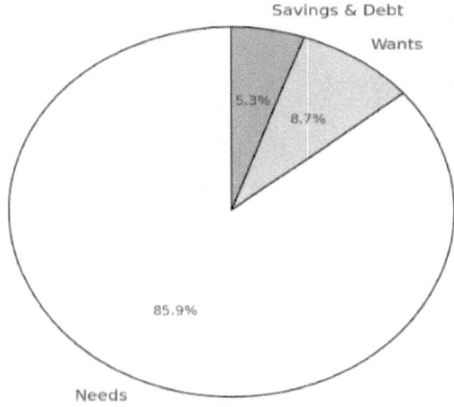

Maria's budget allows her to cover all her essential expenses and save a small amount each month. She spends about 86% ($1,375) of her take-home pay on needs, such as rent, bills, food, and transportation. For wants, including entertainment and clothing, she sets aside 9% ($140). Lastly, she contributes 5% ($85) toward savings and debt payments.

While Maria is able to manage her daily expenses, she is not saving enough to build long-term financial stability. Now that she understands her budget, she wants to reduce her spending on needs and bring it closer to the recommended 50%. This would allow her to increase her savings and have more flexibility for things she enjoys.

Budget Adjustment

Since her rent and bills are too high, Maria decides to make changes. She switches to a cheaper phone and internet plan (now $50) and finds a roommate to split the cost of rent and utilities (now $479.50), which were taking up too much of her income. These changes allow Maria to bring her spending on needs closer to 50%, save more money, and still enjoy occasional entertainment.

By following the 50/30/20 rule, Maria is working toward a more balanced budget. These small but important changes can improve her financial situation, helping her build stability and enjoy more freedom in the future.

Saving for Retirement

Many immigrants believe family will support them in retirement, but it is important to be financially independent.

Case Study: Indira's Story

Indira worked tirelessly for 30 years, believing that her husband and children would support her in retirement. She never prioritized saving, assuming that with her husband's income and her children's success, she would be financially secure. At 67 years old, she finally retired, expecting to rest after decades of hard work. However, reality was much different.

Her Social Security check was only $1,000 per month, barely enough to cover basic expenses. The amount was lower than expected due to high healthcare costs and a late start to retirement savings. She had no personal savings, no pension, and no financial backup plan.

Just when she thought she could rely on her husband, he decided to return to their home country, leaving her behind. Their marriage ended, and she found herself alone. She had always believed that her children would help take care of her, but they had moved away several years earlier and were now busy with their own lives, families, and financial struggles. While they still loved her, they couldn't afford to support her. They had their own responsibilities and loved ones to support.

The bills piled up — rent, utilities, food, and healthcare. She had spent her life giving to others, but now no one was there to help her. Every month, she had to choose between groceries and medical bills, between keeping the lights on or buying the medicine she needed.

For the first time in her life, Indira felt helpless. She had trusted that her family would take care of her, but now she was alone, struggling, and afraid. Had she saved even a small amount each month, invested wisely, and planned ahead, she could have avoided this painful reality.

Lesson Learned: Saving is Important

Start saving early, even if it is only $10 per month. Do not depend on others for financial security. In many countries, families support their elders, but in the U.S., retirees are expected to be financially independent. Children often move away for work or school and may not be able to cover your expenses.

Social Security is not enough to cover rent, food, and medical bills. Healthcare is expensive, and without savings, many elderly people struggle or must work longer than they would like. Learn about ways to prepare for a secure retirement and begin saving now, so you do not struggle later in life.

Please make sure that all assets, anything you own or include in your financial plans, are in both your name and your spouse's name. If the worst happens, you may not be able to access accounts or income that are not legally shared, including your spouse's earnings. It's okay to hope for the best, but it's wise to prepare for the worst. Taking these steps ensures that you are protected and provided for, no matter what happens to your spouse.

Retirement Saving Tips

Now that you understand the importance of preparing for the future, it's time to consider your options for where to save your money. Below are some of the main ways to save for retirement.

1. 401(k) Plan: Save with Your Job
   Many employers offer a 401(k) retirement plan where you can save money before taxes are taken out of your paycheck. Some companies will match what you put in, which means free money for your retirement. Always contribute at least enough to get the company match, because it helps your savings grow faster. This is the first and best step toward building your retirement savings.

2. Roth IRA: Save on Your Own
   A Roth IRA is a personal retirement account that grows tax-free. This means you do not have to pay extra taxes when you take the money out in retirement. However, simply putting money into a Roth IRA is not enough. You must manually invest it, such as in an index fund like VOO (which tracks the S&P 500), to ensure your money grows over time. If your company does not offer a 401(k), or if you already contributed enough to get the company match, the next best step is to regularly contribute to a Roth IRA, up to the yearly contribution limit of $7,000. The earlier you start, the better, because your money benefits from compound interest, which means your savings grow on top of the interest you already earned.

3. Avoid Expensive Purchases: Do Not Waste Money
   Many people buy new cars or luxury items instead of saving. A new car loses value as soon as you drive it, so it is better to buy a reliable used car and invest your savings instead. Avoid spending on brand-new electronics, designer clothes, and expensive vacations if you have not saved for retirement first.

4. Buy Assets: Own Things That Grow in Value
   An asset is something that increases in value over time and helps you build wealth. Instead of spending money on things that lose value, focus on buying assets that will benefit you in the long run. Below are three examples of assets:

70

- Rental property: Buying a home or apartment and renting it out can provide extra income.
- Stocks: Investing in companies can grow your wealth over time.
- Small business ownership: Running a business can generate long-term financial success.

Reminder: Avoid spending on things that lose value, such as the latest phone models, brand-new furniture, or expensive vacations, if you have not prioritized saving for your future.

Making Smarter Purchases

When we need to buy things, we can still make smart choices. Being a smart shopper means thinking carefully before spending money. Here are some simple ways to make better purchasing decisions:

- Before you buy something, check a few websites online to see if you are getting a good deal.
- Use coupons and look for sales and discounts, especially during the off-season when items like clothes are cheaper.
- Sometimes, used items are just as good as new ones but cost less. You can find these at thrift stores or online marketplaces.
- Join Facebook groups or community pages where people trade, borrow, or give away items for free.
- If you are only going to use an item once, does it make sense to buy it? Consider saving money by renting or borrowing it instead. For example, you could rent a power washer.
- Outlet stores sell items at lower prices, and shopping here can save you money.
- Even when buying essentials, avoid impulsive purchases by waiting 24 hours to make a purchase. This gives you time to decide if you really need the item or if it was just a momentary desire.
- Remember: just because an item is on sale does not mean you need to buy it. The less we spend now, the more we can save for our future.

Key Takeaways

- Be careful with credit and only spend what you can afford to pay back. Using credit wisely helps you stay financially stable.
- Track your expenses. Spend less than you earn to avoid debt, and start saving early for retirement.
- Save enough money to cover 3 to 6 months of expenses before you start investing.
- Having an emergency fund is very important, so keep your savings in a high-yield savings account where it can earn more interest than a regular savings account.
- Ask for help when you need it. Financial advisors and bank representatives can give you good advice to help you make smart choices.

Reflection Questions

1. What financial mistakes did Indira and Miguel make, and how could they have planned better?
2. Write down everything you spend in a month in a budget. Does your budget follow 50/30/20 rule?
3. Why is it important to have an emergency fund before investing?

References

Consumer Financial Protection Bureau. (2023). *Building Credit and Managing Debt*. Retrieved from https://www. consumer finance.gov

Federal Deposit Insurance Corporation. (2024). *Your insured deposits*. https://www.fdic.gov/deposit-insurance/your-insured-deposits-brochure-english

Internal Revenue Service (IRS). (2023). *Guide to U.S. Taxes*. Retrieved from https://www.irs.gov

U.S. Department of Treasury. (2023). *Understanding U.S. Currency and Banking Rules*. Retrieved from https:// home.treasury.gov

U.S. Department of Labor. (2023). *Minimum Wage Laws*. Retrieved from https://www.dol.go

Chapter 10: Renting and Buying a Home – Understanding Leases, Apartments, and Homeownership

The "American Dream" is the belief that in America, everyone should have the chance to succeed and be happy, no matter where they come from or how much money their family has. It's about having freedom, the opportunity to grow, and the chance to live a good life. For many people coming to America, buying a house is a big goal and a part of the American Dream. Owning a house means you have your own space and can feel more stable. It's also a way to save and grow money over time. But buying a house can be tough because you need to understand a lot about money, loans, and sometimes houses are very expensive. Some people decide to rent a house first, which means they pay to live there every month, before they think about buying one. This way, they can take their time to learn about how it all works and save money for their future house.

Understanding Leases and Renting a Home

A lease is a legal document that sets up an agreement between a landlord (the owner) and a tenant (the renter). According to the American Bar Association (2023), it outlines how long the tenant can stay, the cost of the rent, and the rules for using the property. This agreement is important because it protects both parties involved:

- The landlord gets assurance that the tenant will pay the rent on time.
- The tenant has a guaranteed right to stay in the home without the risk of sudden eviction. Eviction is a legal process in which a landlord can remove a tenant from the property, typically for not paying rent or breaking the lease terms.

If a tenant does not follow the lease rules, such as having a pet when pets are not allowed, the landlord has the right to end the lease early

(National Association of Realtors, 2022). The lease also benefits the tenant by fixing the rent price during the lease period and ensuring that necessary repairs are made.

When looking for an apartment, review all of these before signing a lease:

- Location: Check the distance to stores, schools, and your workplace.
- Budget: Your rent should not be more than one-third of your monthly income (Mayo Clinic, 2022).
- Amenities: Look for useful features like parking, access to public transportation, or extra storage space.
- Rules: Make sure you understand the policies on pets, visitors, and other restrictions.
- Application: Some landlords may charge an application fee. Be sure to ask about this before applying for an apartment to avoid unexpected expenses.
- Credit Score: Many landlords will check your credit score to see if you reliably pay your bills. If you are renting for the first time, you might need a cosigner, a family member or friend who agrees to pay the rent if you cannot (Consumer Financial Protection Bureau, 2023).
- Inspect the Apartment: You can find an apartment though rental websites, real estate agencies, or local listings. It's important to visit the apartment in person before you sign any lease.

Finally, be cautious of scams. If an offer seems too good to be true, it probably is a scam. Do not hand over any money if something feels suspicious (Federal Trade Commission, 2023).

Moving Into an Apartment

Setting Up Utilities

Before moving in, set up electricity, water, and gas. Some landlords include these in the rent, while others do not. Also, arrange services like internet, phone, and cable TV if needed (Federal Communications Commission, 2022).

Renter's Insurance

Many landlords require renter's insurance, which protects belongings if they are stolen or damaged by fire, leaks, or vandalism (Insurance Information Institute, 2023). It is usually affordable and recommended.

Preparing Your Apartment

- Check for repairs – Look for any damage and inform your landlord of what you find before moving in. Take pictures as proof in case there are any disputes later.
- Clean before unpacking – It is easier to clean an empty space.
- Get basic furniture – Most renters need a bed, table, chairs, and kitchen supplies.
- Plan for laundry – Some buildings have laundry rooms, while others require using a laundromat.

Steps to Buying a House

Some people choose to buy a home instead of renting. Buying a home is a long-term financial commitment, but it allows you to build wealth over time (National Association of Realtors, 2022). There are many steps to take to prepare for buying a home.

1. Save for a down payment – A down payment is the amount of money you pay upfront when buying a home. Most lenders require at least three to twenty percent of the home's price (Fannie Mae, 2023).
2. Check your credit score – A higher credit score helps you get a lower interest rate on a loan (Consumer Financial Protection Bureau, 2023).
3. Get pre-approved for a loan – A bank or lender will tell you how much you can afford. Most landers require proof of stable income and good credit score to approve a mortgage.
4. Find a real estate agent – Look for one who comes recommended and is willing to negotiate and lower their fee.
5. Choose a home – Consider location, size, and future value.
6. Make an offer – If accepted, you enter a contract to buy the home.

7. Home inspection – A professional checks the home for problems before you buy it.
8. Close the deal – Finalize the loan and sign the papers. You now own the home!

Buying a home also comes with extra costs like property taxes, insurance, and maintenance (U.S. Department of Housing and Urban Development, 2023). Property taxes are paid each year in the U.S., even when the house is paid off.

Case Study: Helping My Parents Buy a House

At age 16, I helped my parents buy a house because they didn't speak much English. I had to be their translator, assisting with bank communication, negotiations, and paperwork. It was a stressful time, but I was used to handling important responsibilities for my family.

Negotiating the price of the home was challenging. My father wanted to lower the price by pointing out problems like a damaged roof and walls. It was awkward to translate everything, but I ensured the message was clear and professional. This worked; the owner lowered the price!

Another challenge was understanding the mortgage rules. If buyers don't pay at least 20% of the price upfront, they must pay private mortgage insurance (PMI). This would cost at least about $100 extra a month. My father did not want to pay this and was negotiating for a few days with the seller and the bank. Instead of paying PMI, my father negotiated a lower interest rate with the bank by paying a few thousand dollars upfront to reduce the mortgage rate instead. This also saved him money in the long run.

Find out why the house is on the market so you can use that to your advantage. The seller had inherited the house and lived far away. He wanted to sell quickly and avoid maintenance. My father convinced the bank to waive PMI due to the seller's urgency, and the bank was flexible. Waiving PMI saved us a lot of money.

Lessons Learned: Negotiating When Buying a House is Possible

The bank waived PMI, saving us money. Negotiating, while it was a little uncomfortable for me, paid off. The seller accepted our offer, eager to close the deal and get his inheritance. I ensured all paperwork and payments were correct, securing our new home!

Key Takeaways

- Leases protect both landlords and renters. A lease outlines the rules, rent, and rights of both sides (American Bar Association, 2023).
- Renting needs planning. Make a budget, check what amenities are included, and be careful of rental scams before signing a lease (Federal Trade Commission, 2023).
- Take pictures of any damage in the apartment before you move in. This can help avoid problems with the landlord later.
- Renter's insurance keeps your things safe. It covers your belongings from theft, fire, or damage and is often required (Insurance Information Institute, 2023).
- Buying a home is a long-term investment. It needs a down payment, good credit, and careful financial planning (National Association of Realtors, 2022).
- Find a trusted real estate agent. Working with an agent who agrees to a lower fee can save you money.
- Homeownership has extra costs. Property taxes, maintenance, and insurance should be part of your budget (U.S. Department of Housing and Urban Development, 2023).

Reflection Questions

1. What is the difference between renting a home and buying a home? Which one would you prefer to do?
2. What questions should you ask before renting or buying a home?

References

American Bar Association. (2023). *Understanding leases and rental agreements*. Retrieved from https://www.american bar.org

Consumer Financial Protection Bureau. (2023). *Understanding credit scores and rental applications*. https://www. consumerfinance.gov

Fannie Mae. (2023). *Guide to home buying and mortgages*. https://www.fanniemae.com

Federal Communications Commission. (2022). *Setting up internet and phone services*. https://www.fcc.gov

Federal Trade Commission. (2023). *Avoiding rental and housing scams*. https://www.ftc.gov

Insurance Information Institute. (2023). *What is renter's insurance and why do you need it?* https://www.iii.org

Mayo Clinic. (2022). *Financial wellness and budgeting for rent*. https://www.mayoclinic.org

National Association of Realtors. (2022). *Steps to renting and buying a home*. https://www.nar.realtor

U.S. Department of Housing and Urban Development. (2023). *Guide to homeownership and mortgage loans*. https://www.hud.gov

Chapter 11: Job Interview Procedure and Skills for Newcomers

Moving to a new country is exciting but can also be challenging, especially when looking for a job. This guide will help newcomers to the U.S. understand how to apply for jobs, prepare for interviews, and succeed in the workplace. Trusted resources and citations are included for each step, as well as some examples of each step of the process.

Step 1: How to Apply for a Job

First, you will learn the steps to apply for a job. These steps include finding job openings, writing a resume and cover letter, and completing job applications.

Find Job Openings

Search for jobs on these websites for job openings:

- Indeed – www.indeed.com
- LinkedIn Jobs – www.linkedin.com/jobs
- Glassdoor – www.glassdoor.com
- USAJobs (Government jobs) – www.usajobs.gov
- CareerOneStop – www.careeronestop.org

Create a Resume

Create a resume that represents you well. A resume lists your experience and skills. It is a good strategy to customize your resume for the job you are applying for. For example, review the job posting to identify the required qualifications and see if your previous experiences can be tailored to match those qualifications. If the job requires someone who is organized, be sure to specify how you organized aspects of your previous job.

- Zety Resume Builder – zety.com/resume-builder
- Canva Resume Templates – www.canva.com/resumes/templates
- ChatGPT –https://chat.openai.com

A sample resume is included below.

Your Name
Address
Contact phone
Contact Email

Objective
Dedicated and skilled Machine Operator with over 5 years of experience in operating and maintaining various types of machinery, seeking to bring expertise in efficient production techniques and safety procedures to XYZ Manufacturing.

Professional Experience
ABC Manufacturing Co., Reading, USA
Machine Operator
June 2019 – Present
- Operate CNC machines and other manufacturing equipment with precision and adherence to all safety standards.
- Monitor production to ensure compliance with specifications and make necessary adjustments to maintain quality.
- Conduct regular maintenance checks on machinery to prevent breakdowns and prolong equipment lifespan.
- Collaborate with team members to optimize production processes, resulting in a 15% increase in efficiency.
- Train new operators, emphasizing safety, quality, and company standards.

Production Company, Reading, USA
Assistant Machine Operator
May 2015 – May 2018
- Assisted in setting up machinery for operation by adjusting tools and loading materials.
- Helped maintain equipment and troubleshoot minor mechanical issues under supervision.
- Recorded production output and participated in team meetings to discuss improvements.
- Followed strict safety protocols and contributed to achieving the company's safety record of zero incidents during my tenure.

Education
GHI Technical Institute, Anytown, USA
Certificate in Machine Operation
Graduated: May 2015

Skills
- Proficient in operating CNC and PLC systems.
- Strong mechanical and troubleshooting skills.
- Excellent attention to detail and adherence to safety protocols.
- Able to read blueprints and technical diagrams.

- Effective communication and teamwork skills.

Certifications
- Certified Production Technician (CPT)
- OSHA Safety Certification

Write a Cover Letter

A cover letter explains why you want the job, so be sure to create a cover letter for a job you are applying for. A cover letter should have a greeting, say which job you want, explain why you are a good worker for that job, thank the employer, and end with your name. Use Purdue OWL Cover Letter Guide – owl.purdue.edu as a resource.

A sample cover letter is included here.

Your Name
Your Address

Employers Name
Employer Address

Dear [Employer's Name],

I am applying for the [Job Title] position at [Company Name] that I saw advertised on [Where You Found the Job Posting]. I believe that my skills in [mention a key skill or area, such as customer service, technology, etc.] make me a good fit for this job.

I have worked at [Your Last Company or Relevant Experience], where I learned a lot about [mention a relevant skill or task]. I think I can do well at [Company Name] because I am hardworking and learn quickly.

Please find my resume attached for more information about my work history and skills. I am very interested in this job and hope to hear from you soon. Thank you for considering my application.

Sincerely,

[Your Signature (if sending via mail)]
[Your Typed Name]

Submit Your Application

When you apply for a job, you need to fill out a job application. This is a form that asks questions about you to help the employer see if you are a good match for the job. Most applications are online, but some are still on paper.

Before you apply, read the job listing carefully and follow all instructions. Here is what you usually need to include:

1. Personal information: Provide your name, address, phone number, and email. Some jobs may also ask for your Social Security number.
2. Job details: Write the name of the job you are applying for, how much you want to get paid, when you can start, and if you want to work full-time, part-time, or temporarily.
3. Educational background: List the schools you attended, degrees or certifications earned, and any special awards or honors.
4. Work experience: Include the names of places where you worked before, what your job was, what you did, how long you worked there, and the names and phone numbers of your supervisors.
5. Skills and qualifications: Talk about the things you know how to do, like using a computer, speaking other languages, or special training you have had.
6. References: These are people (not family) who can talk about your work. Ask them for permission before writing their name. Tell them about the job you are applying for so they can be ready.
7. Availability: Some applications ask when you are available to work or if you can move to a new place for the job.
8. Legal questions: You may need to answer if you can work in the U.S. or if you have a criminal record.
9. Optional questions: Some forms ask about your gender, race, veteran status, or disability. You do not have to answer these. They are only used to learn more about who is applying.
10. Signature and date: At the end of the application, you must sign and write the date. This shows that your answers are true and correct.

After you finish your application:

- Upload or attach your resume and cover letter if required.
- Check your email often to see if the employer contacts you.

Important: Fill out your application carefully and honestly. This helps the employer see why you are a good person for the job.

Step 2: Preparing for the Interview

In this section, you will learn how to research the company, dress professionally, plan your trip, prepare for interview questions, and get ready for both in-person and online interviews.

Research the Company

Before your interview, be sure to visit the company's website as well as the following websites to gather comprehensive information about the company and its industry. Researching a company before you apply for a job is very important for many reasons. First, it helps you write your application and resume to match what the company is looking for, which makes you a stronger candidate. Knowing about the company also prepares you for the interview, so you can talk confidently about the company's work and ask smart questions. This shows you are really interested in the job. Understanding the company's situation helps you decide if you will enjoy working there and if the job fits your career goals. Plus, when you know more about the company, you can better discuss your salary. Overall, researching a company shows you are serious about the job and helps you make sure it's the right place for you.

- Glassdoor (Company reviews) – www.glassdoor.com
- LinkedIn (Company profiles) – www.linkedin.com

Practice Common Questions

Practicing interview questions helps you feel more confident and ready. When you practice, you learn how to talk about your skills, experience, and goals. It also helps you speak more clearly and understand what the employer might ask. This way, you will not feel as nervous, and you can give better answers during the interview.

Employers may ask:

"Tell me about yourself."

"Why do you want this job?"

"What are your strengths and weaknesses?"

"Why should we hire you?"

"How do you handle stress and pressure?"

Practice answering interview questions until you feel comfortable with your answers, using these resources:

- Big Interview – www.biginterview.com
- Indeed Interview Guide – www.indeed.com/career-advice/interviewing

Dress Professionally

Your clothing should match the job level. The level of professionalism required for each job varies depending on industry, workplace culture, and specific role. Guidelines are included here: The Balance Careers Dress Code Guide – www.thebalancemoney.com/dress-for-a-job-interview-2058432

Plan Your Trip

For in-person interviews, it's good to arrive about 20 minutes early. This helps you feel relaxed and ready. Here's how you can find the best way to get there:

- Google Maps – www.google.com/maps. This tool helps you see different ways to travel, like driving, walking, or taking the bus (Google, n.d.). It also shows you how busy the roads are so you can plan ahead.
- Uber – www.uber.com or Lyft – www.lyft.com. You can book a ride to your interview using Uber or Lyft. Both services allow you to see the cost before you book and track the driver's arrival (Uber, n.d.; Lyft, n.d.). This way, you can ensure you leave with enough time to arrive early for your interview.

Online Interviews

For online interviews, it's important to prepare your setting to make a good impression. Here are some steps to help you get ready:

- Choose a quiet place where you won't be disturbed by noise or interruptions. This helps you focus and allows the interviewer to hear you clearly.
- Make sure your internet is working well. A good connection helps you avoid problems during the interview.
- Test your microphone and camera before the interview. This makes sure the interviewer can see and hear you clearly.
- Pick a simple and clean background. This helps you look professional and organized.
- Log in at least 5–10 minutes before the interview to check your internet, audio, and video. This shows you are on time and well-prepared.

Step 3: During the Interview

Interviewers want to see that you are polite, confident, and can fit into the work culture at their company. Polite and confident people smile, speak clearly, make eye contact, and sit up straight. When you enter the interview, greet the interviewer with a smile and introduce yourself clearly. Speak confidently, maintain eye contact, and show enthusiasm for the job. Practicing these skills will help you feel more comfortable and make a great impression in your interview.

For questions about your experience, use the STAR method (Situation, Task, Action, Result) to describe past work experiences clearly and effectively. Here's how you can use it:

1. Situation – Describe a specific situation or challenge you faced.
2. Task – Explain your responsibility or what needed to be done.
3. Action – Describe the steps you took to solve the problem.
4. Result – Share the outcome of your actions and what you learned.

For example, if you are asked about a time you handled a difficult customer, this is how you can use the STAR method to answer:

- Situation: In my previous job as a cashier, a customer was upset because they were charged twice for an item.
- Task: My job was to stay calm, listen carefully, and fix the mistake.
- Action: I checked the receipt, apologized for the mistake, and refunded the extra charge. I also explained how the issue could be prevented in the future.
- Result: The customer appreciated my help and left satisfied. My manager praised me for handling the situation professionally.

If you want to improve your confidence with answering questions, two helpful resources you can use to practice are Toastmasters (Public Speaking Skills) – www.toastmasters.org and MindTools (Interview Confidence Tips) – www.mindtools.com.

Answer Questions Clearly

Pay attention to the interviewer's questions. Take a moment to think before answering and make sure your responses are clear and to the point. Keep your answers short and focused, and provide examples from your past experience to support your answers. A helpful resource for interview preparation is the Job-Hunt Interview Guide at www.job-hunt.org.

Ask the Interviewer Questions

At the end of the interview, you can ask questions to show your interest in the job. Some good questions include: "What are the next steps in the hiring process?" or "Can you describe a typical day in this role?" For more ideas, you can check out the Harvard Business Review Interview Questions at hbr.org.

Thank the Interviewer

Before leaving, always thank the interviewer. You can say, "Thank you for your time. I look forward to hearing from you." This leaves a positive impression and shows professionalism.

Step 4: After the Interview

Send a Thank-You Email
It is a good idea to send a thank-you email after your interview. Do this within 24 hours after the interview. Be sure to thank the interviewer for their time, mention something specific you discussed, express excitement about the job, and keep it short and professional.

A sample thank-you email is included here.

Subject: Thank You for the Interview

Dear [Interviewer's Name],

Thank you for taking the time to speak with me today about the [Job Title] position at [Company Name]. I appreciate the opportunity to learn more about the role and your team.

I am very excited about the possibility of joining [Company Name] and believe my skills in [mention a relevant skill] would be a great fit. Please let me know if you need any more information from me.

Again, I appreciate your time and look forward to hearing from you soon.
Best regards,

[Your Name]
[Your Email]
[Your Phone Number]

For more step-by-step directions, see the Indeed Thank-You Guide: www.indeed.com/career-advice/interviewing/how-to-write-a-thank-you-email

Follow Up if Needed
Wait about one week before following up after you have sent your think-you email. A follow-up is a short email asking about the next steps. This shows that you are still interested in the job and reminds the employer about your application.

A sample follow-up email is included here.

Subject: Following Up

Dear [Interviewer's Name],

I hope you are doing well. I wanted to follow up on my interview for the [Job Title] position at [Company Name] on [Interview Date]. I am still very interested in the role and wanted to check if there are any updates on the hiring process. Please let me know if you need any more information from me. I appreciate your time and look forward to hearing from you.

Best regards,

[Your Name]
[Your Email]
[Your Phone Number]

For detailed step-by-step directions, see LinkedIn Career Blog – www.linkedin.com/advice

Learn from Rejections

If you don't get the job, you can politely ask for feedback via email. Feedback can be effective in helping you learn what to improve for your next interview. Keep your email short and professional, thanking the employer for their time and asking for any suggestions.

A sample email asking for feedback is included here.

Subject: Thank You and Request for Feedback
Dear [Interviewer's Name],

Thank you for considering me for the [Job Title] position at [Company Name]. While I am disappointed that I wasn't selected, I truly appreciate the opportunity to interview and learn more about your team.

If possible, I would love to receive any feedback on my interview performance. Understanding how I can improve will help me in future opportunities.

Thank you again for your time, and I hope to stay in touch.
Best regards,

[Your Name]

For more detailed guidance, check out The Muse Job Rejection Guide: www.themuse.com.

Step 5: Onboarding – Starting Your New Job

Lastly, once you have been hired, you will still need to know about the onboarding process. This includes completing paperwork, attending orientation (which is a type of training for new employees), understanding workplace rules, improving communication, and learning strategies for career growth.

Complete Paperwork

Each of these documents is designed to help ensure you are legally compliant.

Employers may require:

- I-9 Form (Work Authorization) – www.uscis.gov/i-9-central. This form is used in the U.S. to make sure that employees are legally allowed to work. It involves providing documents that prove you can work in the country (U.S. Citizenship and Immigration Services, n.d.). You can find more information and the form itself at the U.S. Citizenship and Immigration Services website.
- W-4 Form (Tax Withholding) – www.irs.gov. This form is used by employers to determine how much federal income tax to withhold from your paycheck (Internal Revenue Service, n.d.). You provide information about your filing status and any other important information affecting your taxes. You can find this form on the Internal Revenue Service (IRS) website.

Orientation

Orientation is the training you get when you start a new job. Not every company has formal orientation, but many do. It helps you learn about the company, your job duties, and the rules you need to follow. Orientation is a good time to ask questions and understand how to do your job well.

Learn Workplace Rules

Every company has different policies. These may be discussed at an orientation training that some workplaces have. Read:

- EEOC – Workplace Rights – www.eeoc.gov. The Equal Employment Opportunity Commission (EEOC) provides information on your rights as an employee in the U.S., including protections against workplace discrimination (Equal Employment Opportunity Commission, n.d). This information can be found on their website.
- SHRM – Workplace Etiquette – www.shrm.org. The Society for Human Resource Management (SHRM) offers guidance on workplace etiquette, which includes how to behave professionally and interact with colleagues (Society for Human Resource Management, n.d). More details are available on their website.

Improve Workplace Communication

It is a good idea to work on your communication skills for the workplace. Courses for workplace communication:

- Coursera – Business English – www.coursera.org. This platform offers courses designed to help non-native speakers improve their English language skills, particularly in business contexts (Coursera, n.d.). These courses can help with writing, speaking, and understanding English in the workplace.
- Khan Academy – Soft Skills – www.khanacademy.org. Khan Academy provides resources on "soft skills" like communication, teamwork, and problem-solving, which are crucial for success in any job (Khan Academy, n.d.). These skills help you interact effectively with others at work.

Strategies for Career Advancement in Business

Career paths in business and education are different. Teachers often stay in the same job for many years. In business, you might need to change jobs more often to advance in position, especially if there's no more room to grow or learn in your current job.

To advance in business, consider these strategies:

- Learn from Every Job: Each job teaches you new things.
- Start at a Small Company: It might be easier to become a leader in a smaller company.
- Have Support: If you have support from family, friends, or savings, it's easier to take risks and change jobs.

In the U.S., people with more money often use their connections, go to well-known schools, and meet the right people to find better jobs. If you don't have these advantages, you can still succeed by working hard and moving up step by step.

How to Make Your Own Opportunities:

- Meet People in Your Field: Talk to other professionals and make friends with them.
- Get Recommendations: Ask your teachers, professors, or supervisors for letters that support your qualifications, skills, or experience.
- Be Reliable and Dedicated: Show that you are hardworking and dependable before you ask for help.
- Use Your Contacts: Many jobs come from people you know, or from people they know, who tell you about job openings. Go to events, job fairs, and meet-ups to meet more people.
- Be Memorable: When you meet someone new, introduce yourself clearly and confidently.
- Communicate: Use LinkedIn to keep in touch with people you meet. Follow up with a message or email to stay connected. Also, be helpful by sharing your ideas or introducing them to others. When you help someone, they are more likely to help you when you need support.

By networking, finding mentors, and always learning, you can find more opportunities and grow your career. Knowing the right people can be as important as your skills. Building strong relationships with others can support your success.

Key Takeaways

- You can search for jobs and find openings on websites like Indeed, LinkedIn, and Glassdoor.

- Building a strong application is important. You should create a clear resume and a cover letter that fits the job.
- Interview preparation is important. You should learn about the company, practice answering common questions, and dress in a professional way.
- Confidence and communication matter. Speak clearly, make eye contact with the interviewer, and ask questions to show you are interested in the job.
- Follow up after the interview. Send a thank-you email, and if you do not hear back, follow up politely.
- Prepare for your new job. You should learn the rules at work, fill out any necessary forms, and get used to the company's way of doing things.

Reflection Questions

1. Before going to a job interview, it's important to prepare and practice. What are two things you should do before an interview to make a good impression? How can researching the company help you answer interview questions better?
2. Why should you send a thank-you email after an interview? How long should you wait before following up if you don't hear back?

References and Resources

Note: The following websites and resources were either cited in this chapter or recommended for additional support. Some were not directly quoted or paraphrased but are included for transparency and easy access.

Big Interview. (n.d.). *Big Interview*. Retrieved April 8, 2025, from https://www.biginterview.com

Canva. (n.d.). *Resume templates*. Retrieved from https://www.canva.com/resumes/templates

CareerOneStop. (n.d.). *Job search tools*. https://www.careeronestop.org

CareerOneStop. (2024). *Job Search Help for New Immigrants*. Retrieved from www.careeronestop.org

ChatGPT. (n.d.). *ChatGPT*. OpenAI. Retrieved from https://chat.openai.com

Coursera. (n.d.). *Business English communication skills*. Retrieved from https://www.coursera.org/specializations/business-english

Equal Employment Opportunity Commission. (n.d.). *Employee rights*. Retrieved from https://www.eeoc.gov/employees

Glassdoor. (n.d.). *Job search and company reviews*. https://www.glassdoor.com

Glassdoor. (2024). *Company Reviews and Salaries*. Retrieved from www.glassdoor.com

Google. (n.d.). *Google Maps*. Retrieved April 8, 2025, from https://www.google.com/maps

Harvard Business Review. (n.d.). *What to ask the interviewer*. Retrieved from https://hbr.org/2016/05/what-to-ask-the-interviewer

Indeed. (n.d.). *Job search*. https://www.indeed.com

Indeed. (n.d.). *How to prepare for an interview in 11 steps*. Retrieved from https://www.indeed.com/career-advice/inter viewing/ how-to-prepare-for-an-interview

Indeed. (n.d.). *How to write a thank-you email after an interview*. Retrieved from https://www.indeed.com/careeradvice/interviewing/ how-to-write-a-thank-you-email

Internal Revenue Service. (n.d.). *Form W-4, Employee's withholding certificate*. Retrieved from https://www.irs.gov/ forms-pubs/about-form-w-4

Job-Hunt. (n.d.). *Guide to successful interviews*. Retrieved from https://www.job-hunt.org/guide-to-successful-interviews/

Khan Academy. (n.d.). *Soft skills*. Retrieved from https://www.khanacademy.org/career-content/soft-skills

LinkedIn. (n.d.). *Find jobs*. https://www.linkedin.com/jobs

LinkedIn. (n.d.). *Career advice*. Retrieved from https://www.linkedin.com/advice

LinkedIn. (n.d.). *LinkedIn Jobs*. Retrieved from https://www.linkedin.com/jobs

Lyft. (n.d.). *Lyft – Your ride, anytime*. Retrieved April 8, 2025, from https://www.lyft.com

MindTools. (n.d.). *Building confidence for interviews*. Retrieved from https://www.mindtools.com/pages/ article/newCDV_96.htm

Purdue Online Writing Lab. (n.d.). *Cover letters*. Purdue University. Retrieved from https://owl.purdue.edu/owl/job_search_writing/job_search_letters/cover_letters/index.html

Society for Human Resource Management. (n.d.). *Workplace etiquette*. Retrieved from https://www.shrm.org/resources andtools/tools-and-samples/hr-qa/pages/workplace-etiquette.aspx

The Balance Careers. (n.d.). *What to wear to a job interview*. Retrieved from https://www.thebalancemoney.com/dress-for-a-job-interview-2058432

The Muse. (n.d.). *How to handle job rejection & ask for feedback*. Retrieved from https://www.themuse.com/advice/how-to-ask-for-feedback-after-job-rejection

Toastmasters International. (n.d.). *Public speaking tips*. Retrieved, from https://www.toastmasters.org/resources/publicspeaking-tips

USAJobs. (n.d.). *Federal government jobs*. https://www.usajobs.gov

U.S. Citizenship and Immigration Services. (n.d.). *Form I-9, Employment eligibility verification*. Retrieved, from https://www.uscis.gov/i-9

U.S. Department of Labor. (2024). *Employment and Training Administration*. Retrieved from www.dol.gov

Uber. (n.d.). *Ride with Uber*. Retrieved April 8, 2025, from https://www.uber.com

Zety. (n.d.). *Resume builder*. Retrieved from https://zety.com/resume-builder

Chapter 12: Understanding Work Behavior and Culture

Imagine it's your first day at a new job in a new country. You woke up early, changed your outfit a few times, and arrived at work very early. Now, you are sitting in a small, plain waiting area, palms sweaty, heart racing. As you wait, you replay every possible scenario in your head, wondering if you will fit in, understand the rules, or meet the expectations. This kind of nervous anticipation is common when starting a job in an unfamiliar environment. Understanding workplace behavior, social expectations, and professional norms is crucial to easing these nerves and helping you succeed. Although different workplaces have different cultures, there are many common expectations in American work environments. This chapter provides guidance on how to adapt to work culture, handle workplace challenges, and advance in your career.

Workplace Behavior: Professionalism and Respect

In the workplace, it is essential to show professionalism and respect at all times to maintain a good working environment. This helps employees work well together and creates a positive atmosphere. Fitting in is important because people feel more comfortable around others who share similar behaviors and attitudes. By following workplace norms, communicating respectfully, and being professional, you can build good relationships with coworkers and succeed in your job.

Be Professional

Focus on your job and ensure you complete your tasks on time while treating everyone at work with respect. For example, if your manager asks you to finish a report by the end of the day, make sure to meet the deadline to show that you are reliable. Being professional also means dressing appropriately for the job. The way you dress reflects your respect for your work and helps create a strong, positive impression in the workplace.

Be Punctual (On Time)

Coming to work on time shows respect for your job and your coworkers. This is considered an important part of being professional. For example, if your job starts at 9:00 AM, try to arrive by 8:55 AM. If you think you will be late, let your manager know as soon as possible.

Be Polite and Respectful

Always use polite language, such as "please" and "thank you," when speaking with coworkers and managers. For example, you can ask for help by saying, "Can you help me with this, please?" and then say, "Thank you" to show your appreciation.

Communicate Clearly

Clear communication is important to avoid misunderstandings and make sure tasks are done correctly. If you are unsure about a task, ask for clarification by saying, "Can you explain this again? I want to make sure I do it correctly.

Understanding Work Culture in the U.S.

Work culture in the U.S. may be very different from the one you are used to experiencing. It often focuses on teamwork, respect for hierarchy, and flexibility.

Teamwork Is Important

Collaboration is highly valued in many American workplaces, encouraging employees to work together and respect each other's contributions. For instance, if working on a group project, listen carefully to your teammates and share your ideas respectfully.

Respect Workplace Hierarchy and Culture

It's important to understand and respect how authority works in U.S. workplaces. Employees should follow the instructions from their managers to help maintain order and efficiency. For example, when you are given a task, focus on completing it as directed.

In the workplace, a hierarchy means that some people have more responsibility and more power to make decisions than others. For example, a manager is usually above employees, and a company director is above the manager. In the U.S., workplace hierarchy can vary depending on the industry and the size of the company. Some workplaces are more formal and structured, while others are more relaxed and informal.

In many U.S. office settings, employees are encouraged to share their ideas, even with their managers. While job titles like "Manager" or "Director" are important, teamwork and collaboration are highly valued. In fact, it's common for workers to call their managers by their first names instead of using formal titles.

American workplaces often promote open communication. You are expected to speak up, ask questions, and offer suggestions, even to your boss. Feedback is also a normal part of the work culture. It is not meant to be negative, but to help you learn and grow. Teamwork and taking initiative are especially important in most professional jobs.

However, in jobs like manufacturing, retail, or other physically demanding work, managers usually make most of the decisions, and employees are expected to follow instructions rather than share ideas. Work culture can vary depending on the company, so it's helpful to ask a coworker about their experience to understand what to expect.

Flexibility at Work

Some jobs let you choose your work hours and where you work from, while others have fixed schedules that you must follow. Many office jobs allow you to choose when to start and finish work, offering flexible hours, and you might even have the option to work from home. This kind of flexibility can help you balance your personal life with your job. For example, you could start work at 10:00 AM and finish at 6:00 PM instead of the usual 9:00 AM to 5:00 PM. Other jobs, like those in stores or factories, require you to work set hours because these roles need people present at specific times to operate properly. For instance, a store worker might need to be there from 8:00 AM to 4:00 PM to assist customers, and changing these hours is usually not possible.

Understanding whether a job offers flexible or fixed hours can help you choose the right job for your lifestyle.

Handling Workplace Challenges

Dealing with Harassment

Harassment is when someone behaves in a way that makes you feel uncomfortable or unsafe. If someone harasses you at work, stay calm and do not respond in anger. It is important to document what happened, including the date, time, location, and details of the situation. Report the issue to your supervisor or human resources (HR). HR is the part of the company that helps with employee problems, like pay, time off, or feeling safe at work. HR makes sure everyone follows the rules and is treated fairly. If the problem continues, you may need to seek legal help.

Case Study: Be Professional at Work

Steve had just started a new job in the U.S. and was excited to get to know his coworkers. As a way of being friendly and playful, he often blew kisses at female coworkers. In his home country, this type of flirting was seen as a lighthearted compliment and was considered normal in social situations.

However, in his new workplace, two women felt uncomfortable with this behavior and decided to report it to Human Resources (HR). Even though Steve never touched anyone or said anything rude, HR explained that his actions were inappropriate for a professional setting in the United States. Behaviors that may seem harmless in one culture can be seen as unprofessional or even disrespectful in another, especially in the workplace.

Steve received a written warning and was told not to repeat this behavior. He understood the situation and made sure it did not happen again.

Lesson Learned: Use Human Resources

If a coworker is making comments or doing things that make you feel uncomfortable, it's better to report it to HR than to argue or ignore it. Every workplace has rules about respectful behavior, and it's important to speak up when those rules are broken.

Avoid Gossip

Gossiping about coworkers can create problems in the workplace. Talking about others behind their backs can lead to misunderstandings, hurt feelings, and a negative work environment. It is better to focus on your work instead of spreading rumors. For example, if coworkers are speaking negatively about someone's personal life, it is best to stay out of the conversation to avoid unnecessary conflict or drama.

Job Evaluations and Career Growth

Many companies provide job evaluations, also called performance reviews, to give feedback on your work. Employers usually look at different areas, such as punctuality, work quality, teamwork, and communication skills. If your manager says you need to improve your time management, try organizing your schedule better to show that you are making progress.

Asking for a Raise

If you want to ask for a raise, prepare in advance. Keep a record of your achievements, such as successful projects and extra responsibilities. Schedule a meeting with your manager and use professional language when making your request. For example, you can say, "I have taken on additional responsibilities and contributed to the team's success. Can we discuss a possible salary increase?" To support your request, bring documents like performance reviews, letters of recommendation, or a list of your contributions to the company. Being prepared and professional can increase your chances of getting a raise.

Social Norms and Expectations at Work

Different workplaces have different expectations for behavior, dress, and communication. Understanding these norms can help you fit in and feel comfortable at work.

Dress Code (What to Wear)

Different workplaces have different expectations for clothing. Some workplaces require formal clothing, while others allow casual wear. For most professional jobs, business clothes are typically expected. This includes suits, dress shirts, blouses, and dress shoes, especially in offices or meetings. In contrast, service jobs often allow more casual clothes or uniforms. For example, retail or restaurant workers may wear polos, khakis, or simple T-shirts with company logos. While a corporate job may require suits, a tech company might allow jeans and T-shirts. If you are not sure what to wear, it's best to ask your manager or a coworker. Following the company's dress code is important and helps you make a good impression.

Respect Personal Space

In the workplace, it is important to respect your coworkers' personal space. A good rule is to keep about an arm's length of space between you and another person. Do not stand too close, touch their belongings, or touch them without permission. For example, if a coworker is sitting at their desk, give them space instead of leaning over them. Respecting personal space shows professionalism and helps create a comfortable and respectful work environment.

Work-Life Balance

In the U.S., work is important, but so is personal time (Hofstede, 2023). It is common for employees to leave work on time unless overtime is required. For example, if work ends at 5:00 PM, it is normal to leave at that time rather than staying late.

Workplace Norms in Different Countries

In the U.S., workplaces tend to be casual and friendly. Employees may call their bosses by their first names. For example, you might call your boss "Sarah" instead of "Ms. Johnson."

In Mexico, there is a strong respect for hierarchy, and employees usually address managers formally. Workers may socialize with coworkers but remain professional and respectful with supervisors.

Understanding workplace norms can help you communicate better and succeed in different work environments.

Constructive Criticism and How It's Given

Constructive criticism is meant to help someone improve by providing feedback in a respectful and positive way. It focuses on the behavior or task, not the person. In the U.S., constructive criticism is typically given face-to-face, especially when the feedback is negative. This ensures that the person receiving the feedback can ask questions, discuss the issue, and better understand how to improve. For example, if an employee made an error in a report, the manager might say, "I noticed some mistakes in your report. Let's go over it together so you can avoid those in the future." This approach is respectful and provides a chance for improvement.

However, praise or positive feedback can sometimes be given publicly, such as in meetings or team settings, to motivate and encourage the individual in front of others. For instance, a manager might say, "Great job on the project! You really helped the team meet the deadline." Public praise is often used to recognize achievements and encourage others.

In the U.S., indirect communication is sometimes used by managers to avoid conflict or hurt feelings. Instead of directly pointing out someone's mistake, a manager might say, "I think there's room for improvement in this area," or "Maybe we could try a different approach next time." This kind of communication can help soften the message and make it easier for the person to accept feedback without feeling personally attacked.

Not Everyone Is a Friend for Life

Not all work friendships last forever. A friend at work may not always be a friend outside of work. This is normal, so don't feel disappointed.

To be successful at work, you need to have a good relationship with your coworkers. A positive work environment makes your job easier and more enjoyable. However, your coworkers may have different beliefs, religions, political views, or lifestyles. Even if you don't agree with them, you can still learn something from them.

Every person has value and can teach us something. Some people inspire us to be better. Some people show us what we want to avoid. It is okay if work friends don't become personal friends. Jobs change, and it can be hard to keep in touch with everyone. Some people come into our lives for a short time, while others stay with us for the long ride. Both types of friendships are important. Appreciate the people you meet but keep a few close friends for life.

Key Takeaways

- Professional behavior matters. It is important to be polite, punctual, and respectful in the workplace.
- Work culture varies by country. You should understand the norms for teamwork, hierarchy, and expectations in the workplace.
- Harassment should not be tolerated. You should report it to HR and make sure to document the issue.
- Job evaluations help you grow. Use feedback to improve your performance.
- Negotiating a raise requires preparation. You should keep records of your achievements to support your request.

Reflection Questions

1. Why is punctuality important in the workplace? What should you do if you will be late?
2. How can understanding workplace culture help you adjust to a new job?
3. What steps should you take if you experience harassment at work?

References

Hofstede, G. (2023). *Workplace culture and behavior in the U.S.* Retrieved from https://www.hofstede-insights.com

Chapter 13: Understanding Work Ethic and the Economic System in the U.S.

The idiom "pull yourself up by your bootstraps" means to succeed through hard work and determination, without relying on others for help. It reflects the strong belief in self-reliance in American culture, where many people think success comes from personal effort rather than outside support. This idea is closely tied to the American Dream, where people believe that, with enough hard work, they can improve their lives and achieve financial stability. However, not everyone starts from the same place in life, which can make success more difficult for some.

This phrase also speaks to the idea that Americans generally do not like paying for others' expenses. Many people believe that individuals should take care of themselves financially rather than depending on government aid or assistance from others. This belief influences attitudes toward social programs, taxes, and workplace expectations. While some argue that hard work alone is enough to succeed, others point out that education, family wealth, opportunities, and support systems also play a big role in success.

Understanding this idiom helps explain why independence and personal responsibility are highly valued in the U.S., especially in the workplace and economy.

What is Work Ethic?

In the U.S., hard work and personal responsibility are very important (Hofstede, 2023). Work ethic is a set of values that guide how a person performs their job and takes responsibility for their work. It includes being reliable, working hard, and taking responsibility. A strong work ethic means coming to work on time, finishing tasks when they are due, staying focused, and trying your best. Many people in the U.S. believe that success comes from effort, being responsible, and planning for the future.

Hard Work Matters

Many Americans believe that success comes from hard work. If you put in effort, you can achieve your goals. Many people see education as proof that studying can lead to a degree and a better job with higher pay. There are many inspiring stories of people who worked hard and became successful.

One example is Oprah Winfrey, who grew up in poverty and faced many challenging situations as a child. Despite these challenges, she focused on her education and worked hard in the media industry. She eventually became one of the most successful talk show hosts and businesswomen in the world.

Being Responsible

Taking responsibility for your actions is important in the workplace. If you promise to complete a task, you should make sure you finish it on time. Being someone who others can rely on helps build trust with your employers and coworkers.

Punctuality (Being on Time)

Arriving on time is a sign of respect and dedication. If a meeting starts at 10:00 AM, arriving at 10:05 AM is considered late. Being punctual shows that you are reliable and value other people's time.

Motivation and Goals

Americans set goals and plan for the future (U.S. Department of Labor, 2023). Many students work part-time jobs to save money for college or to buy a car. Having clear goals helps people stay motivated and work toward success.

Employers look for workers who are dependable, take responsibility for their actions, and show motivation to improve. Having a strong work ethic can help you succeed in your job and build a good reputation in the workplace. Understanding work ethic in the U.S. can help you adapt to the workplace and achieve your career goals.

The Economic System in the U.S. (Capitalism)

The U.S. economy is based on capitalism, which means that businesses compete with each other, and people can earn money through hard work (Federal Reserve, 2023). In a capitalist system, individuals have the freedom to own property, choose what to buy, and work in different jobs to earn money.

Free Market Economy

In the U.S., businesses sell products and services that people want, and customers get to decide what to buy. For example, if you need a phone, you can compare different brands and choose the best one based on price, quality, or features. This freedom of choice allows businesses to improve their products to attract more customers.

Private Property

People in the U.S. can own homes, businesses, and land. This means that if you work hard and save money, you can buy a house or even start your own business. Private ownership gives people control over their property and financial future.

Earning Money (Jobs and Careers)

Most people earn money by working a job or starting a business. Different jobs pay different salaries depending on skills and experience. For example, a doctor, a cashier, and a mechanic all earn money for their work, but their earnings depend on education, experience, and demand for their job.

Competition

Businesses compete with each other to attract customers by offering better products, services, and prices. For example, grocery stores may offer discounts or special deals to bring in more shoppers. Competition helps keep prices fair and encourages businesses to provide better quality.

Why Work Ethic is Important in the U.S.?

In the U.S., hard work is seen as the key to success. People believe that putting in effort and being dedicated can lead to better jobs, promotions, and new opportunities. The idea is that anyone can improve their life if they work hard and stay focused on their goals. Hard work can also bring financial stability, helping people afford necessities like housing, education, and healthcare. For example, a student who studies hard in school can earn a scholarship for college. This allows them to get a good education and, in the future, a better job. Having a strong work ethic is important because it helps people reach their goals and build a successful life.

Case Study: Work Your Wage, but Remember Your Worth

"Work your pay" doesn't mean doing as little as possible. It means understanding that while you should take pride in your work and do your best, you should also remember that your job is not your whole identity. At work, you can be replaced, but to your family and loved ones, you are irreplaceable.

One of my friends often reminds me of this when my perfectionism, strong work ethic, and desire to help too many people at once take over. Overworking not only stresses me out but also makes me feel like I am giving too much to a job that would replace me quickly if I left or if I died. It is important to work hard, especially in your twenties, and set career goals. This is a time when you have enough energy to juggle many commitments and the least family responsibilities. However, working too much for too long leads to burnout and stress.

Lesson Leaned: The New Generations Want Work-Life Balance

Younger generations, especially after COVID-19, are teaching us the importance of work-life balance. The pandemic changed how people think about work. Some people prefer working from home to avoid wasting time on travel. Others need social interaction and enjoy dressing professionally for the workplace.

Technology has also forever changed the way we work. Not all jobs require us to be on-site anymore. Many companies now allow remote work, and virtual meetings have become the new norm. This has given workers more flexibility, but it has also blurred the lines between work and personal life.

Setting Boundaries to Avoid Burnout

To protect my personal time, I have made small but important changes. I now set aside uninterrupted time on the weekend, when I do not check my email. I also turn off my notifications when I am with my children after work. My messages will still be there when I check them later, but my family time is something I can't get back.

One big lesson from COVID-19 is this: When everything shuts down, we are left with ourselves and our families. This reminds us that while work is important, our relationships, health, and happiness matter more.

It's okay to work hard, but don't forget to live your life. Your job can replace you, but your family cannot. And if work is making you constantly stressed, it may be time to set boundaries.

Key Takeaways

- Work ethic means being hardworking, responsible, and punctual.
- The U.S. follows the economic system of capitalism, where businesses compete and individuals can earn money through work.
- By understanding work culture and the economy, you will know how people think about jobs and success in the U.S. Working hard and being responsible can help you achieve your goals!

Reflection Questions

1. In the U.S., having a strong work ethic means working hard, being responsible, and arriving on time. Why is being on time important at work or school? How can being responsible help someone do well in their job?
2. In the U.S., people believe that hard work can lead to success. How can setting goals and planning for the future help someone achieve their dreams? Can you think of a personal goal you have and explain how hard work could help you reach it?

References

Federal Reserve. (2023). *The U.S. economic system and capitalism.*
   Retrieved from https://www.federalreserve.gov
Hofstede, G. (2023). *Workplace culture and behavior in the U.S.*
   Retrieved from https://www.hofstede-insights.com
U.S. Department of Labor. (2023). *Understanding work ethic in
   America.* Retrieved from https://www.dol.gov

SECTION 4: SCHOOL LIFE AND YOUTH CULTURE

Chapter 14: Understanding the School Environment in the U.S. for Newcomer Students and Parents

Starting school in a new country can be exciting, but it can also be confusing. School culture, rules, and daily life in the U.S. may be different from what you are used to back home. Learning about these differences can help you adjust more quickly and avoid surprises.

In this chapter, you will learn about how U.S. schools are structured, what to expect each day, how grades work, and how to succeed in a new school environment as a newcomer.

A Personal Story: My First Snow Day Surprise

Imagine my surprise when, during my first week of school in the United States, I arrived at the front doors, only to find them locked. I knocked, hoping someone would let me in, but no one answered. I peered through the windows, expecting to see students walking in the halls, but the school was completely empty. My heart pounded. *Was I late? Had school moved to another location? Had I misunderstood something?*

There was only one inch of snow on the ground, so I didn't think much of it. Back home, school would never close for such a small amount of snow! But after waiting outside in the cold, I later found out that in the U.S., schools sometimes close due to weather conditions, even for a little snow.

I felt confused, nervous, and a little scared, but it was a learning experience. I realized that in the U.S., school closings are announced on the news, school websites, or through text alerts. Now, I always check before heading out in bad weather!

Lessons Learned: Learn from My Experience

In the U.S., schools may close due to snow, storms, gas leaks, or extreme weather. Always check the school website, local news, or phone alerts before leaving home. Schools may also close early for special events, teacher training, or emergencies. Pay attention to announcements and communications sent home. Don't be afraid to ask questions when you do not know something. If you are unsure about school schedules or rules, ask a teacher, school staff member, or a classmate. It's okay not to know everything at first!

The Structure of the U.S. Education System

Compulsory education refers to a period in a child's life when they are legally required to attend school. The purpose of compulsory education is not only to promote literacy and basic skills but also to help children develop critical thinking, social skills, and civic responsibility. The typical age range for compulsory education is from about 5 or 6 years old until the age of 16 to 18, depending on the country, and in the U.S., even the specific state. For instance, in the United States, children must start school by age 5 or 6 and continue until they are at least 16, with some states requiring attendance until age 18.

Education can be provided through public schools, private schools, or at home through homeschooling, depending on what is legally accepted in the country. The U.S. education system is divided into different levels based on age (U.S. Department of Education, 2021):

Elementary School – Education can be provided through public schools, private schools, or at home through homeschooling, depending on what is legally accepted in the country. The U.S. education system is divided into different levels based on age (U.S. Department of Education, 2021):

- Elementary School – Kindergarten (K) through 5th grade (ages 5-11). It focuses on basic subjects like math, reading, science, and social studies.
- Middle School – 6th to 8th grade (ages 11-14). Students begin to switch classes for different subjects.
- High School – 9th to 12th grade (ages 14-18). Students take more specialized courses and prepare for college or work.
- College/University – After high school (ages 18+). Students can attend higher education and pursue a degree.

School Schedule and Daily Routine

School Hours – Schools typically start between 7:30 AM and 9:00 AM and finish between 2:30 PM and 4:00 PM (NCES, 2022). Schools are typically in sessions from late August to early June.

Class Periods – Classes last between 45 minutes and 1 hour, with breaks in between. Some schools have block scheduling, where classes last about 90 minutes.

Lunch – Schools have cafeterias where students can buy food or bring lunch from home. Some students qualify for free or reduced-price lunches (USDA, 2023).

After-School Activities – Schools offer clubs, sports, and activities to help students make friends and learn new skills (Harvard Graduate School of Education, 2022). Most of the time after school clubs are free, but some schools may have fees for sports.

School Subjects and Grading System

Governments set a basic curriculum that all schools must follow to ensure that fundamental subjects are taught to all students.

- Core Subjects – Math, English, science, and social studies.
- Electives – Optional courses like art, music, physical education, and technology (U.S. Department of Education, 2021).
- English as a Second Language (ESL) services are designed for students whose first language is not English. These services help them improve their language skills so they can succeed both academically and socially.
- MLL, ESL, and ELL – MLL (Multilingual Learner), ESL (English as a Second Language), and ELL (English Language Learner) are terms often used interchangeably to describe students who are learning English in addition to their native language.
- Individualized Education Plan (IEP) – A plan for students who need special education services due to learning disabilities, physical disabilities, emotional challenges, or other needs. Parents may need to advocate for these services.

112

Understanding Grading System in the U.S.

Understanding how grades work in the U.S. can help students track their progress and set academic goals. Teachers typically provide both written feedback and letter grades, as shown below, to help students understand how they are doing in class.

A = Excellent (90-100%)
B = Good (80-89%)
C = Average (70-79%)
D = Below Average (60-69%)
F = Failing (below 60%)

Some schools use a GPA (Grade Point Average) system to measure overall academic performance. A GPA of 4.0 is the highest, and a 2.0 or below may indicate academic struggles (College Board, n.d). A weighted GPA can be higher in high schools due to honors or Advanced Placement courses. Competitive colleges are more likely to accept students who have higher GPAs. Directions on calculating GPA can be found in Chapter 18.

School Behavior and Expectations

Schools set clear rules to create a safe and positive learning environment (National Education Association, 2023). Some common expectations are explained below.

Respect for Teachers and Peers – Follow instructions and listen when others speak.

Participation – Ask questions and contribute to discussions. Standing out in class is seen as a good thing in the U.S.

Homework – Complete assignments on time. Teachers may have different rules about late work, so it's important to understand their expectations.

Turn in Work – Teachers expect graded work to be turned in on time. This could mean uploading work online or handing it in physically. This process can be confusing for students who are not used to turning in assignments regularly or who may not know how to use technology. For example, after a teenager from Egypt started school, teachers called for a parent meeting because he was not turning in his work. The student was upset because he is very dedicated to his studies and had never caused problems for his parents. In his old school in Egypt, students only took exams at the end of the year. He did not know that in the U.S., students are expected to turn in assignments every day, nor did he know how to use an iPad for schoolwork.

Punctuality – Arriving late may lead to warnings, detention or other consequences.

Attendance – Going to school regularly is required by law. Parents are legally responsible for making sure their children attend school. If a child misses school without a valid reason, the parents or guardians may face legal consequences. These can include fines or other penalties.

Technology Use – Schools often use computers or tablets for classwork (Harvard Graduate School of Education, 2022). Get help if you do not know how to use these devices.

Academic Excellence – Academic excellence means doing your best in school and working hard to earn high grades. It's not just about test scores. It also includes understanding what you learn, thinking critically, and building strong study habits. Some schools give awards like Student of the Month, Perfect Attendance, or subject-specific honors to encourage students. I remember receiving several awards during a junior high assembly. Even though I knew it was a good thing, I felt uncomfortable being in the spotlight and didn't want my friends to see me differently. Still, students should not be afraid to work hard and reach their full potential.

Dress Code – Some schools require students to wear a specific uniform. However, most schools without a specific uniform expect students to wear clothes that cover from the shoulders down to at least an inch or two above the knees. This means that revealing clothes should not be worn. For example, short-sleeved t-shirts are acceptable, while spaghetti-strapped shirts are not. Skirts are permitted but should extend to about two inches above the knees. Most students wear jeans, t-shirts, or sweatshirts, as schools typically maintain a cooler temperature, making the extra layer useful even when the weather is warmer. Brightly colored clothing and very busy patterns are not very common. Inappropriate images or words are not allowed.

School Safety Drills

Schools in the U.S. practice safety drills, or safety practice, to keep students and teachers prepared for emergencies. These drills help everyone know what to do in dangerous situations so they can stay safe.

One of the most common drills is a fire drill, where students and teachers practice what to do if there is a fire in the school. When the fire alarm rings, everyone must quickly and calmly leave the building. Teachers lead students outside to a safe area. Schools do this drill a few times a year so students can learn the fastest way to exit the building and stay safe.

Other drills may include:

- Shelter-in-place drill – Students stay inside the classroom for safety.
- Lockdown drill – Students stay in one area and remain quiet if there is a possible danger inside the school or nearby.
- Severe weather drill – Students move to a safe area in case of severe weather, such as a tornado or hurricane.

These drills are not real emergencies, but they help students and teachers practice staying safe. It is important to listen to teachers and follow instructions during drills so that everyone knows what to do in an emergency.

It is also important to warn newcomer ESL students about these drills so that they do not panic, especially if they have experienced trauma in the past. Helping students understand the purpose of drills can make them feel safer and more prepared when they happen at school.

Understanding the Role of School Staff in the U.S.

For newcomers to America, adjusting to a new school system can be challenging. Understanding the roles of school staff can help students know who to go to for help and support. Several roles are important to know including teachers, ESL teacher, school counselor, administration, nurses, librarians, office staff, and support workers.

Teachers are responsible for teaching subjects, assigning homework, and helping students learn. During early grades you may have one main teacher, as you move up in grades, each teacher you have may only teach one subject. They provide guidance, answer questions, and give feedback on assignments. Newcomer students should feel comfortable asking teachers for help with schoolwork or language difficulties.

ESL (English as a Second Language) teachers help students improve their English skills in speaking, reading, writing, and listening. They also assist with understanding class lessons, homework, and American culture. If English is difficult, ESL teachers can provide extra support to help students understand the content.

School counselors help students with personal, academic, and career concerns. They assist with class schedules, college planning, and emotional support. If ESL students feel stressed, confused, or have a personal issue, they can talk to their guidance counselor and ask for help. Counselors also help students plan for life after high school, including college, vocational training, or finding a job.

The principal is the leader of the school and ensures everything runs smoothly. Assistant principals help enforce school rules and assist students when needed. If there is a major concern about safety, bullying, or school policies, students can speak to an administrator.

School nurses help students who feel sick or get injured at school. If an ESL student has a headache, stomachache, or needs medication, they can visit the nurse's office for care.

Librarians or resource specialist manage the school library and help students find books, use computers, and research information. Some school libraries have books in different languages to support ESL students.

The office staff answers phone calls, helps with paperwork, and gives information to students and parents. If ESL students need to report an absence or ask about school events, they can visit the school office.

While custodians keep the school clean and take care of the building, cafeteria workers prepare and serve meals for students. If ESL students have questions about food choices or meal programs, they can ask the cafeteria staff for help.

Understanding the roles of school staff can help ESL students feel more comfortable and confident in their new school environment. Each staff member is there to support and guide students as they adjust to life in an American school.

Making Friends and Social Life

Joining clubs and activities helps newcomer students make friends and feel included. Don't be afraid to try new things. You may end up enjoying the activity and making friends. Some students form social groups based on shared interests. For example, students who become friends in their English as a Second Language (ESL) class may feel more comfortable sitting together at lunch.

There are also behaviors to avoid in schools. Most schools have strict policies against bullying, which means doing something repeatedly that hurts, threatens, or mistreats another person on purpose (CDC, 2023). If you experience bullying, it's important to report it to a teacher or school staff.

However, sometimes what feels like bullying may be a classmate's awkward way of trying to connect and make friends. Some students may use gentle teasing or ask personal questions because they are unsure how to make friends or lack social skills. This happened to me in junior high school. I thought a student didn't like me because she asked intrusive questions about my culture. Later, I realized she was simply curious and truly interested in learning about different cultures. I had misunderstood her at first, but we are still friends today.

School Calendar

The school calendar is a helpful tool because it shows which days students are expected to be in school, usually around 180 days per year. It also lists early dismissal days, when students leave school earlier than usual. Many schools include dates for family conferences, special events, and school closings. This information helps students and families plan ahead more easily.

School Holidays in the U.S. and What Happens at School

In the U.S., schools have different holidays throughout the year. Some holidays are national, meaning all schools close, while others depend on the state or local school district. Schools often have special activities before a holiday to teach students about its meaning or to celebrate in fun ways. Understanding school holidays helps students prepare for days off and school celebrations. Every school may have slightly different traditions, but these are common practices across the U.S.

Labor Day (First Monday in September)

Labor Day honors workers and their contributions to society. Schools are closed for the day, and some teachers talk about different types of jobs and why they are important before the holiday.

Halloween (October 31st – Not a Day Off)

Halloween is a fun holiday, but schools usually stay open on that day. Many schools allow younger children (usually ages 5–10) to wear costumes. Some elementary schools have Halloween parties or parades, where students walk around in their costumes. In the evening, children go trick-or-treating between 6:00 PM and 8:00 PM. They knock on doors in their neighborhoods to get candy. People who want to participate in this event leave their porch lights on, while those who do not want visitors turn their lights off.

Thanksgiving Break (Late November, Usually a Few Days Off)

Thanksgiving is a major holiday in the U.S. Schools usually teach about the history of Thanksgiving and why it is celebrated. Some schools hold a "Thanksgiving Feast," where students share food. Most schools close for 2–5 days, including Thanksgiving Day, which is the fourth Thursday in November. Thanksgiving is a time for family and friends to come together, eat a big meal, and give thanks.

One common view of Thanksgiving focuses on the story of unity and gratitude. This version comes from a harvest feast in 1621 between the Pilgrims (English settlers) and the Wampanoag Native Americans in Plymouth, Massachusetts. The Pilgrims had a hard time surviving when they first arrived in America. The Wampanoag people helped them grow food, fish, and hunt. After a good harvest, they shared a big meal to celebrate and be thankful. This version of the holiday highlights cooperation, friendship, and thankfulness.

However, there is another perspective that reflects the painful history of Native Americans. Many people remember that after the Pilgrims arrived, Native Americans lost much of their land, culture, and way of life. For some Native American families, Thanksgiving is not a happy celebration; it is also a time to honor their ancestors and reflect on the hardships their communities have faced.

Today, Thanksgiving includes many traditions. People usually eat turkey, mashed potatoes, stuffing, cranberry sauce, and pumpkin pie. Some families watch football or the Macy's Thanksgiving Day Parade. Others volunteer to help people in need. While the holiday has a complicated history, many people use it as a time to show gratitude, spend time with loved ones, and share kindness.

Winter Break (Mid to Late December – Early January)

Winter break lasts about 1–3 weeks, depending on the school district. Before the break, some schools hold holiday concerts, plays, or classroom parties. Many schools teach students about different religious holidays, including Christmas, Hanukkah, and Kwanzaa. Some elementary schools also have a "Secret Santa" gift exchange, where students bring small gifts for their classmates.

They may put up a holiday tree and organize fundraising activities to support a good cause.

Martin Luther King Jr. Day (Third Monday in January)

Schools are closed for one day to honor Martin Luther King Jr., a leader of the Civil Rights Movement. Before the holiday, students learn about his work for equality and justice in the U.S.

Presidents' Day (Third Monday in February)

Many schools close for one day to honor past U.S. presidents, including George Washington and Abraham Lincoln. Some schools teach about the role of the president and the U.S. history.

Spring Break (March or April – Usually One Week Off)

Spring break is a one-week vacation that gives students time to rest before finishing the school year. Not all schools have spring break, but many do. Some families use this time to travel, while others stay home and relax. Schools usually do not have major celebrations before spring break, but students may have tests or projects due before the break begins.

Easter (March or April – Not Always a School Holiday)

Easter is a Sunday holiday, so schools usually do not need to close since they are not in session on Sundays. However, some elementary schools or preschools may have an Easter egg hunt before the holiday. During this activity, children search for plastic eggs filled with candy or small prizes. Not all schools celebrate Easter, as it is a religious holiday. Still, some schools may give students a day off on the Friday before Easter (called Good Friday) or the following Monday.

Memorial Day (Last Monday in May)

Schools close for one day to honor military members who died in service. Some schools teach about Memorial Day and the importance of remembering those who served in the U.S. military.

Summer Break (June – August, Dates Vary by School)

Summer break is the longest school vacation, lasting 2–3 months. Before summer break, students take final tests, return books, and sometimes have class parties or graduation ceremonies. Many families go on vacation, and older students may take summer jobs or attend summer programs.

Independence Day

Another important U.S. holiday is Independence Day, also called the Fourth of July. Schools are usually not in session during this time, since it is in the summer. However, summer school sessions typically close for this holiday. Independence Day celebrates the date in 1776 when the United States became independent from Britain. The holiday is about freedom and national pride, and it is common to see fireworks, parades, and barbecues with family and friends.

Case Study: Omid's Journey to Graduation

Omid arrived in the U.S. as a refugee from a war-torn country. He had no school transcripts to prove he had completed 9th grade. Despite this, Omid was a smart and hardworking student who wanted to graduate on time.

He lived with his older sister, who supported him. Since his previous school could not send his records, he had to find another way to earn credit. A high school credit is a unit that measures the completion of a course. Students need a certain number of credits in subjects like math, English, and science in order to graduate. Fortunately, Omid's English was strong, and he took extra classes after school and over the summer to catch up.

By the end of 11th grade, Omid had made up his 9th-grade year and graduated on time. He was later accepted into college and is studying to become an engineer.

Lessons Learned: Ask Your School for Your Options

Missing school records can be a challenge, but options exist. Many schools offer ways to earn missing high school credits through summer school, online courses, or extra classes. Ask your guidance counselor what your options are if you are in this situation.

A support system helps students with their school. Omid's sister, teachers, and school staff guided him to find solutions. Also, after school tutoring and ESL services were helpful to him.

Hard work and determination are often the keys to success. Omid's efforts allowed him to graduate on time and continue his education.

Key Takeaways

- Learn about the differences in school culture, rules, and daily routines in the U.S. This will help you adjust faster and avoid surprises.
- Be aware that U.S. schools may close suddenly because of weather or other emergencies. Always check the school website, local news, or phone alerts before leaving home.
- Get to know how the U.S. education system is organized.
- Understand the roles of different school staff members, such as teachers and librarians, who can help you as you adjust to the new environment.
- Learn the school rules about being on time, attendance, homework, and using technology to avoid problems and do well in school.
- Ask for help when you face challenges in school or your personal life, and use resources like ESL teachers and school counselors.
- Keep track of the school calendar. Learning about U.S. school holidays and their meanings can help you feel more connected to the school community.

Reflection Questions

1. How does school in the U.S. compare to school in your home country?
2. What problems might students face if they do not have school records, and how can they overcome these challenges?

3. What steps can you take to succeed in a new school environment?

References

Centers for Disease Control and Prevention (CDC). (2023). *Bullying Prevention and School Policies*. Retrieved from https://www.cdc.gov/violenceprevention/youthviolence/bullyingresearch

College Board. (n.d.). *How to calculate your GPA on a 4.0 scale*. BigFuture. Retrieved from https://bigfuture.collegeboard.org/plan-for-college/get-started/how-to-calculate-gpa-4.0-scale

Harvard Graduate School of Education. (2022). *Helping Newcomer Students Adjust to U.S. Schools*. Retrieved from https://www.gse.harvard.edu

National Center for Education Statistics (NCES). (2022). *Fast Facts: Public School System Structure*. Retrieved from https://nces.ed.gov

National Education Association (NEA). (2023). *School Discipline and Behavior Expectations*. Retrieved from https://www.nea.org

U.S. Department of Education. (2021). *Education in the United States*. Retrieved from www.ed.gov

Chapter 15: Parent Participation in U.S. Schools

First-generation immigrants may be very busy balancing work and family responsibilities. My parents worked separate shifts and were not able to check on me at school. I had to navigate my education mostly on my own. However, my experience with my own children has been different. I have been able to volunteer in the classroom, help my children with fundraising activities, email teachers when needed, and support their extracurricular activities.

In the U.S., parents and guardians are expected to be part of their child's education. Schools encourage families to attend events, talk to teachers, and help with learning at home. Studies show that children do better in school when their parents are involved (Harvard Family Research Project, 2020).

Case Study: Turning Struggles into Success Through Family Support

Some students struggle when they first arrive in the U.S. because they must adjust to a new school system, language, and expectations. Family support can make a big difference in a student's success.

José and his family moved to the U.S. when he was in high school. His first year was difficult. He struggled with assignments, often forgot to turn in his homework, and his grades started to drop. His parents, who worked different shifts, were not always able to help him with schoolwork. They wanted him to do well but weren't sure how to support him.

After talking to his teachers, they realized he needed more structure and accountability. They set up weekly meetings at home to review his assignments and progress. If he fell behind, they emailed his teachers for regular updates until he caught up on his work. To help him focus, they took away his phone when he wasn't keeping up with his work. At first, José was frustrated, but over time, he learned to manage his responsibilities better. His grades improved, and he started turning in assignments on time.

Like José, Omid also faced challenges in school while working to support himself, make up classes from his 9th grade year, and completing high school in just three years. He was a bright student but had no school transcripts from his home country to prove he had completed ninth grade. Since he was in the U.S. with his older sister as his guardian, he did not have parents available to support him. His sister worked long hours but still found ways to help. She:

- Checked his grades and attendance online.
- Sent emails to teachers in her native language, which they were able to translate and understand. This kept both the teacher and her informed of Omid's progress and things he needed to do.
- Encouraged him to use school resources like tutoring and English Language Learner club.

Because of guardians' involvement, both José and Omid overcame challenges, improved their grades, and successfully graduated. Today, José is planning for college, and Omid is studying engineering. Their stories show that even when parents or guardians are busy, small actions can make a big difference in a child's success.

Parent Involvement Helps Children Perform Better

When parents are involved in their children's education, it can lead to many positive outcomes:

- Better Grades – Children do better in school when parents are involved (Harvard Family Research Project, 2020).
- Stronger School Community – Parents, teachers, and students work together to improve education (U.S. Department of Education, 2022).

- More Information – Parents stay updated on school events and their child's progress (NEA, 2021).
- Transportation – Some parents choose to drive or walk their children to school during elementary years, while older children might walk with friends or take the school bus if provided. Transporting children to school can also be a valuable time for families to talk and support their children's goals.

Ways to Be Involved: Attend These School Events

There are many ways for parents and guardians to help their child do well in school. One way is to attend school events.

- Parent-Teacher Conferences – These meetings give you information about how your child is doing in school. Some schools can meet with you online if needed.
- Open Houses – You can visit the school, meet the teachers, and learn about school rules and what your child will study.
- School Activities – You can go to sports games, music concerts, or talent shows. This shows your child that you care about their interests.

Volunteer at School

Parents can actively participate in school life in many ways. Helping in the classroom allows parents to assist teachers with different activities, which can greatly improve the classroom experience. This usually happens in elementary schools. Parents can also join field trips to help supervise students and ensure their safety during school outings. Another way to help is by supporting fundraisers, such as bake sales or charity events that raise money for school programs. This type of involvement is common at all levels of K–12 education.

A very important way to get involved is by joining the PTA or PTO (Parent-Teacher Association/Organization). By attending meetings, parents work together with teachers to improve the school community. PTA members often help plan and organize events such as school festivals, family nights, and fundraisers.

Parents can also join school committees, where they help make decisions about school programs and policies. All these efforts help create a stronger, more supportive learning environment for students.

Talking to Teachers and School Staff

Parents have several ways to communicate with teachers about their child's progress. They can email, call, or schedule meetings to talk about how their child is doing in school. If parents do not speak English, many schools offer translation software or access to over-the-phone interpretation to support communication. Teachers usually appreciate when parents take an active interest in their child's education by asking questions and staying involved. This kind of support helps improve the student's learning experience (Harvard Family Research Project, 2020).

Reading School Newsletters

Schools regularly send out newsletters to keep families informed about upcoming events, important dates, and any changes to school rules. These newsletters are an important resource for parents to stay connected with the school community and stay updated on what is happening in their child's education. Newsletters can be on paper or sent by email.

Using Online Portals

Many schools now offer websites or apps that allow parents to check their child's grades, attendance records, and homework assignments online. While it's important to trust your child, verifying their academic progress can be helpful. Parents are encouraged to talk with their children about schoolwork and ask them to show their grades. This helps build trust, encourages responsibility, and shows support for their academic success.

Helping Your Child at Home

Creating a good environment for homework is very important. Give your child a quiet place to study, encourage the use of a calendar to track assignments, and check their homework, providing help when needed. This support structure helps them manage their responsibilities effectively.

Reading Together

Reading is a powerful tool for expanding vocabulary and improving thinking abilities (AAP, 2021). You can read to your children in your native language, which is beneficial for their language development. Discussing the story as you read can help deepen their understanding and improve comprehension skills.

Setting Expectations

Encourage good study habits. Talk with your children about the importance of education and explain how their efforts in school can lead to long-term success.

Understanding School Rules and Programs

Knowing school rules and available programs can help parents support their child's success and feel more involved in the school community.

School Calendar

Schools provide calendars that list holidays, testing days, and parent-teacher meetings, which are helpful for planning and participation.

School Rules

Schools have rules for attendance, behavior, and dress codes (expectation for school appropriate clothes). Parents should review rules with their child to make sure they understand the expectations.

Special Programs

Schools offer programs for English learners, tutoring, and special education. If your child needs extra help, ask about the support programs available at their school. Schools often welcome ideas that support English language learners. You can advocate for new programs that may benefit your child and other students.

Adjusting to School Culture in the U.S.

Adjusting to a new school culture takes time, but understanding how things work in U.S. schools can help you and your child feel more comfortable and confident.

Be Open to New Ideas

The teaching styles in the U.S. may differ from those in your home country. If you are unsure about anything, do not hesitate to ask the teacher for clarification.

Language Support

For non-English-speaking parents, many schools provide interpreters or bilingual staff. Some schools also use services that offer real-time translation over the phone to help with communication. In addition, translation apps can be useful tools for communicating with teachers.

Making Connections

Going to school events is a great way to meet other parents and integrate into the school community.

Helping Schools in Other Ways

Participate in school life beyond just attending meetings. You can support your child's school by helping with fundraisers, donating supplies like books or classroom materials, or volunteering as a guest speaker. Sharing your immigration story or culture, and even bringing a traditional dish from your country, can be a meaningful experience for both you and the students. It encourages cultural understanding and appreciation within the school community.

Key Takeaways

- Parent involvement helps children do better in school.
- There are many ways to support schools, even if you have a busy schedule.
- Parents can talk to teachers in their own language using email, translation apps, or interpretation services.
- Even if you cannot attend school events, you can stay connected online.

Reflection Questions

1. How can you get more involved in your child's school?
2. What school events or activities interest you the most?
3. How is parent involvement in schools in the U.S. different from how parents are involved in schools in your home country?

References

American Academy of Pediatrics. (2021). *Reading with Children: Benefits and Strategies*. Retrieved from www.aap.org

Harvard Family Research Project. (2020). *Parent Involvement in Schools: Key Findings*. Retrieved from www.hfrp.org

National Education Association (NEA). (2021). *Parent and Community Engagement in Schools*. Retrieved from www.nea.org

U.S. Department of Education. (2022). *How Families Can Support Student Success*. Retrieved from www.ed.gov

Chapter 16: How to Behave at a Dance: A Guide for High School and Middle School Students

Going to a high school dance in the U.S. can be exciting, but if you are new to American culture, it may feel confusing. Whether it is prom, homecoming, or a casual dance, knowing what to expect can help you feel comfortable and have fun.

There are some experiences in life that stay with us forever, no matter how much we wish to forget them. We can try to bury them in our minds, or we can embrace them, laugh about them, and use them to teach others so they don't make the same mistakes. We learn either by making mistakes ourselves, by watching others, or by reading stories. I learned this lesson the hard way.

It was the end of 8th grade, and I had been in the U.S. for about two months. My family had arrived with only two bags of clothes for all five of us. Our sponsors were kind. They donated clothes and tried to help. But some of the clothes they gave us were dresses from the 1980s, with big ruffles and very bright colors.

When I heard about the school dance, I worried about what to wear. I knew enough not to wear the outdated dresses I had received. Of course, I was grateful for everything we were given, but with only my father working, we could not afford new clothes.

A friend from Jamaica agreed with me about the dresses, so we decided that I would wear a floral jumpsuit, long before jumpsuits were considered fashionable. Looking back, I still feel a bit embarrassed. Neither of us knew how casual the dance was, and all the stress I felt could have been avoided if we had been informed about school dances. If I had known better, I would have just worn jeans and a T-shirt instead.

So, learn from my mistake. Don't stress too much about what to wear, and if you are unsure, ask someone!

Types of Dances

Prom is a formal event where students wear fancy clothes and enjoy a decorated venue. It usually takes place in the spring, between April and June, depending on the school. Prom is a special dance mostly for 12th grade students (seniors), but some schools also invite 11th grade students (juniors). It is a special celebration before graduation, allowing students to dress up, take pictures, and enjoy a memorable night with friends. Girls usually wear a long dress or a fancy short dress. Boys wear a suit or a tuxedo.

Homecoming is a semi-formal dance that happens in the fall. It includes many events such as a football game, parade, pep rally, and a dance. The homecoming football game is the biggest event, where students, former students (alumni), and the community come together to support their team. Before the game, schools may have a parade with decorated floats, marching bands, and school clubs. A pep rally is held to get students excited, featuring cheerleaders, music, and speeches. After the game, students attend a semi-formal dance to celebrate. For homecoming, students dress nicely but not as formal as prom. Girls often wear short or semi-formal dresses. Boys usually wear dress shirts and pants, sometimes with a tie or jacket.

Some schools have informal dances (casual dances) where students can wear jeans and t-shirts instead of formal clothing. Choose clothes that allow you to dance easily. These dances are usually more relaxed and fun, allowing students to enjoy music and social time without dressing up. Wear a shorter dress, skirt, slacks, or a button-up shirt.

Before the Dance

Students can go to the dance with friends, with a date, or by themselves. Some prefer to go as a group, while others may attend with a special someone. Either way, everyone is welcome to enjoy the event.

Many students take group pictures before the dance. Some go to a photography studio, while others take pictures at home, in a park, or at a nice location with friends and family. These photos create lasting memories of the special night.

At the dance, it is important to be friendly and talk to others. Saying hello, smiling, and being open to conversation can help make the night more enjoyable. Whether dancing, chatting, or just enjoying the atmosphere, being social can make the event even more fun.

During Dance

Let's take a look at what happens at a school dance and how to behave so you can feel more comfortable.

Dancing and Personal Space

At school dances, it is important to respect personal space and give others room to dance comfortably. Everyone should feel safe and enjoy themselves.

For casual dancing, students can move to the music and have fun. It is common for friends to dance in groups, especially at fast-paced songs. Boys often jump up and down together in a circle or crowd, following the beat and cheering each other on. This makes the dance fun and energetic.

For slow dancing, some students may feel unsure at first. If you are not sure how to dance, it can help to watch others first before trying. Slow dancing is usually done with a partner, but it's also perfectly fine to sway back and forth alone or with friends.

If you want to slow dance with someone, always ask for permission before dancing, touching or moving closer. This shows respect and politeness. If the person does not want to dance, that's okay. Please respect their wishes. You can find a friend to talk to or dance nearby instead. Some students enjoy being at a dance but may not feel comfortable dancing with a partner, and that's completely normal.

Most importantly, be yourself at the dance. No one expects perfect dance moves, so just relax and enjoy the music. The goal is to have fun, make memories, and celebrate with friends.

Being Polite and Respectful

At school dances, it is important to be polite and respectful to others. Everyone is there to have fun, so following simple rules of good behavior helps create a positive experience for everyone. There should be no rough behavior, such as pushing, shoving, or loud yelling. The dance floor can get crowded, so it is important to be aware of others and keep things safe.

Students should also respect boundaries. If someone does not want to dance or says no to a request, their choice should be respected without pressure. Likewise, you should not be pressured to do anything that you do not wish to do. Alcohol and drugs are not allowed at school dances. Schools have strict rules to ensure a safe and fun environment, and bringing these substances can lead to serious consequences. Dancing for a long time can make you tired.

Take a short break, drink water, and rest if needed. Most importantly, be kind. Do not make fun of how others dance or dress. Everyone has their own style, and showing kindness helps make the dance enjoyable for all.

Asking Someone to Dance

Asking someone to dance can feel scary, but it is a normal part of school dances. The most important thing is to be polite when asking. A simple phrase like "Would you like to dance?" is a respectful way to invite someone.

If the person says no, don't take it personally. There are many reasons someone might decline. It's best to smile and move on without feeling bad. You can talk to a friend, ask someone else to dance, or simply enjoy the slow song by standing nearby or swaying with a group of friends.

Feeling nervous at the dance is completely normal. Many people feel shy at dances, but it is important to remember that everyone is there to have fun. A helpful tip is to remind yourself that most people are too focused on themselves to remember what you do. So, relax, enjoy the music, and don't let self-consciousness stop you from having a great time!

At the End of the Dance

As the dance comes to an end, it is a good idea to say goodbye and thank your friends and dance partners for a fun night. Showing appreciation makes the experience more meaningful. Many students also like to take group photos before leaving to capture fun memories of the evening. These pictures can be great reminders of the special event. Lastly, it is important to plan your ride home ahead of time. Make sure you have a safe way to get home, whether it's with a parent, guardian, or a trusted friend. Ending the night on a positive and responsible note ensures that the dance is both enjoyable and safe.

If There is a Problem

If you ever feel uncomfortable at the dance, it is important to tell a teacher or chaperone right away. School staff are there to keep students safe and can help if there is an issue. If you see someone in trouble, such as a student feeling unwell or being treated unfairly, try to help them if you can or inform an adult. Looking out for each other ensures that everyone has a safe and enjoyable time at the dance.

Key Takeaways

- Wear the right clothes for the type of dance you are attending.
- Be polite and respect personal space.
- Dance in a way that feels comfortable for you.
- Stay hydrated and take breaks.
- Have fun and enjoy the moment!

Reflection Questions

1. At a school dance, respecting personal space is important. What are two ways you can make sure you respect others while dancing?
2. If you want to ask someone to dance, what is a polite and respectful way to do so? How should you respond if they say no?

Chapter 17: After-School Activities – A Guide for Newcomer Students and Parents

After-school activities matter. In the United States, many students join after-school activities, which take place after the regular school day ends. These activities help students learn new skills, make friends, and have fun. Research shows that participating in extracurricular activities improves teamwork, leadership, and time management skills (National Center for Education Statistics [NCES], 2021).

In addition to these benefits, colleges look for well-rounded students. Being involved in a few well-selected activities can make a big difference when applying to universities. Schools value students who can balance academics with extracurricular activities, as it shows dedication and responsibility.

This guide explains what after-school activities are, why they are important, and how parents can help their children choose the right activities.

What Are After-School Activities?

After-school activities are structured programs that take place outside regular school hours. Activities happen at schools, community centers, or local organizations. They include sports, clubs, arts, volunteering, and academic programs (Afterschool Alliance, 2020). Each school will have a list of programs they offer.

Examples of After-School Activities

Basketball: A team sport where players score points by shooting a ball into a hoop.

Soccer: A game where two teams try to score goals by kicking a ball into a net.

Track and Field: Events where students run, jump, or throw.

Swimming: Students race in the water or practice different strokes like freestyle or backstroke.

Football: A team sport where players try to carry or kick the ball into the other team's end zone.

Robotics Club: A school club where students work together to design, build, and program robots. Students learn about engineering, coding, and problem-solving while having fun creating machines that can move, complete tasks, or even compete in challenges.

Overcoming Challenges and Trying New Activities

Some students may feel nervous about joining a new activity, especially if they have never tried it before. You do not have to be great at something to enjoy it. For example, I had never played soccer before my 10th-grade year, but I decided to try it. I was not great at it, but I made friends, had fun, and learned teamwork skills. Later, I also joined color guard, which was something completely new for me, but I enjoyed performing with a team.

In larger schools, athletics can be very competitive, and not everyone who tries out will make the team. For students whose identity is tied to a single sport, not making the team can feel heartbreaking. However, disappointment is a normal part of life and learning. If you don't make the team, consider joining another activity or trying again next year.

For example, a student who doesn't make the soccer team could join the cross-country team, a recreational league, or a fitness club to stay active and involved. According to the U.S. Department of Education (2022), extracurricular activities help students build skills and improve their chances for college admission.

Why Are After-School Activities Important?

After-school activities help students learn and grow in ways that go beyond the classroom. They provide opportunities to gain new skills, meet friends, and develop confidence. These activities also help students stay active, learn responsibility, and even improve their chances of getting into college.

After-school activities teach students important skills such as teamwork, creativity, and communication. For example, drama club helps students improve their acting and public speaking skills, while soccer teaches teamwork and fitness. These activities allow students to explore new interests and develop talents they might not learn in regular classes.

Joining after-school activities helps students meet others who share their interests. For example, if a student loves music, joining the school band allows them to meet people who enjoy playing instruments or singing. These friendships can make school more enjoyable and create lasting connections.

Succeeding in an activity can make students feel proud of themselves. When students achieve something, like learning a new basketball move or performing in a school play, they gain confidence. This self-belief can help them in other areas of life, including school and social situations.

Being part of a team teaches students the importance of commitment and accountability. For example, in a volunteering program, students learn how to be responsible by helping others and caring for their community. These experiences prepare students for future jobs and responsibilities.

Sports and physical activities help students stay active and improve their overall well-being. Activities like football, swimming, or dance keep students fit while also teaching discipline and teamwork. Staying active also helps with stress relief and mental health.

Colleges look for students who are involved in activities because it shows dedication, leadership, and responsibility. Participating in a few well-chosen activities is better than joining too many and not being committed. For example, a student who participates in student council, a sport, and a volunteer program shows that they have leadership and teamwork skills, which can help them stand out in college applications.

Extracurricular activities help students learn life skills and make it easier to get into college (U.S. Department of Education, 2022). After-school activities not only make learning fun but also help students prepare for their future.

How to Choose the Right Activity

Choosing the right activity depends on a student's interests, schedule, and goals. Ask yourself these three questions to help you decide which activity to join: *What do I enjoy? What do I want to learn? How much time do I have?*

Pick an activity that seems fun. If you love art, join an art club. If you enjoy sports, try basketball or soccer. Some activities build specific skills. Debate club helps with public speaking, and coding club teaches computer skills. Some activities require more time than others. Make sure the activity fits with your schoolwork and family schedule.

How Parents Can Support Their Children in After-School Activities

Parents play an important role in helping their children succeed in after-school activities. Encouraging your children to try different activities allows them to discover what they enjoy. Parents should support their children by making sure they have transportation to and from activities and helping them create a schedule that balances school and extracurriculars.

Being positive is also important. Sometimes, an activity may feel difficult at first, but children should be encouraged to keep going and given time to adjust. Parents can remind their children that trying new things helps them learn and grow.

Getting involved is another great way to support children. Parents can volunteer for school events, help with practices, or attend performances and games to show they care about their child's interest. According to the Harvard Family Research Project (2021), parental involvement in extracurricular activities can positively impact student success.

By encouraging participation, providing support, staying positive, and getting involved, parents can help their children enjoy and benefit from after-school activities.

Key Takeaways

- After-school activities are an important part of student life in the U.S.
- They help students learn new skills, make friends, gain confidence, stay healthy, and prepare for college.
- For both students and parents, after-school activities offer great opportunities to get involved and connect with the school community.
- By participating in after-school activities, students can grow, explore their interests, and develop lifelong skills.

Reflection Questions

1. After-school activities help students learn new skills, make friends, and build confidence. What is one activity you might enjoy, and how could it help you?
2. Some activities require more time and effort than others. Why is it important to choose an activity that fits your schedule? How can parents help students balance school, activities, and free time?

References

Afterschool Alliance. (2020). *Benefits of Afterschool Programs*. Retrieved from www.afterschoolalliance.org

Harvard Family Research Project. (2021). *Parental Support and Extracurricular Activities*. Retrieved from www.hfrp.org

National Afterschool Association. (2021). *The Impact of After-School Programs on Student Development*. Retrieved from www.naa.org

National Center for Education Statistics (NCES). (2021). *Extracurricular Participation and Student Achievement.* Retrieved from www.nces.ed.gov

U.S. Department of Education. (2022). *How Extracurricular Activities Support Student Success.* Retrieved from www.ed.gov

Chapter 18: Post-High School Plans – A Guide for Students and Parents

Graduating from high school is a big milestone, but it also comes with an important question: What should I do with the rest of my life? In the past, earning a college degree often meant securing a good job, but today, that is no longer guaranteed. Job placement is not automatic with a college diploma, and student loans can prevent people from buying homes or reaching financial stability (National Center for Education Statistics [NCES], 2022).

Planning for the future requires careful thought about career paths, education costs, and financial well-being. This chapter explores different options for life after high school and how to make the best decision for your future.

Going to College or University

Attending college or university is an important step for many students in the U.S. Higher education provides opportunities for personal growth, career advancement, and specialized knowledge in different fields. However, getting into college requires meeting certain admission requirements. Your guidance counselor is a great resource who can help you understand the steps you need to take during this process. While specific requirements vary by school, most colleges consider several key factors when reviewing applications, such as GPA, test scores, extracurricular activities, personal statement, and letters of recommendations.

High School GPA

A student's Grade Point Average (GPA) is one of the most important factors in college admissions. Many colleges require a minimum GPA for admission, but competitive schools expect higher GPAs. A strong GPA shows that a student has worked hard in high school and is prepared for college-level coursework (National Center for Education Statistics [NCES], 2022). In the U.S., letter grades are given a number value and these values are used to determine high school GPA:

A = 4.0
B = 3.0
C = 2.0
D = 1.0
F = 0.0

To find your high school GPA (Grade Point Average):

1. Convert each letter grade into a number using the GPA scale (for example, A = 4.0, B = 3.0, C = 2.0, etc.).
2. Add all the numbers from your classes together.
3. Divide the total by the number of classes you took.

Example:
If you took 4 classes and received the following grades: A, B, B, and C, here's how to calculate your GPA:

Step 1: Convert each letter to a corresponding number → A (4.0), B (3.0), B (3.0), and C (2.0).
Step 2: Add the scores → 4.0 + 3.0 + 3.0 + 2.0 = 12.0
Step 3: Divide the total by the number of classes → 12.0 ÷ 4 = 3.0 GPA
A GPA of 3.0 is equal to a B average.

It is important to note that college grades and GPA may follow a slightly different grading scale.

Standardized Test Scores

Some colleges require students to take standardized tests, such as the SAT or ACT, to measure their academic abilities. However, in recent years, many schools have made these tests optional, meaning students can choose whether to submit their scores (College Board, 2023). If a school requires test scores, students should prepare by studying in advance and taking practice exams before the real test.

Extracurricular Activities

Colleges look for students who are involved in activities outside of the classroom. Participating in clubs, sports, volunteering, or leadership roles shows that a student is well-rounded and engaged in their community (U.S. Department of Education, 2022). These activities help students develop important skills like teamwork, leadership, and time management, which colleges value.

Personal Statement or Essay

Many colleges require students to write a personal statement or essay as part of their application. This essay allows students to share their background, goals, and reasons for wanting to attend that specific college (Common Application, 2023). A well-written essay can help students stand out, especially at competitive schools. Teachers can review your essay and help guide you through the writing process.

Letters of Recommendation

Some colleges ask for letters of recommendation from teachers, mentors, or counselors. These letters provide insight into a student's character, work ethic, and academic abilities. Strong recommendation letters can help support a student's application and make a positive impression on admissions officers.

Application Deadlines

Each college or university has specific application deadlines that students must follow. Some schools offer early decision or early action options, allowing students to apply and receive a response earlier than the regular deadline. Meeting deadlines is important to ensure applications are considered and processed on time.

Applying to college requires planning, preparation, and attention to detail. Understanding the admission requirements can help students stay organized and increase their chances of getting accepted into their desired schools. Most colleges use online applications, and some even use a Common Application, which sends information to multiple schools of your choice.

What is College or University?

Colleges and universities offer higher education, where students continue learning after high school. In college, students study different subjects and earn degrees that help them prepare for future careers. Each degree takes a different amount of time to complete and provides different levels of knowledge and skills.

Types of Degrees

There are two common types of college degrees. The first is an associate's degree, which takes two years to complete. It is usually offered at community colleges and can prepare students for jobs that require some college education. Some students also use an associate's degree as a step toward earning a higher degree.

The second type is a bachelor's degree, which takes four years to complete at a university or college. This degree provides more advanced education in a specific subject and is required for many professional careers. Students can choose from a variety of majors, such as business, healthcare, or engineering, depending on their interests. After a bachelor's degree, there are additional degrees such as master's, doctorate, and professional degrees.

Why Go to College?

Going to college provides many benefits that help students prepare for their future. One of the biggest benefits is gaining specialized knowledge in a subject that interests them. College allows students to study fields they are passionate about and develop expertise in areas that lead to career opportunities.

Many jobs require a college degree, and earning one can lead to better job opportunities and higher salaries. Employers often look for candidates with higher education because it shows that they have learned important skills and knowledge needed for the job.

College also helps students build connections with professors, classmates, and professionals. These connections can provide guidance, support, and even job opportunities in the future. Networking in college can be important for career success, as many jobs are found through personal and professional relationships.

Attending college is a great way for students to learn new skills, explore their interests, and work toward their career goals. Whether they choose an associate's degree or a bachelor's degree, higher education can open doors to many opportunities.

Scholarships and Financial Aid

College can be expensive, but there are ways to reduce the cost. Many students receive scholarships and financial aid to help pay for tuition, books, and other expenses. Scholarships are free money that does not have to be paid back. Financial aid includes grants and loans, which can help students cover costs based on their financial situation.

Types of Scholarships

There are different types of scholarships available for students. Merit-based scholarships are awarded to students who have good grades, athletic skills, or artistic talent. Need-based scholarships are given to students who have financial need (Federal Student Aid, 2023).

Many local businesses, community groups, and organizations offer community and local scholarships to help students in their area. Some scholarships are available for specific groups, such as minorities, women in STEM (science, technology, engineering, and math), first-generation college students, and those pursuing certain careers. Students who excel in sports may also receive athletic scholarships to play on college teams. Some schools may have career or guidance counselors who help students find these scholarships and grants, but in many cases, it is up to the student to search for and apply for these opportunities. Grants are free money for education. They do not need to be repaid (except in rare cases, like if a student withdraws from school early or doesn't meet the requirements).

Many students also rely on college loans to pay for their higher education, which must be paid back. It is important that parents do not take on too many loans for their children, as this can put their own financial future at risk.

Where to Find Scholarships?

There are many ways to search for scholarships. One of the most important steps is filling out the FAFSA (Free Application for Federal Student Aid). This form helps determine who qualifies for federal grants, loans, and scholarships. All students who plan to go to college should fill out the FAFSA every year.

Students can also use scholarship search engines, such as Fastweb, Scholarships.com, and College Board's BigFuture, to find scholarships that match their interests and background. Many states offer grants and scholarships for students who attend college in their home state. Additionally, some businesses provide scholarships for their employees or their children.

Finding scholarships takes time and effort, but it can help students save a lot of money on college costs. Applying for multiple scholarships can increase the chances of receiving financial help for education.

Jobs That Pay for College

Many companies recognize the value of an educated workforce and offer tuition assistance programs for their employees. These programs allow workers to earn a degree while working, often at little or no cost. Examples of well-known companies that offer tuition benefits at the time of this publication include:

- Starbucks – Covers tuition for full-time and part-time employees through Arizona State University's online program (Starbucks, 2023).
- Chick-fil-A – Provides scholarships and tuition assistance for eligible employees (Chick-fil-A, 2023).
- Walmart and Sam's Club – Pays 100% of college tuition and books for employees at selected universities (Walmart, 2023).
- Amazon – Offers tuition support through the Amazon Career Choice program for most of tuition for high demand fields. (Amazon, 2023).
- UPS – Provides tuition assistance through its Earn & Learn program (UPS, 2023).

- McDonald's – Offers education benefits through its Archways to Opportunity program (McDonald's, 2023).
- Hospitals and Healthcare Systems – Many hospitals provide tuition reimbursement for employees studying nursing or healthcare-related fields (American Hospital Association, 2023).

Please always check carefully into the benefits package of an employer before accepting a job, as these can change.

How to Qualify for Employer Tuition Assistance

Many companies offer tuition assistance programs, but employees must meet certain requirements to qualify. Most employers require workers to stay with the company for a certain period before becoming eligible for tuition benefits. Some programs only cover specific colleges or degree programs, so it is important to check which schools and courses are included. Additionally, employees may need to maintain good academic standing, such as keeping a minimum GPA, to continue receiving tuition support. This is a great option for students who want to gain work experience, earn an income, and reduce college costs at the same time.

Vocational or Trade School

A vocational or trade school teaches students specific job skills needed for certain careers. These schools train people for hands-on jobs such as electrician, mechanic, chef, plumber, or watchmaker. Unlike traditional colleges, trade schools offer shorter programs, usually lasting between six months and two years. Students receive practical training that helps them learn job skills quickly and start working sooner. Many trade jobs are in high demand and offer good salaries without requiring a four-year college degree (National Association of Career Colleges, 2021). For students who enjoy working with their hands and want a fast and affordable path to a career, vocational school can be a great option.

Entering the Workforce (Full-Time Job)

Starting a full-time job after high school is a great way to gain work experience and financial independence. Working full-time helps individuals develop job skills such as time management, teamwork, and problem-solving, which are important in any career.

To find a job, applicants can apply online or in person, depending on the employer's hiring process. Preparing for interviews by practicing common questions can help job seekers feel more confident. Some jobs also require certifications, such as a food safety certification for restaurant positions (U.S. Bureau of Labor Statistics, 2022). By gaining experience and building skills, full-time workers can create opportunities for career growth and future success.

How AI is Changing the Future of Work

The world of work is changing quickly because of artificial intelligence (AI). AI is already replacing some repetitive jobs, such as data entry and manufacturing, and in the future, it will impact even more industries (U.S. Bureau of Labor Statistics, 2023). While AI will eliminate some jobs, it will also create new opportunities and change the skills needed in the workplace.

How AI Will Change Jobs

AI will eliminate some jobs by replacing roles that involve repetitive tasks. For example, assembly line jobs in factories and customer service chatbots that answer basic questions are already being handled by AI. However, AI will also create new jobs in areas such as AI development, AI ethics, and human-AI collaboration. As technology advances, job requirements will change, and workers will need to adapt by learning AI-related skills, such as data analysis and programming.

What This Means for Students

Many future careers do not exist today, so students should focus on learning how to adapt to new technology. Problem-solving and critical thinking skills will become even more important, as workers will need to think creatively and work with AI instead of being replaced by it. Lifelong learning will also be necessary, meaning students must continue building new skills throughout their careers to stay competitive in the job market.

AI is transforming the workplace, but those who are willing to learn and adapt will find new opportunities and exciting career paths.

Key Takeaways

- A college degree does not guarantee a job, and student loans can create financial challenges.
- Scholarships and grants are available for students who qualify, reducing the cost of higher education.
- Some companies offer tuition assistance to employees, making college more affordable.
- Parents should avoid taking on unmanageable debt for their child's education and instead find other ways to support them.
- Trade schools and apprenticeships provide high-demand skills and are an alternative to traditional college.
- AI will change and eliminate some jobs, so students must focus on adaptability and lifelong learning.

Reflection Questions

1. What are two factors that students should consider when choosing their post – high school path?
2. How can students get ready for jobs that keep changing because of new technology like AI?
3. What are some ways to make college more affordable without taking on large amounts of debt?

References and Resources

Note: The following websites and resources were either cited in this chapter or recommended for additional support. Some were not directly quoted or paraphrased but are included for transparency and easy access.

Amazon. (2023). *Career Choice Program*. Retrieved from www.amazon.com

American Hospital Association. (2023). *Tuition Reimbursement in Healthcare*. Retrieved from www.aha.org

Chick-fil-A. (2023). *Scholarships & Education Assistance*. Retrieved from www.chick-fil-a.com

College Board. (n.d.). *BigFuture: Plan for college*. https://bigfuture.collegeboard.org

College Board. (2023). *SAT and ACT Testing Policies*. Retrieved from www.collegeboard.org

Common Application. (2023). *How to Write a Personal Statement*. Retrieved from www.commonapp.org

Fastweb. (n.d.). *Find scholarships for college*. https://www.fastweb.com

Federal Student Aid. (2023). *Types of Financial Aid*. Retrieved from www.studentaid.gov

McDonald's. (2023). *Archways to Opportunity Program*. Retrieved from www.mcdonalds.com

National Association of Career Colleges. (2021). *Vocational and Trade School Education*. Retrieved from www.nacc.ca

National Center for Education Statistics (NCES). (2022). *Post-High School Outcomes: Trends and Statistics*. Retrieved from www.nces.ed.gov

Scholarships.com. (n.d.). *College scholarships, grants & financial aid*. https://www.scholarships.com

Starbucks. (2023). *College Achievement Plan*. Retrieved from www.starbucks.com

U.S. Bureau of Labor Statistics. (2022). *Employment and Training Outlook for Young Workers*. Retrieved from www.bls.gov

U.S. Department of Defense. (2022). *Military Career Pathways*. Retrieved from www.defense.gov

U.S. Department of Education. (2022). *Higher Education and Career Pathways*. Retrieved from www.ed.gov

UPS. (2023). *Earn & Learn Tuition Assistance Program*. Retrieved from www.ups.com

Walmart. (2023). *Live Better U Tuition Program*. Retrieved from www.walmart.com

Chapter 19: Gender Roles and Expectations at School and Work: A Simple Guide for Students and Parents

Personal Story: Learning About Gender Roles

Many of us realize at some point that gender roles are something we practice every day. Gender roles are the ideas or expectations that a society has about how people should behave based on whether they are male or female. We are often raised, or socialized, to act in ways that match our culture's expectations for boys and girls. For example, girls are often told to like pink, while boys are told to like blue. These roles are taught to us from a young age and come from many places, such as family, media, school, and religion.

I remember the first time I understood that I had to start acting differently because of my gender.

I was twelve years old, playing with my male cousins and one of my female friends, when I was suddenly called to speak to my father. Usually, I translated for my father when foreign aid workers brought supplies to the refugee camp, so I thought he needed my help. However, this time was different. My friend, her brother, and I were listening to American music in one of the aid workers' vehicles. I usually wasn't disturbed while playing unless it was time to eat, so being called over was unusual.

When I reached my father, he spoke to me sternly in front of everyone and told me that I should not be hanging around the trucks. I was confused because I had done nothing wrong. I felt that I should be allowed to do what my male cousins were doing. However, my uncle and father saw things differently. They believed that, as I was turning into a young lady, certain behaviors were no longer appropriate for me. I think I was the last one to realize this change in expectations, maybe because I still looked like a boy with long hair. I just remember feeling embarrassed and different.

Understanding gender roles is important when adjusting to life in a new country. In the United States, men and women have equal rights at school and work. Boys and girls can participate in the same activities, take the same classes, and pursue any career they choose (U.S. Department of Education, 2022). However, some gender expectations still exist. Learning about gender roles can help you understand what to expect at school, at work, and in social situations.

Gender Roles at School

In the U.S. schools, boys and girls have the same opportunities to learn, play sports, and participate in different activities. Schools encourage equality, meaning that all students can explore their interests without being limited by traditional gender expectations. Students are encouraged to follow their interests and abilities, no matter their gender.

Boys and girls can play the same sports, such as soccer, basketball, baseball, and even football or wrestling. Schools typically have teams for males and females to promote fair competition and safety. This allows all students to enjoy athletics and compete based on their skills and interests.

All students are encouraged to take math, science, art, music, and other subjects. It is okay for girls to be good at science and for boys to enjoy art or music. In the U.S., students are not expected to follow traditional gender roles when choosing subjects or career paths.

In the U.S., boys and girls can be friends without judgment. Coed friendships (friendships between boys and girls) are common, and students often work together on school projects, join the same clubs, and spend time together outside of class.

Gender Roles at Work

In the workplace, men and women can have the same jobs and receive equal pay for equal work (U.S. Equal Employment Opportunity Commission [EEOC], 2022). However, research shows that men and women do not always earn the same amount for similar work, despite laws promoting equal pay.

Studies show that women earn about 82 cents for every dollar a man earns (U.S. Bureau of Labor Statistics [BLS], 2023). This gap is even larger for women of color and remains even when comparing men and women with the same job, education, and experience (BLS, 2023). The pay gap impacts families negatively.

Understanding the Gender Pay Gap

There are several reasons why the wage gap continues to exist. One major factor is career choices. Women are more likely to work in lower-paying fields such as education and healthcare, while men dominate higher-paying fields like engineering and finance (U.S. Department of Labor, 2022).

Another reason is discrimination, or unequal treatment. Some employers still pay men more than women for doing the same work (EEOC, 2022). Women also face what is known as the "motherhood penalty". Many women take time off for caregiving, which can hurt their chances for promotions and higher salaries (American Economic Association, 2021). More women stay home to care for the children.

Also, taking time out of the workforce can negatively impact women's careers. Women who leave their jobs for extended periods, such as to raise children, may find it difficult to return to the same salary level or advance in their careers after they come back to work (Pew Research Center, 2022).

Although progress has been made toward equal pay, the gender pay gap still exists due to career differences, discrimination, and time away from work. Understanding these factors can help workers advocate for fair pay and workplace equality.

Staying Home and Career Impact

Some families decide that one parent should stay home to take care of the children. Usually, this is the parent who earns less at work.

Staying home can help the family, but it may also bring financial challenges (U.S. Bureau of Labor Statistics, 2023).

Taking a long break from work can make it harder to find a job later. When people stay home, they may miss chances for pay raises, bonuses, and promotions. This can negatively affect how much money they earn in the future. Also, they may save less for retirement. Retirement savings usually come from the money people earn at work. Social Security benefits and retirement plans from jobs depend on how much money a person makes and how long they work.

Another problem is that some employers do not like long job gaps. This can make it harder to find a good job after staying home for many years. Employers may worry that a person with a long job gap has lost some skills or is not used to working anymore. They might also think the person will need more training. Because of this, employers may choose to hire someone who has been working recently instead.

Families should think carefully before deciding if one parent should stop working. If the decision is made for one parent to stay home, the family should plan to help that parent return to work more easily in the future. To stay connected to a career, parents can try part-time jobs, freelance work, volunteering, or online classes. These options help parents keep learning, gain experience, and make it easier to find a job later (Pew Research Center, 2022).

Fixing the Pay Gap

Men and women should be paid the same for doing the same job. However, this does not always happen. To fix the pay gap, companies should share salary information, support women in getting high-paying jobs, and support women when they negotiate salaries (National Women's Law Center, 2023).

Jobs are not limited to men or women. Anyone can pursue any career they choose. But in some workplaces, men still get paid more or have more chances to get promotions than women. When people learn about these problems, they can speak up for fair pay and ask for what they deserve.

Respecting Gender Differences

Everyone is different, and personal interests are not determined by gender. It is important to avoid generalizing people such as saying, "Boys don't cry" or "Girls can't play sports." People should be free to express themselves without being judged based on gender.

In school and at work, it is also important to support each other. If someone is treated unfairly because of their gender, speaking up can help create a more equal and respectful environment. Respecting all people equally helps schools and workplaces become more positive, welcoming, and fair for everyone.

Key Takeaways

- In the U.S., it is generally believed that males and females should be treated equally.
- Workplace gender pay gaps still exist, and it is important to advocate for fair pay.
- Families must consider the financial impact of one parent staying home to care for children.
- Supporting gender equality in schools and workplaces benefits everyone.

Reflection Questions

1. Why is it important for everyone to have the same opportunities, no matter their gender?
2. How can schools and workplaces promote equality for all people?

References

American Economic Association. (2021). *The motherhood penalty: How career breaks affect earnings.* https://www.aea web.org

National Women's Law Center. (2023). *Wage transparency and closing the gender pay gap.* https://www.nwlc.org

Pew Research Center. (2022). *Gender gaps in employment and income.* https://www.pewresearch.org

U.S. Bureau of Labor Statistics. (2023). *The gender wage gap.* https://www.bls.gov

U.S. Department of Education. (2022). *Gender Equality in Schools.* https://www.ed.gov

U.S. Department of Labor. (2022). *Understanding equal pay laws.* https://www.dol.gov

U.S. Equal Employment Opportunity Commission. (2022). *Workplace Gender Equality.* https://www.eeoc.gov

SECTION 5: DAILY LIFE AND PRACTICAL SKILLS

Chapter 20: Keeping Yourself and Your Environment Clean

Why is cleanliness important? Keeping yourself and your surroundings clean is important for health, confidence, and respect. Good hygiene helps prevent illness and makes you feel good about yourself. A clean environment in homes, schools, and public places improves the quality of life for everyone (Centers for Disease Control and Prevention [CDC], 2021).

Personal Hygiene: Taking Care of Yourself

Personal hygiene means keeping your body clean to stay healthy and avoid bad smells (CDC, 2021). Good hygiene helps you stay healthy and feel confident in daily life. In the United States, personal hygiene is very important. Many Americans believe that being clean shows self-respect and respect for others. Practicing good hygiene habits helps people feel good and fit in at school, work, and in social situations.

Bathing or showering regularly is important to wash away dirt and sweat. Many people shower or bathe daily, using soap, water, and shampoo to clean their bodies and hair. In cold weather, applying lotion helps keep the skin from becoming dry (Mayo Clinic, 2022).

Brushing your teeth is another key part of hygiene. Brushing twice a day helps prevent cavities and bad breath. Using toothpaste and mouthwash removes bacteria and keeps the mouth fresh and healthy (American Dental Association [ADA], 2020).

Washing your hands often is important to stop the spread of germs. Hands should be washed with soap and water for 20 seconds before eating, after using the bathroom, or after coughing, sneezing, or touching dirty surfaces (CDC, 2021).

To prevent body odor, people apply deodorant after showering. However, it is best to avoid too much perfume because strong smells can bother others (American Academy of Dermatology [AAD], 2019).

Hair care is also important. Washing your hair a few times a week keeps it clean and healthy. Brushing or combing your hair daily prevents tangles and helps keep it neat (AAD, 2019).

Keeping nails clean is another part of personal hygiene. Trimming nails regularly prevents dirt and bacteria from collecting underneath, which can cause infections (Mayo Clinic, 2022).

Wearing clean clothes is an important part of good hygiene. Most families in the U.S. do laundry about once a week. Changing clothes every day helps people stay fresh and avoid body odor (CDC, 2021).

Practicing good personal hygiene is important for staying healthy, preventing illness, and feeling confident in school, work, and social situations.

Keeping School and Workspaces Clean

A clean school and workspace help students and employees focus, stay healthy, and respect their environment (National Education Association [NEA], 2018). Keeping areas clean is important for several reasons.

First, cleanliness shows respect for teachers, classmates, coworkers, and staff. When everyone takes care of shared spaces, it creates a positive environment where people feel comfortable.

Second, a clean space reduces germs and prevents sickness. Schools and workplaces have many people in one place, making it easy for illnesses to spread. Cleaning up and following hygiene practices help keep everyone healthy.

Lastly, cleaning up teaches responsibility and independence. When students and workers take care of their own space, they learn good habits that will help them in daily life. Being responsible for keeping spaces clean also shows that a person cares about their surroundings and respects others.

Cleaning Up Shared Spaces

Keeping shared spaces clean and organized is important in schools and workplaces. A clean environment helps everyone focus, stay healthy, and work more efficiently.

One way to keep spaces clean is by organizing your desk or workspace. Always put away books, supplies, or tools after using them. Throw away trash, such as papers, wrappers, and food scraps, to prevent clutter. Wiping down your workspace regularly helps keep it neat and free of germs.

If a spill or mess happens, it is important to clean it up right away. Use paper towels or cleaning wipes to clean small spills. If the mess is too big, ask for help to make sure it is cleaned properly.

Taking care of shared materials is also part of keeping a space clean. Always return books, computers, and supplies to their proper places so others can find and use them. If you borrow something, make sure to put it back when you are done. Keeping shared spaces clean and organized helps everyone work better and feel comfortable in their environment.

Keeping the Home Clean

A clean home makes life healthier and more comfortable for everyone. Parents and children can work together to keep the house tidy. Some tasks should be done daily, while others can be done weekly or monthly to keep everything fresh and clean.

Daily cleaning includes washing dishes, wiping kitchen counters, sweeping or vacuuming high-traffic areas, and making the bed. Picking up clutter every day helps keep rooms tidy. Weekly cleaning involves cleaning the bathroom, including the sink, toilet, shower, and mirrors. It's also important to change bed sheets, dust furniture, mop floors, and take out the trash to prevent bad smells.

For monthly cleaning, tasks like deep cleaning the fridge, washing windows, and organizing closets help maintain a clean and fresh home. It is also a good idea to wipe down doors, light switches, and baseboards to remove dust. By following a cleaning routine, your home will stay fresh, organized, and comfortable for you and your family.

Cleaning Chart Example

Using a cleaning schedule can help everyone take responsibility for different tasks. Many parents use a schedule to assign chores, or cleaning duties, to each family member. Even young children can learn to help by putting their toys away after using them. Here is an example of a simple weekly cleaning chart:

Task	Person Responsible	Day to Complete
Wash dishes	Ann and Sam	Daily
Vacuum floors	Maria	Tuesday
Take out trash	Dad	Monday and Thursday
Laundry	Mom	Saturday
Clean bathroom	Everyone	Sunday

Creating a cleaning routine at home helps children learn responsibility and keeps the house organized (Mayo Clinic, 2022).

Building Responsibility and Respect Through Daily Cleaning Habits

Developing good cleaning habits helps keep homes, schools, and workplaces clean and comfortable for everyone. It is important to take responsibility by cleaning up after yourself whenever you make a mess. Paying attention to when something needs cleaning, such as dirty floors or cluttered spaces, helps maintain a neat environment. Being respectful of school and home property means treating furniture, supplies, and shared spaces with care.

Additionally, helping others by offering assistance when someone needs help cleaning shows kindness and teamwork. Practicing these habits will create a cleaner, more organized, and more enjoyable space for everyone.

Cleanliness is Important

Keeping spaces clean and organized is important for learning, working, and staying healthy. When a place is neat, it is easier to focus at school or work without distractions. Helping others by cleaning up shared spaces makes the environment better for everyone and shows respect for classmates, coworkers, and family members. A clean environment also improves health by reducing germs and sickness, keeping people safe from illness. By maintaining cleanliness, individuals can create a more productive, pleasant, and healthy space for themselves and others.

Case Study: "You Live Here, You Work Here"

In Bosnia, when I was growing up, traditional gender roles were expected. My grandmother did not work outside the home, but she took care of all household responsibilities, and her children helped her as they grew older. My parents lived in the city, where the cost of living was higher, so both of them typically worked sperate shifts to help raise us. However, in the last few years before we came to the U.S., my mother had stopped working due to the war. As a result, our family dynamic changed, and she took on most of the household responsibilities.

Moving to the U.S. was a huge adjustment for all of us. I remember our first week here. While our sponsors were still preparing an apartment for us, we lived with a host family. They were very kind and helped us adjust to American customs.

My father was used to being the one who worked outside the home, while my mother stayed home to raise my younger brother. She did most of the housework, with my sister and me helping. Because of this, it was normal for my father to finish eating lunch and leave his plate on the table. My sister and I would clean up after him, or if we weren't available, my mother would do it.

However, the mother in our host family must have noticed this. One day, she politely and with a smile said to my father, "You live here, you work here." Since my father didn't speak much English at the time, I had to translate this phrase for him, which made me feel a little uncomfortable because showing respect for my father was important to me.

But he got the message, and he cleans up after eating now. Sometimes, he even jokes with me when he cleans up, saying, "You live here, you work here."

Lesson Learned: Adapt to Cultural Expectations

In different cultures, household roles and responsibilities can vary. In some families, tasks are divided based on traditional gender roles, while in others, responsibilities are shared more equally. Moving to a new country often means adjusting to different expectations.

This experience taught me that adapting to new customs doesn't mean losing respect for our traditions, but it does mean learning to balance them with the expectations of the culture we now live in.

Key Takeaways

- Good hygiene keeps you healthy and confident in your new environment.
- Keeping spaces clean shows respect for others.
- Cleaning up after yourself is part of being responsible.
- A clean environment makes learning and working easier.

Reflection Questions

1. What are two daily hygiene habits you should follow to keep yourself clean? How do these habits help prevent sickness?
2. Why is it important to clean up after yourself in shared spaces like schools, workspaces, and homes? How does this help others?

References

American Academy of Dermatology (AAD). (2019). *Personal Hygiene and Skin Care Guidelines*. Retrieved from www.aad.org

American Dental Association (ADA). (2020). *Brushing and Oral Hygiene Recommendations*. Retrieved from www.ada.org

Centers for Disease Control and Prevention (CDC). (2021). *Handwashing and Personal Hygiene Practices*. Retrieved from www.cdc.gov

Mayo Clinic. (2022). *Healthy Hygiene Habits for Children and Teens*. Retrieved from www.mayoclinic.org

National Education Association (NEA). (2018). *Creating a Clean and Respectful*. Washington, D.C.: National Education Association.

Chapter 21: Shopping in the United States: A Guide for Newcomers

Shopping in the U.S. may be different from what you are used to experiencing. This guide will help you understand important parts of shopping, such as going to stores, using self-checkouts, talking to customer service, understanding measurements, and avoiding unnecessary spending (Federal Trade Commission, 2022).

How to Shop in a Store

Shopping in the U.S. is easy and convenient. Store hours are usually posted online and at the entrance, so you can check when the store is open. Here are some things you should know:

- Shopping Aisles: Stores are divided into aisles, which are long rows where products are displayed. Each aisle has different types of products, such as food, clothes, or electronics. You can walk through the aisles to find what you need.
- Prices: Prices are marked on tags or labels on the shelves or products. The amount listed is the cost of the item before sales tax.
- Sales Tax: In most states, the price you see does not include tax. Sales tax is added at checkout and depends on the state you are in (U.S. Department of the Treasury, 2023). For example, if a shirt is priced at $20 and the sales tax is 7%, the total cost will be $21.40 at checkout.

Customer Service

Customer service is very important in American stores. Employees are available to help shoppers.

- Greeting: When you enter a store, employees might say "Hello" or "Welcome!" This is a friendly way to greet customers.

- Asking for Help: If you can't find something, it's okay to ask a store employee for help. You can say, "Excuse me, where can I find [item]?" or "Can you help me?"
- Checkout Process: After collecting everything you need, go to the checkout counter. The cashier will scan your items, tell you the total cost, and ask how you want to pay.

Prices in stores are not negotiable because they are determined by barcodes. Bargaining is not common in most U.S. stores (Consumer Financial Protection Bureau, 2022). However, it is a good idea to compare prices at multiple stores, especially for expensive items, before making large purchases.

Self-Checkout

Many stores have self-checkout machines that let you scan and pay for your own items.

Using self-checkout is easy if you follow these steps:

1. Scan Your Items: Place each item's barcode under the scanner.
2. Check the Price: The machine will show the price on the screen.
3. Pay for Your Items: Choose how you want to pay, such as with cash, credit card, or debit card.
4. Take Your Receipt: After payment, grab your receipt and place your items in bags before leaving.

If an item does not scan properly, you can press the "Help" button to ask a store employee for assistance.

Common Shopping Manners

Here are some shopping etiquette tips to follow:

Respect Personal Space: People like to have space while shopping. Avoid standing too close when others are looking at products. Also, if you are shopping with another person, do not block isles by walking, or standing side by side.

167

Queuing (Standing in Line): In the U.S., it is important to wait your turn in line. Always stand in line and wait until it's your turn at the register.

Using a Shopping Cart: If you have many items, you can use a shopping cart (a large basket with wheels). When finished, return the cart to the designated area outside the store.

Paying for Items

There are several ways to pay in U.S. stores:

Cash: You can pay with dollars ($) and cents (¢). The cashier will give you change if you pay more than the total amount.

Credit or Debit Cards: Most people use credit cards or debit cards to pay. Insert, tap, or swipe your card in the machine to complete the transaction. Some stores allow contactless payment using phones or smartwatches. Tap the device near the reader to pay.

Coupons and Discounts: Some stores offer coupons (paper or digital) that lower the price of an item. Coupons can be found in newspapers, store apps, or online.

Returns and Exchanges

If you need to return or exchange an item, here's what to do:

Check the Store's Return Policy: Stores have different rules for returns. Some allow returns within 30 days, while others may not accept returns for certain items (Federal Trade Commission, 2022).

Keep Your Receipt: You usually need the receipt to return or exchange an item. Some stores allow exchanges for a different item instead of a refund if you do not have a receipt.

Consumer Culture and Materialism

One of the first things newcomers notice is how American culture encourages shopping. This is called consumer culture where businesses constantly advertise products to encourage sales. As soon as September begins, stores start selling Halloween decorations. In November, Christmas products appear, even though Thanksgiving hasn't happened yet. Seasonal sales and promotions are everywhere, inviting people to buy more.

Advertisements constantly encourage people to spend money. From pumpkin spice lattes in the fall to massive Black Friday sales, American culture connects holidays and emotions to shopping (U.S. Department of Commerce, 2023). While shopping can be fun, it can also lead to unnecessary spending and financial stress (Consumer Financial Protection Bureau, 2022). Additionally, products today are often designed to be eventually replaced, allowing companies to benefit from ongoing sales. Saving money and making smart purchases will help you manage your finances better.

Smart Shopping Tips

There are many ways to save money when making a purchase. Here are several suggestions:

- Shop at discount stores: Grocery outlet stores, thrift shops, and dollar stores sell many items for lower prices than big supermarkets.
- Buy items off-season: Stores discount holiday and seasonal products once the season is over. For example, winter clothes are cheaper in spring, and summer items go on sale in the fall.
- Use coupons and discounts: Some stores offer paper or digital coupons that lower prices of items. Many grocery stores have loyalty programs that give discounts.
- Make a shopping list: Only buy the items from your list. Do not go grocery shopping when hungry because you will buy more items.
- Clearance Sections: Look for "Clearance" sections in stores. These are areas where products are sold at the lowest price. Always ask yourself, "Do I really need this item, and is it in my budget?"
- Be mindful of sales tricks: Just because something is "on sale" doesn't mean you need it.
- Wait 24 Hours: If you see something in the store that isn't on your list, wait 24 hours before buying it. If you truly need

it, you will come back. If not, not buying it will help you save money.

Understanding Weight and Measurement in the U.S.

The United States uses a different measurement system than many other countries. The most common system is called the U.S. Customary System (also known as the Imperial System). The metric system is still used in science, medicine, and some industries.

Weight Measurements

- Ounces (oz): Small items like snacks or drinks are often measured in ounces. For example, 1 pound (lb) is 16 ounces.
- Pounds (lbs): Heavier items like fruits, vegetables, and meats are usually measured in pounds.

Volume Measurement

- Gallons and Quarts: Liquids like milk, juice, and water are often sold in gallons (gal) or quarts (qt). For example, a small bottle of soda may be 16 ounces (oz), while a large bottle of milk may be 1 gallon (gal) (U.S. Department of Commerce, 2023).
- Cup (c): A common unit used in cooking and for measuring drinks. For example, you might use 1 cup of rice or milk in a recipe.
- Quart (qt): A larger unit for liquids. One quart has four cups. For example, a bottle of juice or a soup container is often one quart.
- Fluid Ounce (fl oz): A small unit for measuring liquids. One cup has eight fluid ounces. For example, a small juice box is about 6 fl oz.

These measurements are useful when cooking or following a recipe. Recipes also use teaspoons (tsp) and tablespoons (tbsp) to measure smaller amounts of ingredients.

Length Measurements

In the United States, people measure length using inches, feet, yards, and miles. Here are the basics:

- Inch – This is a small unit. A paperclip is about 1 inch long.
- Foot – 1 foot = 12 inches. A ruler is usually 1 foot long.
- Yard – 1 yard = 3 feet. A door is about 2 yards tall.
- Mile – 1 mile = 5,280 feet. We use miles to measure long distances, like driving or walking far.

For example, if you need to buy a curtain for a window, you will need to know the measurements. You must find out how wide and how tall the window is to buy the right size curtain. In the U.S., these measurements are usually in inches or feet. This helps you buy the right size curtain that will fit your window.

Understanding Temperature Measurements

In the United States, temperature is usually measured in degrees Fahrenheit (°F). People use Fahrenheit to describe how hot or cold the air, food, or objects feel. Fahrenheit is commonly used in the U.S. when talking about weather, cooking, and food storage. For example:

- A hot summer day might be 85°F.
- A typical oven temperature for baking is 350°F.
- A freezer should stay at 0°F or lower.
- A refrigerator is usually kept around 40°F.

Room temperature, which is typically between 68°F and 72°F, is too warm for food that needs to be refrigerated. If food gets too warm, it can spoil. That's why stores and food packages include temperature instructions in Fahrenheit (°F) to help keep food safe and specify whether it should be stored in the refrigerator or freezer.

Key Takeaways

- Be friendly when shopping. It's common to say "Hello" or "Excuse me" when talking to store workers.
- Check store hours before you go shopping. Many stores close in the evening.

- In some stores, you may have to pack your own groceries into bags.
- Understand how advertising can make people spend money, and try to avoid buying things you don't need.
- Shopping in the U.S. is easy once you understand how it works. Be polite, take your time, and don't be afraid to ask for help when you need it!

Reflection Questions

1. What is different about shopping in the United States compared to your home country?
2. What can you do to save money and make smart choices when you go shopping?
3. What measurements in the U.S. (like inches, pounds, or Fahrenheit) are new or confusing for you?

References

Consumer Financial Protection Bureau. (2022). *Understanding U.S. payment systems*. Retrieved from https://www. Consumer finance.gov

Federal Trade Commission. (2022). *Consumer rights and shopping rules*. Retrieved from https://www.ftc.gov

U.S. Department of Commerce. (2023). *Weights and measures in the United States*. Retrieved from https://www.com merce.gov

U.S. Department of the Treasury. (2023). *Sales tax in the United States*. Retrieved from https://home.treasury.gov

U.S. Department of Agriculture. (2023). *Grocery store shopping and food budgeting tips*. Retrieved from https:// www.usda.gov

Chapter 22: Doctor's Office Visits

Going to the doctor is an important part of staying healthy. Whether you need a check-up, treatment for an illness, or a physical exam for work or sports, understanding how doctor's offices and medical care works in the United States will make your visit easier.

Unlike some countries where you can just walk in, most doctor's offices in the U.S. require an appointment, which is a scheduled time to see the doctor. Knowing what to expect will help you feel more prepared and confident.

Making an Appointment and Being On Time

Making an appointment and being on time are important aspects of visiting a doctor in the U.S. Here's a guide on how to schedule a doctor's visit and what to expect:

Appointments Are Required: To see a doctor, you usually need to make an appointment ahead of time. You can call the doctor's office or use their online health portal. This portal allows you to schedule appointments, view your medical results, and communicate with your doctor.

Arrive On Time: Doctors are often on a tight schedule, and if you arrive late, you might have to reschedule. It's a good idea to get there 10-15 minutes early. This gives you enough time to check in and fill out any necessary paperwork.

Bring Important Documents: Always take your identification, insurance information, and a list of any medications you are taking. This helps the office have all the information they need for your visit.

Prepare Questions in Advance: Doctors typically have limited time for each patient. Writing down your questions beforehand ensures that you don't forget to ask about something important during your visit.

Answer Questions Honestly: Be honest when answering questions about your health and symptoms. This helps your doctor diagnose you correctly and recommend the best treatment. If they ask, *"How do you feel today?"* you can answer, *"I have a headache,"* or *"I feel fine."*

Follow Office Rules: Pay attention to the rules of the doctor's office. For example, you might be asked to turn off your cellphone or to keep noise to a minimum in the waiting area.

Ask for Clarification: If you don't understand something your doctor says, ask the doctor to explain it in simpler words. You can say, *"Sorry, I don't understand. Can you say it in a different way?"*

These steps will help you navigate your doctor's visit more smoothly and ensure you get the care you need.

Who You Will Meet at the Doctor's Office?

Different healthcare professionals work together to take care of patients. When you visit a doctor's office, you will meet several healthcare professionals, and each plays a role in your care:

Receptionist: This is the first person you meet. They help you sign in, take your insurance details, and set up your next visits. They make sure all your papers are ready for your appointment.

Nurse: Before seeing the doctor, a nurse will check things like your weight, height, temperature, and blood pressure. They get your health information ready for the doctor.

Doctor: The doctor checks you, talks about what you feel, and decides on your treatment. They are the main person you talk to about your health.

Medical Assistant: This person helps the doctor by getting the room ready and writing down notes during your visit. They make sure everything is noted correctly.

Billing or Insurance Clerk: After your visit, this person takes care of the money matters. They handle payments and work with your insurance to make sure all costs are covered.

Remember, only doctors and nurse practitioners can tell you what illness you have and give you medicine (American Medical Association, 2023). Everyone you meet at the doctor's office is there to help you get the best care possible.

Asking for an Interpreter

If you need help understanding English at the doctor's office, you can ask for a professional interpreter (US. Department of Health and Human Services, 2023). It's important not to use your children as interpreters because medical language can be complex, and it's a lot of pressure for them. Depending on the doctor's office, they might have an interpreter who can come in person or someone who can help over a video call or phone. This service is very helpful because it helps you talk with your doctor and understand important information about your health care.

Doctor's Office vs. Urgent Care vs. Emergency Room (ER)

This chart can help you determine where to go when needing medical care.

Place	When to Visit	Examples
Doctor's Office	Regular check-ups, minor illnesses	Cold, flu, allergies, prescription refills
Urgent Care	Quick care when your doctor is unavailable	Minor injuries, fever, ear infection

Emergency Room (ER)	Life-threatening emergencies	Car accident, breathing problems, severe chest pain

The ER is for serious emergencies. If you go there for a minor issue, you may have to wait a long time (Centers for Disease Control and Prevention, 2023).

What to Expect at Each Place

At the doctor's office, you need to schedule an appointment ahead of time. When you arrive, you will check in and wait until it's your turn to see the doctor for routine health issues like a cold or annual check-ups.

At urgent care, you don't need an appointment. It's quicker than the emergency room for non-life-threatening issues but can still be busy. You might go here for things like fevers, ear infections, or minor injuries like a sprained ankle. You still need to wait your turn to be seen.

The emergency room (ER) is for serious, life-threatening conditions. Patients with the most severe problems are treated first, which means if your issue is less urgent, you might wait a long time. Use the ER for major issues like severe pain, breathing problems, or significant injuries.

If you are not sure where to go for your health problem, it's a good idea to call your doctor's office first to get advice on the best place to seek care. Also, going to urgent care or the emergency room (ER) can cost more money.

Case Study: A Family's Tough Choice

A cancer patient was brain dead and kept alive by machines because his family couldn't agree on whether to stop his treatment. Despite the doctors trying everything, there was no chance he would get better. This sad situation made his family very upset and cost a lot of money.

If he had an advance directive, his wishes would have been clear, and his family would not have had to make such a hard choice. An advance directive tells doctors what to do if you get very sick and can't talk for yourself.

Lesson Learned: Stay in Control of Your Health Decisions

If you are over 18, it's a good idea to make an advance directive. Talk to your doctor and your family about it. This paper tells others what kind of medical care you want if you cannot speak or decide for yourself in the future. It can help your family feel less stressed during difficult times.

Advance Medical Directives: Planning for the Unexpected

An Advance Medical Directive is a legal document that tells doctors what kind of medical care you want if you are too sick to speak for yourself. It can be difficult to think about this, but having this document helps make sure your wishes are followed, even if you cannot make decisions later. Without clear instructions, your family might have to make hard choices during a stressful time.

There are different types of Advance Directives including the following:

- A Do Not Resuscitate (DNR) order is a legal document that tells doctors not to perform CPR (chest compressions or rescue breathing) if your heart stops or you stop breathing.
- A Living Will is a document where you explain what medical treatments you want or do not want.
- A Medical Power of Attorney is a document where you choose a trusted person to make medical decisions for you if you are not able to make them yourself.

Using Health Portals to Manage Your Care

Many doctors' offices and hospitals have online health portals that help you manage your medical care from home. These portals let you schedule appointments, see your test results, send messages to your doctor, and look at your medical records. Using a portal can save you time and make it easier to keep track of your health without always having to go to the doctor's office. To start using a portal, ask someone at your doctor's office to help you sign up.

Understanding Health Insurance in the United States

Health insurance helps people pay for medical care. This includes doctor visits, hospital stays, medications, and check-ups. In the United States, medical care can be very expensive. That is why health insurance is important. It can protect your health and your money.

Some people do not think about health insurance until they are sick. However, it is better to plan ahead. Health insurance also covers preventive care such as vaccines, tests, and regular check-ups. Preventive visits can help find problems early and keep you healthy. Having insurance can also reduce stress because you know that help is available if you need it.

For serious illnesses like cancer, health insurance is especially important. It can help pay for treatments such as surgery, chemotherapy, hospital care, and prescription medicine. These treatments cost a lot of money. If you do not have insurance, you might not be able to get the care you need. You could also end up with money problems or big medical bills. Some insurance plans also pay for mental health care and other support during recovery. Without insurance, it can be very difficult to get the care you need.

If You Do Not Have Insurance

If you do not have health insurance, there are still options that can help. Government programs like Medicaid and the Children's Health Insurance Program (CHIP) offer free or low-cost insurance for people with low income. You can also apply for health insurance through the Affordable Care Act (ACA). If you qualify, you may receive financial help to pay for your plan.

Some people use short-term insurance plans. These plans do not cover everything, but they can provide temporary help while you look for a better plan. Many hospitals also have financial assistance programs. If you need medical care, ask the hospital if they can help you apply for aid or set up a payment plan. There are also non-profit organizations that support people who cannot pay for treatment. Also, be sure to ask for interpretation services and assistance with filling out the paperwork.

Many hospitals can help you in your language. Do not let fear of paperwork stop you from getting insurance. Without insurance, you and your family could be in danger. I have personally known people who waited too long to get medical care. They did not have insurance and were afraid of casing money problems for their families.

Annual Enrollment: What You Need to Know

In the United States, most people must review or renew their health insurance every year. This time is called annual enrollment or open enrollment. It is the period when you can choose a new plan or make changes to your current plan.

If you get insurance through your job, your employer will let you know when open enrollment begins. If you buy insurance through the Affordable Care Act marketplace, the government will post the dates. Open enrollment usually takes place in the fall. It is important to pay attention to these dates because you may not be able to make changes later.

Medicare Enrollment for Older Adults

People who are 65 years old or older, or who have certain disabilities, may be able to get Medicare. This is a government health insurance program. Medicare has different parts. Part A pays for hospital care. Part B pays for doctor visits. Part D helps pay for prescription medicines.

When you first qualify for Medicare, you can choose a plan that fits your needs. After that, you can make changes once a year during the Medicare open enrollment period. This happens between October 15 and December 7. It is important to choose a plan carefully. If you start with a plan that does not cover what you need, it may be difficult, impossible, or expensive to change it later.

Why Is Important to Review Your Insurance Each Year?

Your health needs may change from year to year. Your plan may also change. For example, the cost of your plan may increase. Your medicine may no longer be covered. You may want to see a new doctor or receive care from a specialist.

During open enrollment, you can review your current plan and compare it to others. If you select the same plan, your coverage will stay the same. However, this could be a problem if your needs have changed. If you miss the enrollment period, you may lose your insurance coverage. Reviewing your plan helps ensure you have the right coverage for your situation.

Emergency Rooms Use by Uninsured Patients: Not for Long Term Care

Some people without health insurance go to the emergency room when they are very sick or injured. This is because hospitals must treat patients in an emergency, even if they do not have insurance or money to pay. This rule is part of a law called the Emergency Medical Treatment and Labor Act (EMTALA).

Emergency rooms provide care for serious and life-threatening problems. These include chest pain, broken bones, breathing problems, and severe infections. If someone is in danger, the emergency room will try to help right away. However, the emergency room is not the right place for long-term care. It also costs more money to use the emergency room compared to regular doctor visits.

While emergency rooms treat urgent problems, they do not provide care for chronic illnesses. Chronic illnesses are long-term health conditions, such as diabetes or cancer. Emergency rooms can give temporary help, such as pain medicine or tests, but they cannot give full treatment for conditions that need ongoing care.

For example, if someone has symptoms that may be related to cancer, the emergency room can do tests and provide pain relief. However, the person will still need to see a cancer specialist, called an oncologist, for full treatment. This includes chemotherapy, surgery, and long-term follow-up care. These services are not available in the emergency room. They require a care team and health insurance.

What Happens If You Need Cancer Treatment Without Insurance?

If a person is diagnosed with cancer and does not have health insurance, the cost of treatment can be very high. Hospitals may try to help by offering financial assistance or by helping the person apply for Medicaid, which is a government program for people with low income. There are also non-profit organizations that help patients pay for cancer treatment. However, without insurance, it is difficult to get all the care you may need.

In the United States, the total cost of cancer treatment for one year can range from $100,000 to over $300,000. This includes testing, surgery, chemotherapy, hospital stays, and follow-up care. If you have health insurance, your out-of-pocket costs may still be between $5,000 and $10,000 per year, depending on your plan. This is why it is important to have health coverage before a serious illness happens. Having a good insurance plan can make it easier to get the care you need and protect your family from financial hardship.

Plan Ahead for Your Health and Your Future

Health insurance protects your health, your family, and your finances. Medical problems can happen at any time. If you have insurance, you can get care when you need it without worrying about large medical bills.

Every year, take time to look at your plan. Think about what has changed in your life. If you need help, talk to someone you trust or contact a community resource center, where people can assist you.

There are often individuals and programs available to support your needs.

If you do not have insurance yet, learn about your options. It may take some time, but it is worth it. Having insurance can help you stay healthy and reduce the stress that comes with medical bills. Planning ahead is a smart way to take care of yourself and your loved ones.

Key Takeaways

- Doctor's offices require an appointment. Do not just walk in.
- Arrive ten to fifteen minutes early for your appointment.
- Ask for an interpreter if you do not understand English well. Do not use children to interpret important medical information.
- Go to the right place for medical care. The emergency room is for life-threatening emergencies only.
- Consider advance medical directives to help your family make decisions in an emergency.
- Use a health portal to check test results and schedule appointments online.
- Having no insurance can limit your access to care and create serious financial problems.
- It is important to choose a health insurance plan that fits your needs before a medical emergency happens. Remember to re-enroll each year during the annual enrollment period.

Reflection Questions

1. Why is it important to ask for an interpreter instead of relying on family members to translate?
2. How can an Advance Medical Directive help your family if there is a medical emergency?
3. Have you ever avoided going to the doctor because of cost or fear of medical bills? What support or information might help you feel more confident about getting care?

References

American Medical Association. (2023). *Understanding medical roles*. Retrieved from www.ama-assn.org

Centers for Disease Control and Prevention. (2023). *Emergency room visits and when to seek care.* Retrieved from www.cdc.gov

United States Department of Health and Human Services. (2023). *Your right to an interpreter at the doctor's office.* Retrieved from www.hhs.gov

Chapter 23: Managing Stress and Building Wellness – A Guide to a Healthy Mind and Body

Stress is a normal part of life. It happens when you feel worried, overwhelmed, or pressured. Stress can come from school, work, family, or big life changes. Some stress is positive, like feeling excited before a big event. However, too much stress or long-term stress can harm your health (American Psychological Association, 2023). Newcomers to the U.S. experience high levels of stress from the adjustment so it is important to learn to manage this stress.

This chapter will help you understand different types of stress, ways to manage stress in the moment, and strategies to prevent and control stress in the future. You will also learn about five areas of wellness and how improving your self-esteem can help you handle stress and problems better.

Types of Stress

People experience different types of stress in daily life. Understanding these types can help you recognize and manage stress more effectively.

Acute Stress (Short-Term Stress)

Acute stress is short-term stress that happens in response to a specific event. It can come from things like taking a test, riding a roller coaster, or speaking in front of a crowd. This type of stress usually goes away quickly after the event is over (Mayo Clinic, 2022).

Chronic Stress (Long-Term Stress)

Chronic stress lasts a long time and comes from ongoing problems such as family conflicts, moving to a new country, or school pressure. Over time, chronic stress can harm your health and increase the risk of illness (National Institute of Mental Health [NIMH], 2023).

Moving to a new country is a big change and is an example of a chronic stressor. Everything is different, including the language, food, and customs. You might feel overwhelmed, lonely, or homesick. This kind of stress can cause headaches, stomach aches, or trouble sleeping, as your body reacts to the changes (Jones & Lee, 2019). Additionally, adjusting to a new language and adapting to school or work can lead to chronic headaches and other health issues if not managed properly. I remember experiencing persistent headaches during my first year in the United States.

Coping with Stress in the Moment

There are many ways to cope with stress, such as deep breathing, exercise, grounding techniques, and talking to someone you trust. Finding the right way that works for you can help you feel more in control and improve your well-being. Below are some effective strategies to manage stress in the moment when it happens.

The 90-Second Emotion Rule

When we feel strong emotions, such as anger, sadness, or fear, our brain releases chemicals that create these feelings (Taylor, 2008). This reaction lasts only for about 90 seconds. After that, the emotion will fade unless we keep thinking about it (Taylor, 2008).

How This Rule Works:
1. Something Happens: You get a bad grade, someone says something mean, or you feel embarrassed.
2. Your Brain Reacts: Your body changes, and you may feel a fast heartbeat or sweaty hands.
3. The Ninety-Second Cycle: The feelings start to fade if you do not keep thinking about them.
4. You Control It: If you keep thinking about what happened, the feelings will return again and again.

Notice how you feel the next time you are triggered by a negative event, and remind yourself that the feeling will pass. Then take deep breaths and wait for 90 seconds. During that time, choose to focus your attention on something else, like your breath, the sounds around you, or something calming. This helps you stay calm and in control, instead of letting the emotion take over.

Deep Breathing Meditation Strategy

Practicing deep breathing or meditation can calm the mind and relax the body when we feel stressed. One simple technique is the 4-7-8 breathing method (Weil, 2018):

- Inhale for 4 seconds.
- Hold your breath for 7 seconds.
- Exhale slowly for 8 seconds.
- Repeat these steps several times.

This breathing strategy can lower your heart rate and reduce the anxiety you may experience during stressful moments. You can add a word or phrase, such as "I am safe," "I am calm," or even say your favorite prayer while practicing deep breathing. The goal is not to worry about any thoughts that come to you, as these are normal, especially when practicing deep breathing for several minutes. Instead, gently notice the thoughts and redirect your attention back to your breath. After a few repetitions, you can stop holding your breath and simply focus on slow, steady inhaling and exhaling, which is a core part of meditation. With regular practice, this can become a powerful tool to improve emotional balance and mental clarity.

Managing Negative Emotions with the RAIN Strategy

Sometimes, stress lasts longer, and we experience more lasting negative emotions. When this happens, the RAIN method can help you understand and manage your emotions that were caused by stress (Brach, 2019). The benefits of the RAIN strategy are that it helps calm the nervous system, build emotional resilience, increase self-awareness, and interrupt patterns of reactivity and self-criticism. It also helps create a space between the emotion and your response, giving you time to choose how to act instead of reacting automatically.

How the RAIN Method Works:

1. Recognize what you are feeling. For example, you may think, "I feel nervous about my test."
2. Allow yourself to feel the emotion instead of ignoring it. Say to yourself, "It is okay to feel this way."
3. Investigate why you feel this way. Ask yourself, "Did I study enough?"
4. Nurture yourself with kindness. Say, "I did my best, and I will try my hardest. This feeling will pass."

Physical Techniques to Help You Feel Safe

There are physical practices that can calm your body and mind withing a few minutes of using them when you feel triggered by an event. These simple actions help you care for yourself with kindness.

1. Hand-on-Heart Strategy:
   Place both hands over your heart, with your palms facing your body. Take slow, deep breaths while saying kind words to yourself, such as, "I am safe." Try this for 20 seconds to up to three minutes. Even a short time can help you feel more present and allow your body and mind to return to a calmer, more peaceful state.
2. Self-Hug Strategy:
   Gently wrap your arms around your shoulders and give yourself a warm, comforting hug. Try to hold this position for 1 to 3 minutes while focusing on positive thoughts or intentions. Take deep breaths. Your body will begin to release oxytocin, a "feel-good" hormone that helps lower cortisol, the stress hormone. This can slow your heart rate and create a sense of comfort and emotional safety.

These small nurturing actions are powerful. They can help you treat yourself with the same kindness and care that you would offer a close friend (Brach, 2019).

Case Study: Mira's Journey to the 5-4-3-2-1 Grounding Strategy

Mira was very close to her father. When he passed away unexpectedly, the grief was overwhelming. One day, while she was at home, she suddenly felt short of breath, dizzy, and had a racing heart. She thought something was seriously wrong and was rushed to the emergency room. After several tests, the doctor told her she had experienced a panic attack (American Psychological Association [APA], 2023).

After that day, Mira worried that another attack would happen. Her doctor recommended that she try a grounding technique called the 5-4-3-2-1 method, which helps people focus on their senses when they feel panic starting (Verywell Mind, 2023). This method involves paying attention to your environment and silently naming several things you notice using each of the five senses.

How Mira Used the 5-4-3-2-1 Method:
- 5 Things She Could See – Books, a window, a cup of tea, a chair, and a clock.
- 4 Things She Could Touch – The warmth of her tea, the fabric of her sweater, her desk, and the cool air.
- 3 Things She Could Hear – Birds, a car passing by, and the ticking clock.
- 2 Things She Could Smell – Her lavender candle and her tea.
- 1 Thing She Could Taste – A sip of her tea.

By using this technique, Mira calmed her mind by focusing on the present moment and prevented another panic attack. Over time, she also changed her daily habits to include getting enough sleep, practicing deep breathing, and exercising regularly (Manhattan Mental Health Counseling, n.d.). Since using the 5-4-3-2-1 method, she has not had another panic attack.

Mira's story shows that grounding strategies can be helpful with managing stress and anxiety.

Daily Ways to Prevent Stress

It is also important to prevent stress from building up by using daily stress management strategies. Here are some simple ways to reduce stress and maintain a healthy mind and body:

- Exercise: Moving your body releases stress and increases energy (Anderson & Patel, 2016).
- Eat healthy foods: Eating a variety of colorful fruits and vegetables, lean proteins, and whole grains can improve your mood (Williams, 2019).
- Relax: Listening to music, meditating, or taking a walk in nature can be calming (Gonzalez, 2020).
- Do what you love: Hobbies and spending time with friends help reduce stress (Park, 2018). Set aside at least 20 minutes each day for yourself to relax and practice self-care.
- Talk to someone: Sharing your worries with a friend, family member, or teacher can help.
- Know your limits: Do not take on too much at once. Learn to say no when needed to protect your well-being (Davis, 2021).

The Five Areas of Wellness

Taking care of your well-being is about more than just avoiding illness. To feel your best, you need to focus on different parts of your life: your mind, emotions, relationships, body, and sense of purpose (World Health Organization [WHO], 2023). When all these areas are balanced, you are more likely to feel confident, manage stress better, and enjoy life. Below, we explore five key areas of wellness and how they can help you live a healthier and happier life.

Mental and Emotional Wellness

Your thoughts and feelings play a big role in how you handle stress, make decisions, and interact with others. To stay happy, it's important to keep your mind active and manage your emotions in a healthy way. You can do this by trying new activities like puzzles, games, or learning a new skill. It's also helpful to stay curious by reading and writing regularly. Don't keep your feelings inside; talk about them. And remember to learn from your mistakes and focus on moving forward (Harris, 2016).

Social Wellness

Having strong friendships and good relationships with others helps you feel supported and connected. To build these connections, spend time with friends and family. You can also join clubs, sports teams, or social groups to meet new people. Being open to different ideas and cultures will help you understand the world better and enrich your interactions (Martinez, 2018).

Physical Wellness

Taking care of your body helps you stay strong and full of energy. To do this, eat healthy meals and drink enough water. Make sure to get enough sleep so both your body and mind can rest. Exercise often to stay active and feel good. For example, plan for a 45-minute brisk walk four times per week, do strength training exercises like lifting weights at least twice per week, practice your balance every day, or every other day, by standing on one foot for a minute or two, and increase your heart rate at least twice per week with short cardio workouts. Don't forget to visit the doctor for regular checkups to stay healthy (White & Kim, 2020).

Spiritual Wellness

Finding meaning in life can help you stay positive and focused, even during hard times. You can practice mindfulness through activities like meditation, prayer, or simply enjoying quiet time. Spending time in nature can also help you relax and feel calm. It's important to discover what makes you happy and gives you a sense of purpose (Nakamura, 2021).

Building Self-Esteem and Problem-Solving Skills

How you feel about yourself is called self-esteem, and it can change based on influences from family, school, friends, social media, or life experiences. Having healthy self-esteem helps you feel strong and confident, which also makes it easier to manage stress. When you believe in yourself, it becomes easier to solve problems, make good choices, and stay calm in difficult situations (Lopez, 2019). You are not born with self-esteem; it develops over time through positive and meaningful actions.

How to Build Self-Esteem

Try the following tips to help you improve your self-esteem:

- Notice what you do well. Everyone has unique talents.
- Be kind to yourself. Making mistakes is part of learning.
- Try new things. This helps you discover strengths and grow.
- Set small goals. Celebrate when you achieve them.
- Keep a list of things you have done well. Look at it when you feel discouraged.
- Remind yourself of your strength and courage, especially the bravery it took to come to a new country and adjust to a new life.
- Share your voice. Don't be afraid to speak up or share your opinions (Reynolds, 2020).
- Practice gratitude. Every day, think about and answer these questions in your head:

    o What went well today?
    o What you are thankful for?
    o Who you are grateful to have in your life?

When you have good self-esteem, you are more likely to feel confident. You believe that you are capable, even when things are difficult.

Solving Problems Also Builds Your Self Esteem

To solve problems in a healthy way, begin by taking a deep breath to stay calm. Break big problems into smaller steps and tackle them one at a time. Think carefully before acting by considering the problem, possible solutions, and their pros and cons. Ask yourself who can help and what the consequences of your choices might be.

Ask yourself these questions to help you decide how to handle a problem:
- What is the problem?
- What are the possible solutions?
- What are the pros and cons of each solution?

191

- Who can help me?
- What could happen if I make this choice?

If you are feeling stuck, take one small action step forward to gain a sense of control. Don't be afraid to ask for help, as talking to someone can provide new perspectives. Learn from your mistakes to find better ways to handle similar situations in the future and stay positive by focusing on solutions rather than problems (Thompson, 2017).

At the end of the day, let go of the things that did not go well, and try again the next day with a new plan. You don't have to be perfect. On most days, a "good enough" effort is good enough.

When you believe in yourself and understand how to approach problems, you will feel stronger and less stressed in daily life. Taking care of your self-esteem is important for maintaining your well-being, helping you remain calm, confident, and happy.

Key Takeaways

- Stress is normal, but it is important to manage it for your health (Brown, 2021).
- The 90-second emotion rule and the RAIN strategy can help you deal with stress in a healthy way (Kabat-Zinn, 2017).
- Moving to a new country can be stressful, but using methods like exercise, talking to others, and taking care of yourself can help (Jones & Lee, 2019).
- Having strong self-esteem makes it easier to solve problems and handle stress (Lopez, 2019).

Reflection Questions

1. What activities help you feel less stressed, and how do you usually react when you feel overwhelmed?
2. How can you use the RAIN method the next time you feel negative emotions?

References

American Psychological Association. (2023). *Stress and health: Understanding the connection.* Retrieved from www. apa.org

American Psychological Association (APA). (2023). *Understanding panic attacks and how to manage them.* Retrieved from https://www.apa.org

Anderson, P., & Patel, R. (2016). *The effects of physical activity on mental health.* Health & Wellness Journal, 12(3), 45-56.

Brach, T. (2019). *Radical compassion: Learning to love yourself and your world with the practice of RAIN.* HarperCollins.

Brown, L. (2021). *Managing chronic stress: A guide to long-term wellness.* Mindful Living Press.

Davis, K. (2021). *Time management for a stress-free life.* Productivity & Wellness Magazine, 8(2), 22-30.

Gonzalez, J. (2020). *Meditation and relaxation techniques for stress relief.* Calming Minds Press.

Harris, T. (2016). *Mental wellness strategies for a healthy life.* Brain Health Research, 4(1), 14-28.

Jones, A., & Lee, S. (2019). *Adjusting to a new culture: The stress of immigration and adaptation.* Social Psychology Review, 15(2), 67-80.

Kabat-Zinn, J. (2017). *Mindfulness for beginners: How to handle stress with RAIN.* Harvard Mindfulness Center.

Lopez, R. (2019). *Self-esteem and confidence building for young adults.* Psychology Today, 11(4), 33-41.

Manhattan Mental Health Counseling. (n.d.). *5-4-3-2-1 grounding technique for anxiety.* Retrieved from https://manhattan mentalhealthcounseling.com

Martinez, C. (2018). *The importance of social connections for mental health.* Community Wellness Studies, 7(1), 12-19.

Mayo Clinic. (2022). *Stress management: How to reduce and relieve stress.* Retrieved from www.mayoclinic.org

Nakamura, H. (2021). *Finding meaning and purpose through spiritual wellness.* Japan Wellness Research, 10(3), 55-70.

National Institute of Mental Health. (2023). *Coping with stress and mental health.* Retrieved from www.nimh.nih.gov

Park, Y. (2018). *The impact of hobbies and recreation on stress reduction.* Lifestyle & Health Journal, 9(1), 29-38.

Reynolds, D. (2020). *Boosting self-esteem through positive thinking.* Self-Help Today, 14(2), 19-35.

Taylor, J. B. (2008). *My stroke of insight: A brain scientist's personal journey.* Viking Press.

Thompson, M. (2017). *Developing problem-solving skills for success.* Educational Strategies Journal, 6(2), 41-57.

Verywell Mind. (2023). *Feeling anxious? Try the 5-4-3-2-1 grounding technique.* Retrieved from https://www.verywellmind.com

Weil, A. (2018**).** *Breathing: The master key to self-healing.* Weil Integrative Medicine Library.

White, L., & Kim, B. (2020). *Healthy living: Nutrition, exercise, and self-care.* Wellness & Health Publishing.

Williams, S. (2019). *Nutrition and mental health: The link between diet and emotions.* Mind-Body Health Press.

World Health Organization. (2023). *Mental health: Strengthening our response.* Retrieved from www.who.int

SECTION 6: SOCIAL EXPECTATIONS AND CULTURAL ADAPTATION

Chapter 24: Religious Practices in a Diverse Society

The United States is home to people from many different religions and cultures. Religious freedom is protected in the U.S., and people have the right to practice their faith without discrimination (American Civil Liberties Union, 2022).

When I first moved to the U.S., I was surprised by the diversity of religious beliefs and practices. Some people wore crosses, others wore headscarves, and some had dietary restrictions. I learned that understanding religious practices helps us show respect and build friendships with others. There is something beautiful about sharing a small part of your religion with others and enjoying learning about theirs. This is not done with the hidden intention of changing someone's beliefs, but to simply share and enjoy together a part of your culture without feeling any pressure or expectations.

For example, even if you are not Christian, you can enjoy having a holiday tree or sharing a Christmas meal with your neighbor and even participating in a small gift exchange for fun. Or, if your Muslim friend invites you to break their fast with them by sharing a meal for "Iftar" (even though you were not fasting, you can still eat), you will still experience delicious food, friendship, and community. These times are great for building an understanding of others' customs and finding things you value about their practices. During these times of togetherness, it is a good time to ask questions and build your understanding of the religious ways of others. After all, many religious beliefs share the same values of trying to be a good person, helping others, and respecting your parents and neighbors. This chapter will explore different religious traditions, ways to show respect, and why religious freedom matters in a diverse society.

Religious Practices

Religious practices are the ways people show their faith and include various activities:

- Praying: Some individuals pray daily or at specific times according to their religion.
- Fasting: In some religions, fasting is required at certain times. For example, Muslims fast during Ramadan, and Jews fast on Yom Kippur.
- Celebrating Holidays: There are many religious holidays like Christmas for Christians, Ramadan for Muslims, Hanukkah for Jews, and Diwali for Hindus.
- Worship Places: People often visit places of worship like churches, mosques, synagogues, and temples to pray.
- Dietary Rules: Different religions have specific dietary restrictions. For instance, many Muslims and Jews do not eat pork, and Hindus often avoid beef.
- Religious Clothing: Some followers of religions wear specific clothes as part of their faith, such as hijabs in Islam, kippahs in Judaism, and turbans in Sikhism (Pew Research Center, 2022).

Although religious practices can vary widely, it is important to respect each person's way of expressing their faith.

Religious Traditions

There are many different religions around the world, each with its own customs and beliefs. Here are some examples:

- Christianity: Followers believe in Jesus Christ. They celebrate holidays like Christmas and Easter and gather in churches for worship.
- Islam: Muslims believe in Allah (the Arabic word for God) and pray five times a day. They observe Ramadan and gather in mosques for prayer.
- Judaism: Jews follow the Torah, celebrate holidays like Passover and Hanukkah, and worship in synagogues.
- Hinduism: Hindus worship many gods and goddesses, celebrate festivals like Diwali and Holi, and pray in temples.
- Buddhism: Buddhists follow the teachings of Buddha, focusing on meditation and kindness.

These are just a few examples. Many other religions are practiced in the U.S. and around the world, each with its own unique traditions.

Respecting Religious Differences

Understanding and respecting different religions helps make our society more inclusive and peaceful. You may ask polite questions if someone is comfortable sharing about their beliefs. But you should mostly learn about different religions by reading about them. Avoid making fun of religious practices. It's important to respect what others believe, even if it's different from your beliefs. Try to be open-minded.

Always treat people with kindness, regardless of their religious beliefs. Respect religious holidays. If a friend or coworker celebrates a holiday that's new to you, ask about it respectfully. Showing understanding and acceptance is key to building a community where everyone feels valued and respected. Small actions, like showing curiosity and kindness, help create a respectful community. Also, just because someone identifies with a certain religion does not mean that they observe every part of their religion's teachings.

Examples of Respecting Religious Differences

At work, Emily's team plans a Christmas party. Her coworker Ahmed does not celebrate Christmas because he is Muslim, but he invites his coworkers to learn about Ramadan. Emily takes an interest and asks respectful questions, which helps the team build a stronger work relationship.

A Muslim woman wears a hijab, and a Jewish man wears a kippah. Instead of staring or asking uncomfortable questions, people respect their choice and understand it is part of their faith.

A workplace cafeteria offers pork and vegetarian options. A Hindu employee avoids beef, and a Jewish coworker follows kosher food rules. The cafeteria ensures there are many meal options, so everyone feels included.

All these examples show respect toward people whose beliefs may be different from your own. In the U.S., the first Amendment guarantees religious protection.

Case Study: Religious Respect in Everyday Life

Jorge recently started a new job and noticed that his coworker Samir left the office at certain times each day. Curious, he asked, "Why do you leave for a few minutes?" Samir explained that he prays at specific times as part of his faith.

Jorge had never met someone who practiced daily prayer and was interested. Instead of making assumptions, he asked polite questions. Samir appreciated the respect and was happy to share. Over time, they became good friends.

Lesson: Respect Helps Build Relationships

It is okay to ask questions respectfully to learn about different religions. Everyone's beliefs are different, but we can learn from each other. Respecting religious differences helps us build better relationships.

Respecting Religion Matters

Being open-minded toward people of different religions is a valuable approach to building understanding and respect in diverse environments. Here's are several ways you can use to grow this openness:

1. Learn About Religions: Start by learning about different religions. Read books, visit websites, watch documentaries, or take classes to learn about what people believe and how they practice their faith.
2. Look for Similarities: Find things that your beliefs have in common with other religions, like kindness or honesty. You will quickly see that many core values may be similar. This can help you feel more connected to others.
3. Celebrate What's Different: It's also good to appreciate what makes each religion special. Learn about different festivals and traditions. You can ask questions or even watch or join in celebrations if you are invited.
4. Talk to Others: Have conversations with people who follow different religions. Be curious and open, not judgmental.

You can talk during meetings, community events, or just with friends. Most people are happy to discuss their values.

5. Think About the Good Things: Often think about what you like or find interesting about other religions, like how they help their community or their peaceful practices. Consider how the community-building aspects of religious practices help people live more social and healthier lives.

6. Try to Understand Others: Try to see things from other people's point of view. This will help you understand why their beliefs are important to them.

7. Be Respectful: Always be respectful when you talk about or deal with religious differences. Never assume or joke about someone's religion.

By using this strategy, you can better understand and appreciate people from different religious groups, which makes your experiences richer and helps everyone get along better. Respecting different beliefs creates a welcoming environment where everyone feels safe and accepted. It encourages learning and friendships across different cultures, enriching our understanding of the world. Respect for diverse beliefs helps people live and work together more peacefully in workplaces, schools, and communities. This creates a community where all individuals feel valued and integrated, regardless of their cultural or religious backgrounds. Now, isn't that a society you want to live?

Key Takeaways

- Religious freedom is protected in the U.S., and respecting differences helps create an inclusive society.
- Being open-minded and respectful helps build friendships and positive relationships.
- Learning about different religions promotes kindness and understanding.

Reflection Questions

1. Why is it important to respect religious differences at work, school, and in daily life?
2. How can you show respect to someone with a different religious belief?

References

American Civil Liberties Union. (2022). Religious freedom in public spaces. Retrieved from www.aclu.org

Pew Research Center. (2022). Religious diversity in America. Retrieved from www.pewresearch.org

Chapter 25: Personal Space and Social Customs in the U.S.: A Guide for Newcomers

Every country has different customs regarding personal space, communication, and daily interactions. In the United States, people follow certain social behaviors that may be different from those in your home country.

When I first moved to the U.S., I noticed that people stood farther apart when talking, and strangers smiled at me in public. At first, I was confused. Did they know me? Should I say something to them? I could not remember where I would have seen them, and this added to my confusion. Later, I learned that personal space and friendliness are part of American culture. Understanding these customs will help you feel comfortable in school, at work, and in your community.

Personal Space

Personal space is the area around a person where they feel comfortable. In the U.S., people value their personal space and usually stand farther apart than in some cultures. When talking to someone, stand about an arm's length away from the other person. Standing too close might make them uncomfortable (Hall, 1966). In a crowd, try to leave space between you and others even when walking. Do not touch other people when trying to pass them. Americans avoid physical contact with strangers on buses or trains unless the space is overcrowded. If you are unsure how much space to give someone, watch what others do. If someone steps back, that is a sign they want more space.

Saying "Excuse Me"

In the U.S., it's important to use polite words like "Excuse me" or "Sorry" in everyday situations. If you need to walk past someone, especially in crowded places or when going to your seat in a movie theater, it's nice to say, "Excuse me, please." Also, in busy places like school hallways, you should say "Excuse me" instead of pushing through people. If you accidentally bump into someone, saying "Sorry" or "Excuse me" quickly shows you didn't mean to do it. Lastly, if you need to ask someone a question or start talking to someone you don't know, always start by saying "Excuse me." Using these polite words helps show respect and makes it easier to get along with others.

Greetings and Handshakes

Greetings and handshakes are important ways to show respect and friendliness in many situations, especially formal ones. When you meet someone like a teacher, employer, or a professional contact, offering a handshake is a common sign of respect. Children and teenagers might not always need to shake hands; simply saying "Nice to meet you" is usually enough. However, remember that some people may choose not to shake hands because of their religious beliefs or cultural practices. In these situations, it's perfectly okay to give a polite nod or a friendly smile instead. If you do shake hands, remember to grip the other person's hand firmly but gently, and make sure to make eye contact to show your sincerity and confidence (Knapp & Hall, 2013).

Using "Please" and "Thank You"

Using polite words like "Please" and "Thank you" is very important because it shows respect and appreciation. When you ask for something, always say "please." For example, you can say, "Can I have some water, please?" When someone gives you something or helps you, you should say "thank you." For instance, "Thank you for helping me!" is a great way to show your gratitude. If someone says "thank you" to you, the best response is "You're welcome." These simple words can make a big difference in school, at work, and when you are with friends, helping everyone feel respected and appreciated.

Waiting Your Turn (Taking Turns)

In the U.S., it's important to follow the rule of taking turns in different situations to show respect and fairness. For example, when you are standing in line at a store, cafeteria, or bus stop, it's considered rude to cut ahead of someone who was there before you. Always wait your turn by standing behind the last person. Similarly, in a classroom setting, if you want to speak or answer a question, you should raise your hand and wait for the teacher to call on you. Interrupting others or speaking out of turn is discouraged because it can disrupt the class and shows a lack of respect for both the teacher and your classmates. Following these simple rules helps maintain order and shows that you value others' rights and space.

Case Study: Cultural Differences in Communication

When Sam moved to the U.S., he was surprised by how formal conversations were. In his home country, people often spoke loudly, engaged in multiple conversations at once, and interrupted each other as a sign of interest and enthusiasm. A lively, overlapping discussion meant that people cared deeply about what they were talking about, and interrupting someone was not considered rude; it was a way to promote conversation and show engagement.

At school, however, Sam noticed that Americans communicated very differently. They took turns speaking, listened quietly, and used calm, controlled voices in class. Interrupting is discouraged, and conversations follow a structured pattern where only one person speaks at a time, while others are expected to listen and wait their turn to talk.

At first, Sam found this style of communication strange and uncomfortable. He felt that conversations didn't have the same energy and excitement he was used to in his native culture. Over time, though, he learned that neither style was better or worse, just different. He began to adjust to the American way of communicating while still appreciating the liveliness of discussions in his home culture.

Sam also had to prepare his American girlfriend for this aspect of his culture since it was still practiced at home. He explained to her that when his family talked over each other or spoke loudly, it did not mean they were arguing or being disrespectful. Instead, it was their way of showing engagement and enthusiasm in conversations. Since she was used to more structured discussions where people took turns speaking, he wanted to make sure she wouldn't feel overwhelmed or disrespected. By setting these expectations ahead of time, he helped her feel more comfortable when she interacted with his family.

However, Sam also noticed that his family adapted their communication style at work and in professional settings. While they still embraced lively conversations at home, they understood that in the U.S., being too loud, interrupting, or speaking over others at work was seen as unprofessional. Over time, they adjusted by speaking more calmly, listening without interrupting, and taking turns in conversations in workplaces and formal environments.

Lessons Learned: Communication is Culture Specific

Different cultures have different ways of communicating. In some cultures, interrupting shows engagement, while in others, it is seen as rude. Loud conversations and multiple discussions at once can be a sign of enthusiasm in some cultures, while in others, people prefer orderly conversations where one person speaks at a time.

Observing and adapting to new customs helps people adjust to new environments without losing appreciation for their own culture. Cultural adaptation does not mean losing identity. Sam's family still practiced their traditional communication style at home but adjusted in professional settings. However, preparing others for cultural differences can help prevent misunderstandings and make interactions more comfortable.

Individualistic vs. Collectivist Communication Styles

In individualistic cultures, such as the U.S. and countries in Western Europe, communication is more structured, where people take turns speaking and personal space is valued. In collectivist cultures, such as countries in Latin America, the Middle East, parts of Africa, and Southern Europe, conversations can be fast, energetic, and overlapping. Here, interrupting is not typically considered rude but is seen as a sign of enthusiasm, especially when adding to the discussion (Triandis, 1995). Group discussions are often louder and more interactive. If you are in a culture with different communication styles than you are used to, it is helpful to first observe these exchanges and adapt to the situation.

Respecting Privacy

In the U.S., respecting someone's privacy is very important, especially when it comes to personal questions. In general, it's best not to ask about someone's age, salary, or personal relationships unless you are close friends. Questions like "How old are you?", "How much money do you make?", or "Are you married?" are considered too personal for casual conversations. Additionally, when it comes to visiting someone's home, you should never go without an invitation. It's polite to call or text beforehand. For instance, if someone invites you to their house, a respectful response would be to ask, "What time should I come?" This shows consideration for their privacy and schedule.

Dressing for Different Occasions

In the U.S., what people wear depends on the occasion. For school, most students wear casual clothes like jeans and t-shirts. For formal events like dances, graduations, or job interviews, people usually dress up in suits or dresses. For sports, athletes wear comfortable clothes like shorts, jerseys, and sneakers that are easy to move in. Remember that every school and workplace has its own rules for how to dress. It's a good idea to check the rules before you go to make sure you are dressed appropriately for the event.

Tipping in Restaurants

In U.S. restaurants, tipping waiters is expected. A tip is usually 15 to 20 percent of the total bill (National Restaurant Association, 2022). For example, if your meal costs 20 dollars, leave a 3 to 5 dollar tip.

Using Phones and Technology

When using phones and technology, there are some important etiquette rules to follow, especially in social settings. At school, phones are generally not allowed in class unless the teacher says it's okay. This helps make sure that students are paying attention to their lessons and not getting distracted. When eating meals, whether you are at home, a restaurant, or with friends, it's polite to put your phone away. This shows respect to the people you are with and allows everyone to enjoy the meal and conversation more. For example, if you are having dinner with friends, or are on a date, you should avoid texting and focus on the conversation instead. This helps everyone feel more connected and valued.

Key Takeaways

- Personal space is important. Stand about an arm's length away from others.
- Use polite words like "Please" and "Thank you."
- Wait your turn in lines and when talking to others.
- Respect privacy. Do not ask personal questions too soon.
- Different cultures have different ways of communicating.

Reflection Questions

1. Why do you think personal space is important in social interactions?
2. How can watching how others behave help you understand personal space expectations?

References

Hall, E. T. (1966). *The Hidden Dimension: Personal Space in Different Cultures*. New York: Doubleday.

Knapp, M. L., & Hall, J. A. (2013). *Nonverbal Communication in Human Interaction*. Boston, MA: Wadsworth, Cengage Learning.

National Restaurant Association. (2022). Tipping guide for restaurants. Retrieved from www.restourants.org

Triandis, H. C. (1995). *Individualism and Collectivism: Cultural Communication Differences*. Boulder, CO: Westview Press.

Chapter 26: Common Social Mistakes Newcomers Make and How to Avoid Them

Moving to a new country can be exciting, but it can also be confusing. Every culture has different social rules, and what is normal in one country might be rude in another. This chapter will explain some common social mistakes newcomers to America make. It will also provide examples and tips to help you avoid them.

Not Making Eye Contact

In many cultures, looking down or away when speaking to someone is a sign of respect. However, in the United States, eye contact shows confidence and honesty (Smith, 2020). This can lead to confusion. For example, Maria, a student from Japan, avoids looking at her teacher's face when answering a question. The teacher thinks Maria is shy or unsure of her answer. When speaking to someone in the U.S., try to look at their eyes for a few seconds at a time. Do not stare, but do not look away too much either.

Standing Too Close or Too Far

Every culture has a different idea of personal space. In the U.S., people usually stand about an arm's length apart when talking. Standing too close can make others uncomfortable, while standing too far may seem unfriendly (Brown, 2019). But, Ahmed, from Egypt, stands very close to his new classmates while talking. They step back, but he moves closer again. This makes them uncomfortable. Watch how close Americans stand when talking and try to match their distance so that you do not make people uncomfortable. Also, this applies to sitting. Leave space between yourself and another person whenever possible, and make sure you are not touching them when sitting next to them.

Speaking Too Loudly or Too Quietly

Some cultures encourage loud talking, while others prefer quiet speech. In the U.S., people expect a moderate volume. Speaking too loudly in public can seem rude, and speaking too softly can make communication difficult (Johnson, 2021). Li, from China, speaks very quietly in class. His classmates cannot hear him, so they do not respond to what he says. To avoid this mistake, listen to how loud people around you speak and try to match their volume.

Not Saying Please and Thank You

Americans often use polite words. Saying "please," "thank you," and "excuse me" is very important in daily life. Not using them can seem impolite, even if you do not mean to be rude (Davis, 2018). For example, Ivan, from Russia, asks a cashier for food directly by saying, "Give me a hamburger." The cashier feels that he is being demanding and impolite. Always say "please" when asking for something and "thank you" when receiving something. In some languages, this is implied, but it needs to be stated directly in English.

Being Too Direct or Too Indirect

Some cultures encourage being very direct, while others prefer indirect communication. In the U.S., people are usually polite but also direct. They say what they mean without being rude (Hall, 2020). Fatima, from Saudi Arabia, does not like the food at her friend's house. Instead of saying something, she just eats very little. Her friend worries that she is sick. If you do not like something, you can politely say, "It is not my favorite," or "I prefer something else." Avoid saying "I do not like your food," as this sounds too direct and rude. Americans try to provide feedback in a polite way, so as not to be too harsh.

Forgetting to Smile or Greet People

Americans often smile and say hello, even to strangers. Not smiling or not greeting people can seem unfriendly (Miller, 2017). Not knowing about this expectation, Maximilian, from Germany, walks into class without saying hello. His classmates think he is rude, when in fact he just does not know the American custom. Say "hello" when entering a room, and smile when greeting people.

Not Understanding Small Talk

Small talk is casual conversation about topics like the weather or sports. Americans use small talk to be friendly. Not responding to small talk can make people think you are not interested in talking (Taylor, 2021). Sofia, from Brazil, is asked, "How are you?" She only says "Fine" and does not ask anything in return. Her classmates think she does not want to talk. When someone asks, "How are you?", you can reply, "I'm good, how about you?" This is a polite way to interact with others.

Offering Too Much Food

In some cultures, it is polite to offer guests a lot of food and insist they eat. Guests may be offered food multiple times, and even if they accept, they may feel like their hosts keep encouraging them to eat more. People following their hospitality cultures are just being friendly and making sure that they are being gracious and generous hosts. In the U.S., guests usually expect to be offered a drink but not a full meal unless dinner is planned. Forcing food on someone can make them uncomfortable (Williams, 2022). Noor, from India, invites her American friend over and keeps insisting they eat more food, even when they say they are full. Her friend feels pressured and uncomfortable and does not know what to do. With your American guest, offer food once, but if they say no or they are not hungry, respect their answer.

Being Too Honest in a Harsh Way

In some cultures, it is normal to make comments about a person's appearance or weight, especially if you know the person well. However, in the U.S., these types of comments are often seen as too personal and can be considered rude and hurtful (Anderson, 2021). For example, Luka, from Serbia, sees an old friend and pats his belly, saying, "You got fat!" Luka didn't mean to be unkind. He was simply speaking the way people often do in his culture. However, his friend feels embarrassed and uncomfortable.

In the U.S., it is best to avoid making personal comments about someone's appearance or body unless they ask for your opinion. If they do, try to be kind and respectful. You can focus on health or well-being rather than appearance, or say something encouraging like, "I hope you are feeling well," instead of commenting directly on how they look.

Being Late

Being on time is very important in the U.S. for work, school, and social events. Arriving late without notice is considered disrespectful (Anderson, 2021). Amir, from Iran, arrives 20 minutes late to a job interview, thinking it is normal. The interviewer thinks he is irresponsible and does not hire him. Always arrive on time or a few minutes early for work, a scheduled appointment, or an agreed-upon time to meet friends. Punctuality is very important to Americans. If you are running late, call or message the person to let them know.

Not Tipping at Restaurants

In many countries, tipping is not expected because service workers earn higher wages and the cost of service is already included in the price. However, in the U.S., tipping is a common practice. Restaurant workers rely heavily on tips as part of their income (National Restaurant Association, 2022). Ming, from China, eats at a restaurant and leaves without tipping. The waiter is upset because tipping is expected, and he provided good service. In the U.S., it is customary to leave a tip of 15-20% at restaurants. If you choose to eat at a restaurant, be sure to budget for tips.

Smiling Too Much in Serious Situations

In some cultures, people smile to show politeness or respect, even in serious situations. However, in the U.S., smiling too much during serious conversations may seem inappropriate or insincere. A student from an Asian culture is often absent. When her teacher talks to her about the importance of coming to school, she looks down and smiles. In her culture, this is a way to show respect and submission, but the teacher might think she is not taking the conversation seriously. In serious situations, try to match the other person's tone and facial expressions. If someone is discussing an important topic, keeping a neutral expression shows that you are listening and taking it seriously.

Taking Words Too Literally

Some phrases do not translate well word-for-word, especially idioms and sarcasm. Idioms are expressions where the meaning isn't obvious from the individual words, and sarcasm involves saying the opposite of what you mean, often jokingly. For example, "It is raining cats and dogs" is an idiom that means it is raining heavily, not that animals are falling from the sky.

Misunderstanding idioms and sarcasm can lead to confusion. For instance, when Sara asked Steve, "How are you?" and he responded, "Living the dream," he did not literally mean that he was happy or that life was great. Instead, he was being sarcastic to indicate that he was tired, stressed, or frustrated. To recognize sarcasm, pay attention to the speaker's tone and body language, such as sighs or eye rolls, which might indicate they don't mean what they say literally. If you are unsure, it's okay to ask, "Do you mean that literally?" or "Are you being sarcastic?"

Key Takeaways

- Make eye contact to show confidence and honesty.
- Stand about an arm's length away when talking to people.
- Speak at a moderate volume, not too loud or too quiet.
- Always say "Please," "Thank you," and "Excuse me."
- Be direct but polite when talking.
- Smile and greet people to seem friendly.
- Answer small talk questions and ask one back to keep the conversation going.
- Avoid making personal comments about someone's appearance.

- Arrive on time for meetings and social events.
- Remember to tip in restaurants.
- Learn idioms and recognize body language that shows sarcasm.

Reflection Questions

1. Why is making eye contact important in American conversations? How can avoiding eye contact cause misunderstandings?
2. Small talk is an important part of social interactions in the U.S. Why is it important to respond to casual questions like "How are you?" with more than just a short answer?
3. Why do Americans expect tips in restaurants? How does this differ from tipping customs in your country?

References

Anderson, J. 2021. *Cultural Norms and Social Etiquette*. New York: Social Studies Press.

Brown, L. 2019. *Personal Space in American Culture*. New York: Culture Press.

Davis, R. 2018. *Politeness in Everyday Life*. Boston: Social Etiquette Books.

Hall, E. 2020. *Direct and Indirect Communication Styles*. Chicago: Communication Press.

Johnson, M. 2021. *Speaking Volumes: Understanding Speech Norms*. Los Angeles: Language House.

Miller, J. 2017. *The Power of a Smile: Social Etiquette in America*. San Francisco: Friendly Press.

National Restaurant Association. (2022). *Tipping Guide for Restaurants*.

Smith, P. 2020. *Eye Contact and Trust in American Society*. Washington, D.C.: Human Behavior Studies.

Taylor, C. 2021. *Small Talk: The Key to Social Success*. Miami: Conversational Press.

Williams, K. 2022. *Hospitality Norms in America*. Dallas: Cultural Guidebooks.

Chapter 27: Understanding American Values

Moving to a new country means getting used to the way people behave and understanding their beliefs. In the United States, people follow several key values. Values are important ideas that help people decide how to live, work, and treat others. Some common American values are freedom, responsibility, creativity, and respect for different cultures. These values are very important and affect how people in the U.S. behave every day. Even though not everyone thinks the same way, many people agree on these important values. Understanding these values can help you feel more at home in your new environment.

Freedom and Individual Rights

One of the most important values in the U.S. is freedom. Many Americans believe that everyone should be able to make their own choices. This includes freedom of speech, which means people can say what they think, even if others don't agree (Cornell Law School, 2023). However, saying everything you think is not always socially appropriate, especially in places like school or work, or if what you say might hurt someone's feelings.

There's also freedom of religion, which lets people follow any religion they want or not follow one at all (U.S. Constitution, First Amendment). People in the U.S. can also choose their own paths in education, work, and personal life. For example, you can pick your job, what you wear, and what you believe in. Others will respect your right to make choices because freedom is highly valued.

Equality

Many Americans believe that everyone should be treated fairly, no matter their race, gender, religion, or background (National Archives, 2023). For example, if you want to be a doctor, artist, or scientist, you should have the same chance as anyone else. This belief includes the right to pursue the same opportunities, not necessarily that everyone has the same starting points.

Hard Work and Success

Most Americans value hard work and believe that effort leads to success (Weber, 1905). For example, if you study and practice, you can improve in school and achieve your dreams. This is why we love those success stories, or token examples, of people who started with very poor or difficult backgrounds and became successful.

Respect for Others

Respecting others means treating people with kindness, listening to their opinions, and valuing their differences (Harvard Pluralism Project, 2023). For example, even if you do not always agree with someone, listening and being kind still shows respect. Traditionally, this idea is connected to the Golden Rule, which says, "*Treat others the way you want to be treated.*"

Today, many people believe it is even better to treat others the way they want to be treated, recognizing each person's unique needs, experiences, and perspectives. A version of the Golden Rule is found in many cultures and religions throughout history. In the United States, many people try to follow these ideas in daily life, at school, at work, and in public. Respect and fairness are often taught to children at a young age and are important values for building a kind and inclusive community.

Independence and Self-Reliance

Most Americans believe in being responsible for themselves (Tocqueville, 1835). For example, as children get older, they are expected to develop independence by managing their own time, doing their homework, and planning for their future. This reflects the American value of individualism, which means that people are encouraged to be independent, make their own choices, and take responsibility for their actions. In American culture, being independent and self-reliant is often seen as a sign of maturity and success.

Family and Community

While independence is highly valued in the U.S., helping family and the community is also important (Putnam, 2000). People often engage in community service by volunteering, donating, or participating in local events to support their neighborhoods. Many Americans also help family members by babysitting, cooking meals, helping with schoolwork, or caring for older relatives. It is common for neighbors to support each other during difficult times, such as illness or after natural disasters. This balance of individual responsibility and community involvement is a key aspect of American culture, showing that being independent does not mean being alone. It means contributing to the well-being of others while also taking care of yourself.

Fairness and Justice

Most Americans believe that the same rules should apply to everyone (Cornell Law School, 2023). This means everyone should be treated fairly. For example, if two students take a test, they should both be graded the same way. If one student cheats, they will get in trouble. This helps make sure everyone is honest and follows the rules.

Diversity and Inclusion

The U.S. is a very diverse country with many different cultures living together (U.S. Census Bureau, 2023). For example, in school, you might meet students who come from different places and have different traditions. Everyone sharing their backgrounds can make learning more interesting and fun. It helps students understand and respect each other better as they learn about different ways of life from around the world. Many Americans value diversity and believe that learning from different cultures makes communities stronger. This makes schools a great place to learn not just about subjects like math and science, but also about the world and the people in it.

Innovation and Progress

Innovation is highly valued in the United States, where people often look for new and better ways to solve problems (National Science Foundation, 2023). Many individuals in the U.S. appreciate new items, technology, and other innovations because they can improve and offer easier or faster ways to do things. For example, gadgets like smartphones and tablets have made it easier to communicate, learn, and work from anywhere.

People across the U.S. are often excited about new technology because it can bring convenience, fun, and opportunities for success. New devices are sometimes seen as a sign of being modern or professional. In schools, updated technology helps students learn more effectively. In businesses, new tools can lead to greater productivity and better results.

While not everyone values technology in the same way, many communities in the U.S. welcome new ideas and tools that bring innovation, efficiency, and creative solutions. This openness to change reflects a broader cultural interest in progress and continuous improvement.

Responsibility and Accountability

Taking responsibility for one's actions is an important value in many communities across the United States (Covey, 1989). This means that when someone makes a mistake, like forgetting to do their homework, it's better to admit it rather than make excuses. Being honest helps people learn from their mistakes and grow.

For example, if a student forgets their homework, telling the truth and trying to fix the situation shows maturity. The same idea applies to adults at work. If someone misses a deadline or makes a mistake on a project, it is respectful to let the team know and help solve the problem. This kind of accountability is often seen as a sign of honesty, reliability, and professionalism.

By encouraging people to take responsibility, both children and adults can build trust, make better decisions, and improve how they handle challenges. This value helps create stronger relationships in schools, workplaces, and communities.

Final Thoughts

These values shape American society and everyday life. While not every person follows these beliefs, understanding them will help you adjust, make friends, and succeed in school.

Case Study: Lessons Learned from "A Different Mirror"

As a history teacher, I followed the traditional way of teaching American history. I talked about Black history in February and included Native American history more fully into my lessons. I also made sure to discuss the important work of Hispanic Americans, Asian Americans, and other groups throughout the year. But it wasn't until I read a book called "A Different Mirror: A History of Multicultural America" by Ronald Takaki that I really understood how much immigrants have helped build the United States.

Immigrants have had a big impact on America, but they haven't always been welcomed. For example, when Italian Americans and Irish Americans first came, they faced a lot of unfair treatment. Even though they eventually became part of the main society, some people still don't welcome immigrants today.

How immigrants are treated often depends on the state of the economy. When there are plenty of jobs and money, people are usually more welcoming to immigrants. But when the economy is struggling, immigrants are often unfairly blamed for taking jobs, even though they usually work in difficult, low-paying jobs like farming and construction that many others do not want to do.

Reading *A Different Mirror* helped me understand that America's history is deeply connected to the stories of immigrants, their struggles, and contributions (Takaki, 1993). The book shows how the nation's past is intertwined with the experiences of Indigenous peoples, African Americans, and immigrants from Europe, Asia, and Latin America. Together, these diverse communities have helped shape the country and create the multicultural fabric of American society.

Lessons Learned: Immigrants Played a Role in Building of the U.S.

Immigrants have played a crucial role in building America, yet their contributions are often overlooked. Discrimination against immigrants is not new. Historically, groups like Irish and Italian immigrants faced similar challenges. Yet, public attitudes toward immigrants change with the economy; when times are hard, resentment grows. Many immigrants work in very important but low-paying jobs that help industries like farming and building.

Reading "A Different Mirror" helped me see that America's history is closely tied to the stories of immigrants and their struggles and successes (Takaki, 1993).

Key Takeaways

- Freedom, equality, and fairness are important in the U.S. The U.S. has made progress in these areas even though more work is needed to gain equality.
- Hard work and independence are seen as keys to success.
- Respect, diversity, and responsibility help people build strong relationships.
- Innovation and progress drive new ideas and improvements.
- By staying curious, open-minded, and respectful, you will be able to connect with others and feel more comfortable in your new home.

Reflection Questions

1. Freedom and individual rights are highly valued in the U.S. Why is it important to respect others' freedoms, even if they have different opinions or beliefs from your own? Can you give an example of how you might show respect for someone's choices?
2. Hard work and independence are important values in American culture. How can taking responsibility for your own actions, like completing homework or planning for the

future, help you succeed? Can you think of a time when being responsible helped you achieve something?

References

Cornell Law School. (2023). *First Amendment and Fourteenth Amendment of the U.S. Constitution.*

Covey, S. (1989). *The 7 Habits of Highly Effective People. Simon & Schuster.*

Harvard University Pluralism Project. (2023). *Respect for Diversity in the U.S.* Retrieved from https://pluralism.org/

National Archives. (2023). *Civil Rights Act of 1964. Retrieved from www.archives.org*

National Science Foundation. (2023). *Innovation and Scientific Progress in the U.S.*

Putnam, R. (2000). *Bowling Alone: The Collapse and Revival of American Community.*

Takaki, R. (1993). *A different mirror: A history of multicultural America.* Back Bay Books.

Tocqueville, A. (1835). *Democracy in America. University of Chicago Press.*

U.S. Census Bureau. (2023). *Diversity in America Report.*

Weber, M. (1905). *The Protestant Ethic and the Spirit of Capitalism. Routledge Classics.*

SECTION 7: ADVANCED SOCIAL UNDERSTANDING

Chapter 28: Understanding Political Systems in the U.S.

In the United States, there are different political systems or philosophies that guide the way people think about how the government should work. Two of the main ideologies you will hear about are conservatism and liberalism. These terms are often used to describe different views on government, society, and economics (Pew Research Center, 2021). Understanding these political perspectives can help you better understand how people in the U.S. think about laws, policies, and leadership.

Conservatism

Conservatism in the U.S. is a political philosophy that believes in traditional values, limited government, and individual responsibility. Conservatives often believe that people should be free to make their own choices without too much interference from the government (Library of Congress, 2022).

Key Beliefs of Conservatism

- Limited Government– The government should not control too many parts of people's lives.
- Personal Responsibility – People should take care of themselves and their families. While conservatives believe in helping others, they think individuals should work hard to support themselves rather than relying on the government.
- Traditional Values – Many conservatives support religious traditions and traditional family structures.
- Strong National Defense – Conservatives often believe in maintaining a strong military to protect the country.

For example, a conservative might believe that the government should spend less money on social programs and that individuals should take more responsibility for their own health and education (White House, 2023).

222

Liberalism

Liberalism is a political philosophy that believes in progress, social equality, and government involvement to help those in need. Liberals support policies that provide services for disadvantaged groups and promote equality (Pew Research Center, 2021).

Key Beliefs of Liberalism

- Government's Role in Helping People – The government should help struggling individuals by providing resources such as public healthcare and education.
- Equality and Fairness – Liberals often believe in protecting the rights of all people, including racial minorities, women, and the LGBTQ+ community.
- Environmental Protection – Many liberals support policies that fight climate change and reduce pollution.
- Social Programs – Many liberals support government-funded services such as public education, welfare programs, and unemployment benefits (Ballotpedia, 2023).

For example, a liberal might support increasing government spending on healthcare to ensure that all citizens have access to medical care, regardless of their financial situation (Library of Congress, 2022).

Political Parties and Their Ideologies

While there are other political parties, which we often hear about closer to election time, individuals can also be independent, meaning they are not aligned with any party but can still vote in general elections. The two main political parties that compete for influence and election in the U.S. are the Republican Party, which tends to be more conservative, and the Democratic Party, which tends to be more liberal. These parties represent the two major political ideologies in the U.S.:

1. Republican Party (GOP) – Aligned with Conservatism

- Supports lower taxes, smaller government, and fewer regulations on businesses.

- Prioritizes a strong military and law enforcement.
- Favors traditional family values and religious freedoms.
- Advocates for fewer social welfare programs, believing in personal responsibility (Library of Congress, 2022).

2. Democratic Party – Aligned with Liberalism

- Supports higher taxes on wealthy individuals to fund public services.
- Promotes social justice, civil rights, and equal opportunities.
- Advocates for environmental protections and government action on climate change.
- Supports strong social programs, such as universal healthcare and affordable college education (Ballotpedia, 2023).

It is important to know that not everyone within these parties agrees on every issue. Some Republicans may support social programs, and some Democrats may support limited government in certain areas (Pew Research Center, 2021).

Key Differences Between Conservatives and Liberals

Topic	Conservatism	Liberalism
Government Role	Small, limited government	Larger government with more public programs
Personal Responsibility	People should take care of themselves	Government should help people who are struggling
Equality	People should have the same opportunities	Government should ensure fairness and protect minorities
Tradition vs. Change	Preserve traditional values	Support progress and social change

| Defense | Strong military and national security | Focus on diplomacy and international cooperation |
| Social Services | Fewer government programs | More government-funded programs for education, healthcare, etc. |

It is important to note that many people do not fully align with just one side. Individuals can hold a mix of conservative and liberal beliefs, depending on the issue!

Activity

After reading the chapter, circle the values on the chart above that match your views in each of the six topics. This will help you see which of the two major parties you are closer to right now. Remember, your views might change as you get older.

How Can You Participate in Civic Life When You Become a Citizen?

You can actively participate in civic life and learn about the political system in several ways. First, stay informed by reading news articles, watching debates, and learning about current issues. Discussing political issues with family, friends, or teachers can also provide different perspectives and deepen your understanding. Volunteering for community projects is another important way to engage civically, as it helps you contribute to your community's well-being. Voting is a key way to participate in democracy in the U.S. (GPO, 2022). If you are over 18, a U.S. citizen, and registered to vote (though in some states, having a criminal record may affect this), you can participate in elections. Engaging in these activities helps you become a more informed and active member of society.

Staying Safe and Informed as a Green Card Holder

As a green card holder, you have many rights in the U.S., but some protections do not fully cover non-citizens. Your immigration status can be negatively impacted or even revoked if you are connected to political unrest in any way. Even peaceful protests can put you at risk.

Posting strong or controversial political content online, supporting groups under government investigation, or those seen as extreme or hostile to the U.S. can also have negative consequences. These actions can lead to your immigration status being denied or revoked.

Immigration status can be denied if someone is arrested, even without a conviction. It can also be denied if someone is connected to an extremist cause, is accused of disturbing the peace or participating in riots, or fails to show good moral character, which is a requirement for citizenship.

Even if your friends go to a peaceful protest, one mistake could change your entire future in the U.S. You absolutely have the right to care and stay informed. But right now, ask yourself: What matters most: protecting your path to citizenship, or expressing your opinions?

Please think carefully. Your future here may depend on what you decide.

Key Takeaways

- Conservatism and liberalism influence much of American politics.
- Some people strongly follow one system, while others have a mix of beliefs from both.
- Understanding these perspectives can help you join conversations, make informed choices, and become a more knowledgeable citizen in your new home.

- Everyone has the right to their political views, and respecting different opinions is an important part of democracy!

Reflection Questions

1. In the U.S., the Republican Party is usually connected to conservatism, while the Democratic Party is connected to liberalism. What is one key belief of each party, and how do these beliefs influence their views on government policies?
2. People in the U.S. have different political opinions, and it is important to respect different views in discussions. Why is it important to listen to and understand different political ideas, even if you do not agree with them? How can talking about political ideas in a respectful way help build understanding?

References

Ballotpedia (2023). "Republican and Democratic Party Platforms Explained." Retrieved from www.ballotpedia.org

GPO – U.S. Government Publishing Office (2022). "The U.S. Government: How It Works." Retrieved from www. govinfo.gov

Library of Congress (2022). "Political Parties in the United States." Retrieved from www.loc.gov

Pew Research Center (2021). "The Political Typology: Political Divisions in the U.S." Retrieved from www.pewresearch.org

The White House (2023). "American Government 101." Retrieved from www.whitehouse.gov

Chapter 29: Understanding Prejudice, Racism, Stereotypes, Microaggressions, and Bias in Immigrant Experiences

In the United States, understanding terms like prejudice, racism, stereotypes, microaggressions, and bias is important because they impact how people treat each other. This chapter is not meant to place blame. Its purpose is to help immigrants and their communities understand the social situations they may face and to offer guidance on how to respond with confidence, dignity, and awareness. When immigrants move to a new country, they often face these challenges in their daily lives. These barriers make it harder for immigrants to feel accepted, find jobs, and have equal opportunities. Studies show that stereotypes make it harder for immigrants to be treated equally at work and in school (Devine & Sharp, 2009).

For example, when immigrants speak with an accent, they are often less believed than those who do not have an accent. A study found that individuals with accents were perceived as less credible, regardless of what they said (Lev-Ari & Keysar, 2010). Discrimination affects both mental health and economic success of immigrant families (Gee & Ponce, 2010). Another study found that resumes with "foreign-sounding" names were less likely to get job interviews than those with "American-sounding" names (Bertrand & Mullainathan, 2004).

As a newcomer, learning about these concepts will help you navigate American society and respond to unfair treatment at school, at home, and at work in a better way.

What is Prejudice?

Prejudice is when someone has a negative opinion about another person or group without knowing them, often based on their race, gender, religion, or nationality (Dovidio & Gaertner, 2010). It happens when people judge others before getting to know them. For example, if a teacher thinks a new immigrant student from Mexico will struggle in school just because English is not their first language, they might put them in a lower-level class without checking if the student is good at subjects like math. Another example is when someone decides not to be friends with a person from a different country even though they have never met them. This is unfair because prejudice prevents people from being seen for who they really are. It can stop them from getting opportunities and make immigrants feel unwelcome.

What is Racism?

Racism is when people are treated unfairly because of their race or skin color (Tatum, 2017). It can happen between individuals, like one person being unfair to another, or it can be systemic, meaning it's built into laws or policies that disadvantage a whole racial group. Studies have found that facing racism can increase stress, anxiety, and depression among immigrants, making it tougher for them to settle into a new country (Williams & Mohammed, 2013). For example, if a landlord refuses to rent an apartment to an African immigrant because they believe stereotypes, such as thinking the person may be "loud" or "will not pay rent on time," that is racism. Another example is a store employee following a Latino teenager around, thinking they might steal, even if the teenager has done nothing wrong. Racism makes it difficult for immigrants to find jobs and housing and to feel safe in their new country.

What Are Stereotypes?

Stereotypes are ideas about a group of people that are often unfair or untrue (Aronson, 2018). They assume that all people from a certain group are the same and ignore individual differences. For example, some people believe that all Asian immigrants are good at math or that all Middle Eastern immigrants are strict and unfriendly. Another example is when an employer thinks that Latina women can only work as housekeepers and does not offer them jobs in leadership roles. Stereotypes are a problem because they make it harder for immigrants to be seen as individuals. They can affect job opportunities, education, and even medical care (Devine & Sharp, 2009).

What is Bias?

Bias happens when someone unfairly favors or discriminates against a person or group. It can be conscious (when people know they are doing it) or unconscious (when people do not realize they are doing it) (Banaji & Greenwald, 2013). For example, a teacher may show unconscious bias by calling on certain students more often and ignoring others. Another example is when a company reviews two job applications: one from "John Smith" and another from "Ali Mohammed." Even though Ali has the same experience as John, the company picks John because they feel more comfortable with a name they recognize.

Bias is a problem because it makes it harder for immigrants to get jobs, access education, and receive fair treatment. Our brains naturally group things and information from our environment into categories to make sense of the world, so it is normal to have some bias. This also means we must be aware of our biases, so they do not influence us to make unfair or unwise decisions. We can begin unlearning bias by slowing down our thinking, questioning our assumptions, reflecting on our beliefs, and seeking feedback from others. Unlearning bias is a lifelong process that requires patience, self-reflection, and continuous effort.

Microaggressions: Small Words, Big Impact

Microaggressions are small comments or actions that may seem unimportant but can make people feel unwelcome or different. For example, a teacher might say to a student with a foreign-sounding name, "Wow, you speak English so well!" even though the student was born in the U.S. Another example is when a cashier speaks very slowly and loudly to an Asian immigrant, assuming they do not understand English, even though they speak it fluently.

Why do microaggressions matter? Over time, these small actions make immigrants feel like they do not belong. Studies show that microaggressions can lower confidence and increase stress in immigrant groups (Sue et al., 2007). Even if people do not mean to be rude, these comments and actions can hurt others. Learning to avoid microaggressions helps make society more welcoming and respectful for everyone.

Intersectionality: When Multiple Identities Overlap

Intersectionality means that different parts of a person's identity, such as their race, gender, social class, and immigration status, all connect and affect their life experiences. These parts can work together to create different challenges or advantages for each person (Crenshaw, 1989).

The further someone is from the historically dominant social identity — White, property-owning, English-speaking, Protestant, heterosexual men — the more likely they are to face multiple layers of discrimination. This means that people who have more than one minority identity may experience different kinds of unfair treatment at the same time. Here are some examples:

- A Black Muslim woman from Egypt may face racism, religious discrimination, nationality-based bias, and sexism all at once.
- A Latino immigrant may experience bias due to his race and immigration status.
- A wealthy British male immigrant may face obstacles due to his nationality and accent but still has advantages due to his gender, race, and wealth.

From these examples, we can see that an African female immigrant faces even more barriers than the other two individuals because multiple parts of her identity affect how she is treated in the U.S.

Why is this important? The more marginalized identities a person has, the harder it can be for them to receive fair treatment in society. People who experience multiple types of discrimination may face greater challenges in areas like finding jobs, accessing housing, or feeling accepted in their communities. Recognizing intersectionality helps us understand why some groups face more barriers than others. It also allows us to find more effective ways to address unfair treatment and work toward a more equal and just society for everyone. While life in the U.S. can be difficult for anyone, including white, middle-class men, people with multiple marginalized identities often face additional challenges that may require extra support and understanding.

How Prejudice, Racism, Stereotypes, and Bias Affect Us

Prejudice, racism, stereotypes, and bias can hurt people in many ways. They can cause unfair treatment at school or work, making it harder for some people to succeed. These behaviors can also cause emotional harm, making people feel unwelcome, sad, or frustrated. In addition, they create missed opportunities, where people do not get a fair chance to do well in life due to being negatively judged. For example, research shows that Black students in the U.S. are often punished more harshly than White students for the same behavior (Skiba et al., 2011). When people are treated unfairly, it makes life more difficult for them. Understanding these problems can help us treat others with fairness and respect.

How to Address Prejudice, Racism, Stereotypes, and Bias

There are many ways to respond to unfair treatment and help create a more respectful and inclusive society. One way is to speak up calmly when you see racism or prejudice. If a classmate or coworker makes a racist joke, you can respond by saying, "That's not funny. We should respect everyone." Speaking up in a respectful way can help people realize their words or actions are hurtful.

Another approach is to ask questions and learn more. Sometimes, people have biases because they do not know better. Asking thoughtful questions can help them think differently. For example, if someone says, "All people from that country are rude," you might ask, "Why do you think that? I believe every person is different." This encourages people to question their own stereotypes. Similarly, if someone tells a person of color, "You are very articulate," with a surprised expression, it may not be a true compliment. Instead, it shows bias because it suggests they did not

232

expect that person to speak well. It is important for us to be aware of our own biases.

It is also important to stand up for yourself when you experience discrimination. If someone is rude to you because of your race, gender, or background, you can calmly say, "That's unfair. I deserve to be treated with respect." If the situation is serious, you can talk to someone who can help. Seeking support from a trusted adult is another way to address unfair treatment. At school, a teacher, counselor, or parent can provide guidance. At work, a supervisor or human resources coordinator can assist. If a teacher makes a biased comment, you can respectfully bring it up after class by saying, "I felt uncomfortable with what was said. Can we talk about it?"

Another way to fight prejudice is to support others who are being mistreated. If a friend is bullied because of their religion or race, you can stand by them and say, "I support you. That treatment is not okay." Being an ally can make a big difference. Finally, always practice kindness and respect. Avoid making assumptions about people based on how they look or where they come from. Even if you do not know someone well, treat them with kindness rather than making negative judgments about them.

By speaking up, asking questions, standing up for yourself and others, and showing kindness, you can help make the world a fairer and more welcoming place for everyone.

What Can Schools and Workplaces Do?

Schools and workplaces play an important role in preventing discrimination and promoting fairness. Many have rules and policies to protect students and employees from unfair treatment. For example, anti-bullying policies help ensure that students are safe from racist or biased behavior. Diversity training teaches people how to treat others with fairness and respect, helping to reduce prejudice. Additionally, many schools and workplaces have reporting systems where students and employees can safely report discrimination or unfair treatment. These steps help create an environment where everyone feels valued and included.

How Parents Can Help

Parents can also play a big role in teaching their children how to respect others and stand up against unfair treatment. They can encourage their children to respect people from different cultures, races, and backgrounds by setting a good example and having open conversations about diversity. Parents can also teach their children to stand up for themselves and others when they see discrimination or bullying. Encouraging children to be open-minded and challenge stereotypes helps them grow into respectful and fair individuals. When families promote these values at home, it helps build a kinder and more inclusive society.

Case Study: Unequal Discipline and Cultural Perceptions

During gym class at a suburban middle school, a new student from Congo was playing with two other boys. The teacher was explaining how to hold a hockey stick and play hockey. While some boys lifted their sticks and playfully hit each other's sticks in the air, the teacher noticed and immediately disciplined only the boy from Congo.

The boy felt upset and confused because he was not the only one playing but was the only one punished. He also noticed that he was the only Black student in the class, while the other two boys were white. The school decided to suspend him, which deeply frustrated his family.

His parents had not yet spoken to him about how Black people are sometimes perceived in America, but they realized it was now necessary. They sought advice from an ally and were encouraged to speak with both their son and the school about unequal discipline.

In Congo, they would not have had to have this conversation. However, in the U.S., the effects of racial bias are still very real. The parents talked to the school about unfair treatment of their son, hoping to raise awareness and create more equal discipline practices.

Discussion Questions

1. Why do you think the boys were treated differently?
2. How could the school staff and the parents handle the situation differently?

Case Study Analysis

The teacher's decision may have been influenced by implicit bias, meaning they judged the situation unfairly without realizing it which led to differences in treatment. Research shows that Black students are often perceived as more aggressive than their peers, which can lead to harsher punishments for the same behavior. The teacher may have also felt more connected to certain students, leading to unconscious favoritism. Studies have found that Black students are disciplined more harshly than White students for the same actions (Skiba et al., 2011).

Lesson Learned: The School Staff and the Parents Need to Work Together

The teacher and school staff could have taken several steps to ensure fair treatment. First, the teacher should have disciplined all three boys equally or taken more time to carefully assess what happened before deciding on punishment. Schools should also review their discipline policies to make sure that all students are treated fairly, regardless of race. Additionally, teachers should receive bias training to help them recognize and correct unfair discipline practices. Instead of suspending the students, the teacher could have chosen a different approach, such as giving a warning or discussing safe play with them. This would have helped the students understand the situation without unfairly punishing one over the others.

The parents also took an important step by teaching their son about racial bias in American society. However, they could have taken further action by requesting a meeting with district administrators to discuss the issue. Parents could also work with other families and community leaders to encourage anti-bias training in schools. By raising awareness and working together, parents can help create a more just and inclusive learning environment for all students.

Key Takeaways

- Prejudice, racism, stereotypes, microaggressions, and bias can hurt people and society, but understanding them helps create a fair and respectful environment.
- Implicit bias can lead to unequal treatment, even when people do not realize it.
- Intersectionality shows how different parts of a person's identity, like race and gender, can overlap, and create unique experiences of discrimination or advantages.
- Workplaces, schools, and parents play an important role in promoting fairness by setting good examples and addressing discrimination.
- Talking openly helps create fair policies that protect everyone from bias.
- Speaking up, asking questions, and supporting others can help create kindness, inclusion, and equality for everyone.

Reflection Questions

1. Stereotypes and biases can lead to unfair treatment in schools and workplaces. Why is it important to recognize and question stereotypes about different groups of people? Can you think of an example where a stereotype might cause someone to be treated unfairly?
2. How can you respond to racism, stereotype, bias or a microaggression if you witness it?

References

Aronson, E. (2018). *The Social Animal*. Worth Publishers.

Banaji, M. R., & Greenwald, A. G. (2013). *Blindspot: Hidden Biases of Good People*. New York, NY: Delacorte Press.

Bertrand, M., & Mullainathan, S. (2004). *Are Emily and Greg more employable than Lakisha and Jamal?* American Economic Review, 94(4), 991-1013.

Crenshaw, K. (1989). *Demarginalizing the intersection of race and sex: A Black feminist critique of antidiscrimination doctrine, feminist theory, and antiracist politics*. University of Chicago Legal Forum, 1989(1), 139-167.

Dovidio, J. F., & Gaertner, S. L. (2010). *Reducing Intergroup Bias: The Common Ingroup Identity Model*. Psychology Press.

Devine, P. G., & Sharp, L. B. (2009). *Automatic and controlled processes in prejudice.* Psychological Science, 20(10), 1257-1262.

Gee, G. C., & Ponce, N. (2010). *Associations between perceived racial discrimination and health outcomes among Asian Americans.* American Journal of Public Health, 100(8), 1456-1464.

Lev-Ari, S., & Keysar, B. (2010). *Why don't we believe non-native speakers?* Journal of Experimental Social Psychology, 46(6), 1093-1096.

Skiba, R. J., Michael, R. S., Nardo, A. C., & Peterson, R. L. (2011). *The Color of Discipline: Sources of Racial and Gender Disproportionality in School Punishment.* The Urban Review, 34(4), 317-342.

Sue, D. W., Capodilupo, C. M., Torino, G. C., Bucceri, J. M., Holder, A. M. B., Nadal, K. L., & Esquilin, M. (2007). *Racial microaggressions in everyday life.* American Psychologist, 62(4), 271-286.

Tatum, B. D. (2017). *Why Are All the Black Kids Sitting Together in the Cafeteria? And Other Conversations About Race.* Basic Books.

Williams, D. R., & Mohammed, S. A. (2013). *Racism and health I: Pathways and scientific evidence.* American Behavioral Scientist, 57(8), 1152-1173.

Chapter 30: Regulating Emotions

In the United States, controlling your emotions is very important. It helps you stay calm in different situations like at school, at home, or when you are with friends. Many schools in the U.S. teach students how to manage their emotions because emotional regulation is an essential life skill. However, not all schools in other countries teach this, and some parents do not know how to teach their children because they never learned these skills. These skills are called "soft skills." They are very important for doing well both in your personal life and at work. Learning to control your emotions can also help newcomers get used to American culture. For example, not controlling your emotions well can cause someone to lose out on jobs or relationships. While these skills are something we can learn and improve, they take a lot of practice. Once learned, they should be practiced every day.

Emotional Regulation

Emotional regulation means learning how to control your emotions so you can stay calm and not react too quickly. It is normal to feel angry, sad, nervous, or excited. These feelings help us understand what is happening around us. We can think of emotions as signs or feedback. Feelings come and go, but we can choose how to respond. We are not our emotions. The most important part of emotional regulation is handling our feelings in a healthy way. For example, if someone cuts in line, instead of yelling or pushing, you can take a deep breath and calmly say how you feel. It is better to think that the person made a mistake, not that they did it on purpose. Most people will fix their behavior if they realize it was a mistake.

Importance of Emotional Regulation

Managing your emotions is very important because it helps you stay calm in stressful situations. It also helps you solve problems without making them worse and communicate better with teachers, friends, coworkers, and family. When you manage your emotions well, you can build strong relationships with others and create a positive environment around you (Gross, 2023). For example, if someone takes your seat, instead of shouting, you can calmly say that you were already sitting there. Most people are willing to listen if you explain the situation in a respectful way. This helps solve the problem in a peaceful way.

Strategies for Controlling Your Emotions

There are several strategies to control emotions effectively. In this section, we will discuss a few key techniques that can help you manage your reactions and maintain calmness in various situations. Here included are several strategies for controlling emotions, including taking deep breaths (Basic Deep Breath and Box Breathing Method), pausing to think before reacting, talking about your feelings with someone trustworthy, and using positive self-talk to convert negative thoughts into positive affirmations.

1. Take Deep Breaths

When you are feeling upset, deep breathing can be a great way to calm your mind and body, similar to the instant relaxation you feel when yawning. Yawning itself can also be a quick and natural way to relax. Below are two well-known methods you can try. Be sure to repeat these breathing exercises several times until you feel calmer and in control.

Basic Deep Breath:
- Inhale through your nose.
- Hold your breath for a second.
- Exhale slowly through your mouth.
- Repeat these steps several times.

Box Breathing Method:
- Breathe in slowly through your nose for four seconds.
- Hold your breath for four seconds.
- Breathe out slowly through your mouth for four seconds.
- Hold your breath again for four seconds.
- Repeat these steps four to five times.

2. Pause and Think (Meta-moment)

When we experience emotions, the amygdala is the first part of the brain to react because emotions reach the amygdala before they reach the parts of the brain that handle logical thinking. The amygdala processes our feelings, especially strong ones like fear, anger, and pleasure, before the logical part of our brain has a chance to respond. This means we often feel and react emotionally before we think things through.

Emotions can take over quickly, causing us to respond impulsively. Taking a "meta-moment" is a way to pause and interrupt this automatic reaction. By pausing for 10 to 20 seconds when we feel strong emotions, we give our prefrontal cortex, the part of the brain responsible for logical thinking, reasoning, and decision-making, a chance to activate. This short pause allows us to calmly consider our feelings and the situation, instead of reacting right away. During this pause, we can think about the best way to handle the situation. This helps us make decisions based on logic and reason rather than letting our immediate emotions control our actions. Negative emotions are a normal part of life, but allowing them to influence our reactions is avoidable. During the meta-moment, we can name the feeling we are experiencing, and that by itself takes away some of the feeling's control over us. By using a meta-moment, we shift control from the emotional part of the brain to the rational part, leading to more thoughtful and often better choices.

Next time before reacting, pause for 10 seconds and ask yourself:

- "How do I feel?"
- "Why do I feel this way?"
- "What is the best way to respond?"

3. Talk About Your Feelings

Talking about your feelings is a great way to feel better. When you share what is bothering you, it can make you feel less stressed. Keeping feelings inside might make you worry, but talking helps you let them out. Sometimes the person you talk to can help you see your situation differently, which is helpful when you are upset and need clarity. Also, talking to someone who listens and cares can make you feel less alone. It is comforting to know someone understands how you feel.

For example, if school is making you frustrated, talking to a teacher or a friend can help. They might offer advice, or just the act of listening to you might make you feel better. When a friend shares their feelings with you, it is important to know what they need. You can ask them, "Do you want to just vent and have me listen, or would you like my opinion or advice?" Venting means expressing emotions, usually frustration or distress, without expecting a solution. Sometimes, people just need to talk about their feelings to feel better. If a person wants your opinion, they might be looking for a different perspective. If they ask for advice, they are likely looking for help in solving a problem. By asking this question, you ensure you are giving the kind of support your friend really needs. Also, do not hold them to your advice. They may just want a different perspective, but they will make their own decision in the end. Remember to tell your friend what you need too when you talk about your feelings and need support.

4. Use Positive Self-Talk

Positive self-talk helps you feel more confident, stay motivated, and handle challenges more effectively. It is important to use positive self-talk to counteract negative thoughts, which make up the majority of our daily thinking. When you replace negative thoughts with positive ones, your brain begins to believe in your abilities instead of doubting them. This can reduce stress, improve your mood, and help you keep going even when things are difficult. It also helps you focus on solutions instead of problems. This shift also slowly helps to rewire your brain to start seeing more opportunities.

How to Use Positive Self-Talk

- Before a test: Instead of thinking, "I am going to fail," say, "I studied hard, and I will do my best."
- When learning something new: Instead of saying, "This is too hard," say, "I just need more practice."
- During a difficult situation: Instead of saying, "I give up," say, "I will keep trying and find a way."

Using positive self-talk every day can help you feel stronger and more capable, which supports success in school, work, and life. We are all learning and improving each day, so it's important to stay positive and believe that you can grow and improve with the right beliefs and strategies. When we see things more positively, our feelings typically follow.

Emotions in the U.S.

In the United States, people expect others to communicate calmly, even when they are upset (Hofstede, 2023). Speaking in a calm way helps others listen and understand better, rather than feeling attacked or defensive. It is also important to respect other people's feelings and show kindness when they are struggling. Noticing when someone is sad and offering support can make a big difference. For example, if a classmate looks upset, it is better to ask, "Are you okay?" instead of ignoring them. This small act of kindness shows that you care and helps build strong relationships with others. We are all working on handling emptions, and this is not something we can learn all at once.

Sometimes, emotions can feel too strong to handle alone. If you are very upset, talking to someone can help. A teacher, counselor, friend, or parent can listen and give support. Taking a break is also a good way to calm down. Naming what you feel is also a good way to immediately separate yourself from that feeling. Walking around, listening to music, or doing something relaxing can help you feel better. For example, if schoolwork feels overwhelming, taking a short break, drinking water, or stretching can help clear your mind. Finding healthy ways to manage emotions is important for feeling better and staying in control.

Personal Story: It Helps to Share Your Experiences

Sometimes we may have experienced trauma in our lives that makes us more alert to certain noises, for example. I remember when I initially came to the U.S., I was only 14 and had come from a war-torn country, so certain noises were upsetting for me. I did not share my fears with anyone at that time as I felt unprepared to process these fears.

I still do not like balloons because they can pop and suddenly trigger my alertness. The sound makes my heart race when I'm surprised by it. The first time a car backfired (which sounded like a gunshot to me), I ducked down in the middle of the sidewalk. Embarrassed, I looked around to make sure no one noticed. Since then, I have worked through many of those feelings and I have shared them with others as I have grown older, which has helped. But I still feel momentarily uncomfortable when loud noises surprise me. This discomfort may never completely go away, and I can accept that, but I have learned to manage it.

I used a simple strategy to bring my heart rate down by focusing on the present moment. I placed my right palm over my heart and left it there for 10 seconds or more, feeling the warmth of my hand while silently repeating in my mind, *"I am safe"* or *"I am okay"* a few times. This helped lower my sense of alertness and allowed me to relax. Now, I don't need to use this strategy as often because I have become more comfortable with the noise. Strategies like this exist to help people cope with challenges and make life easier, but unfortunately, we are not often taught them.

Other people may be triggered by feelings of not being listened to, feeling powerless, or by loss of control, and they may react by being unkind to others. Family violence is not tolerated here, and if someone is going through this, both the perpetrator and the victim need help. The victim should be taken to safety right away. Having a therapist help you cope with these emotions can be very beneficial. Now, I know some people may not feel comfortable with this, but our brains need to be taken care of just like our bodies. Our bodies also remember and store trauma we have gone through, just like my example with the balloon shows. It is not too extreme to seek help; we owe it to ourselves and our families.

Life Coaching Can Help Immigrants

I know that some people feel more comfortable talking to someone who is not a therapist. That's why having a friend to talk to is important. Friends can offer support, listen without judgment, and help us feel less alone. However, when a friend isn't available or when someone needs more guidance, another helpful option is life coaching. A life coach is someone who helps people learn how to handle problems, make good decisions, and take steps toward a better future, especially if they are new to a country and adjusting to many changes at once.

Life coaches do not ask you to talk about anything you don't want to share. Unlike therapy, which may explore difficult emotions or past trauma, life coaching focuses on what is happening right now and how to move forward. Life coaches often use simple and effective tools to help you solve problems or reach your goals. They also believe that you are the expert in your own life, and their role is to support and guide you, not to tell you what to do. In many cultures, seeking therapy can feel uncomfortable or carry a negative reputation or stigma. For many immigrants, life coaching feels more acceptable because it is seen as training or support, without the same level of emotional pressure. This can make it easier for people to ask for help when they need it. It is also helpful to have a life coach who not only shares the resettlement experience but also has a strong knowledge of the U.S. system and culture. These coaches often share strategies they have personally found helpful, unlike traditional coaching, which focuses more on helping the client find their own solutions.

I started a life coaching program for immigrant and refugee women in 2018 while working for a nonprofit organization. After receiving coaching, most women felt stronger and more confident, using strategies that supported their personal goals and daily lives. Life coaching is action focused. You do not just talk; you learn useful strategies and practice them right away. Even a few sessions can be enough to help someone get through a difficult time or make an important decision. Because the sessions are short term and practical, life coaching is often more affordable than long-term therapy.

I believe that organizations that help immigrants and their families should offer free or low-cost life coaching services when they see families struggling. Life coaching can prevent small problems from becoming bigger by teaching people practical skills they can use in everyday life. These skills might include setting boundaries, managing stress, creating healthy routines, or learning how to ask for help. All of these tools can make a big difference in someone's life, especially when they are adjusting to a new country and culture or working to develop their skills.

Life coaching also helps people feel stronger and more in control of their lives again. It builds self-confidence and gives people steps

244

they can take to reach important goals, such as finding a job, speaking more clearly, or building a new social network. These are common challenges for newcomers, and many need support right away. Coaching also reminds people of their strengths, values, and goals, which are important parts of themselves that may feel lost during a major life change. A coach can guide clients through job searches, interviews, changing careers, or going back to school. These things are often confusing in a new country, but with the right support, immigrants can move forward with more confidence, hope, and a sense of empowerment.

Get Better at Managing Emotions

Improving how you handle emotions takes time and practice. One helpful way is to use relaxation techniques like yoga, meditation, deep breathing, or even prayer. Prayer can provide comfort and help calm the mind when emotions feel overwhelming. It allows you to reflect, find peace, and seek guidance. It is also good to try different emotional control strategies and see which ones work best for you. If one method helps you the most, use it often, but keep others in mind in case you need to switch to a different strategy.

Another helpful strategy is keeping a journal to write about your thoughts and feelings. This can help you understand your emotions better and notice patterns that may lead to solutions. Remember that nobody reacts perfectly all the time. If you respond poorly in a situation, don't be too hard on yourself. Instead, take time to reflect on what happened and think about how you can handle it better next time. We are all learning, and it's okay to make mistakes as long as we keep trying to grow. Learning from mistakes is an important part of managing emotions well.

Case Study: Cultural Differences in Parenting and Dating

George, who is from a Latin American country, married a white American woman. The couple spent a lot of time together, enjoyed dancing, and always found ways to work as a team. However, when they had a daughter and she became a teenager, cultural differences in parenting began to create conflict.

245

When their daughter started dating, George struggled to accept it. In his culture, female purity is highly protected, and he saw it as his role in the family to enforce strict rules. He placed multiple obstacles to prevent his daughter from going out with her boyfriend. His anxiety over her dating sometimes led to heated arguments, and he would demand that she follow restrictive rules, such as always enabling her location on her phone. If she didn't comply, he would yell and forbid her from seeing her boyfriend.

His wife, however, had a different approach. She believed their daughter should be allowed to date if she followed clear rules. These rules included being home on time and letting them know where she would be, who she would be with, and when she would return.

These conflicting views caused tension in their marriage and led to frequent arguments. George felt responsible for protecting his daughter, while his wife wanted to give her more independence within safe boundaries. The family struggled to find a balance, as both parents wanted what was best for their daughter but had very different expectations shaped by their cultures.

Lessons Learned: Bicultural Families Take Negotiation

Parenting styles are often influenced by cultural values, especially regarding gender roles, dating, and independence. Different cultural expectations within a family can cause conflict, especially when raising children. Finding a balance between protection and independence is important in bicultural families. Open communication and a willingness to compromise can help families navigate cultural differences in parenting.

Decision-Making Chart: Dating Rules and Safety

The decision-making charts help parents balance cultural values, safety concerns, and independence when setting rules for their children. Some parents also use a "danger level framework" to compare risks to everyday situations, helping them make more realistic decisions (Arnett, 2016). By combining these strategies, parents can make more informed choices.

This three-step process allows them to consider multiple logical strategies rather than making decisions based only on emotion.

Step 1: Understanding Age Milestones in the U.S.

In the U.S., teen dating and independence happen gradually:

Age	Common Dating Rules in the U.S. (Steinberg, 2017)
12-13	Group outings, school dances, chaperoned events
14-15	Supervised one-on-one dates, parent drop-off/pick-up required
16-17	More independence, driving to dates, later curfews
18+	Full independence, responsible for their own dating choices

Parents may adjust these rules based on their culture and family values while keeping safety in mind.

Step 2: Evaluating Risks Using a Decision-Making Chart

This chart helps parents decide on rules by comparing risks to familiar situations:

Situation	Risk Level	Comparison Example	Possible Compromise
Going to a restaurant with boyfriend (age 16)	Low	Like trying a new restaurant—some unknowns, but not risky	Require check-ins, set a curfew
Boyfriend picking her up in his car	Moderate	Like riding a bike in traffic—depends on driver and road conditions	Meet the boyfriend, set driving rules

Going to a house party with no parents home	High	Like walking alone at night— depends on safety of the place and people	Only allow if parents are home, discuss safety plan
Going on a weekend trip with boyfriend at 17	Very High	Like hiking in an unknown forest—many unpredictable risks	Only allow if trusted adults are present
Skipping curfew and ignoring calls	Severe	Like swimming with sharks—no control over safety	Set clear rules, establish trust-building consequences

Step 3: Using the "Danger Level Framework"

These three questions can be used to help parents and teens agree on fair and clear rules:

1. Is this like walking through a new neighborhood or swimming with sharks?

   If it is like walking through a new neighborhood, it's a reasonable risk. Set boundaries but allow growth. If it is like swimming with sharks, it's too risky. Firm rules and safety measures are needed.

2. Is this a real safety issue or just discomfort with change?

   A safety issue involves clear evidence of harm, lack of supervision, or risky behavior. Discomfort may come from a parent's personal beliefs or cultural values, such as feeling uneasy about dating.

3. What compromise allows safety and independence?

   For example, instead of banning dating, parents can require regular check-ins and set a curfew, which is a time when the teen must be home.

This decision-making process helps parents balance rules and independence while making sure their concerns are realistic and not based on fear (Arnett, 2016). It also encourages open conversations, so teens and parents work together instead of arguing about restrictions.

Discussion Questions

1. How could the couple compromise and express their feelings more positively?
2. What conflict resolution strategies could they use to navigate their differences?
3. How can they agree to disagree while deciding whose parenting approach to follow?

Use Logical Strategies to Make Good Decisions

Sometimes, emotions can make it hard to think clearly and make good decisions. That is why it is important to use different tools to stay logical and make smart choices. One useful tool is a pros and cons list. Pros are all the good things about a choice, and cons are all the negative things. By actively writing down pros and cons and looking at both sides, we can see the full picture before making a decision (Steinberg, 2017).

Other helpful tools are decision-making charts and logical questioning frameworks, which guide us step by step when making difficult choices. These tools help us organize our thoughts and encourage thoughtful reflection before making a decision. For example, parents can use a decision-making chart to set dating rules for their children. Using these tools helps us stay calm, think logically, and make better choices.

Key Takeaways

- Emotional regulation is important because it helps you stay calm, solve problems, and communicate better.
- It also helps you build strong relationships with others and allows you to handle difficult situations in a healthy way.
- Decision making charts and frameworks can guide us in making smart, logical choices.

- By practicing deep breathing, pausing before reacting, using positive self-talk, and applying decision-making frameworks, you can improve your emotional control and adjust more successfully to life in America.

Reflection Questions

1. What is one technique you can use to stay calm in a stressful situation? How does this technique help you make better decisions?
2. Why is it important to pause and think before reacting in an argument? How can practicing deep breathing or positive self-talk help you manage strong emotions?

References

Arnett, J. J. (2016). *The importance of balancing protection and independence in adolescent development. Journal of Adolescent Research*, 31(1), 10-20.

Gross, J. J. (2023). *Emotional Regulation and Social Adjustment.* Retrieved from www.psychologytoday.com

Hofstede, G. (2023). *Cultural Differences in Emotional Regulation.* Retrieved from www.hofstede-insights.com

Steinberg, L. (2017). *Age of opportunity: Lessons from the new science of adolescence.* Mariner Books.

Chapter 31: How to Have Constructive Conversations

Having strategies for conversations is important because it helps people communicate clearly, avoid misunderstandings, and handle disagreements in a respectful way. A constructive conversation is a discussion where people listen to each other, share ideas, and try to understand different opinions. This is important because it allows people to solve problems effectively, learn from one another, and strengthen relationships (Johnson, 2021).

When people use conversation strategies, they can express their thoughts without arguing or hurting others' feelings. For example, using active listening, asking questions, and staying calm during a discussion can help both sides feel heard and respected. These skills are useful in school, at work, and in daily life because they help build trust, improve teamwork, and create positive interactions. Without these strategies, conversations can easily lead to frustration and conflict. By practicing constructive conversations, people can become better communicators and build healthier relationships with others.

Steps for Having a Constructive Conversation

Having specific steps for a constructive conversation is important because it helps people communicate in a clear and respectful way. Without a plan, conversations can quickly become confusing, emotional, or even turn into arguments. Following steps allows people to express their thoughts, listen to others, and solve problems more effectively. These skills are useful in school, at work, and in everyday life. When we practice constructive conversations, we build stronger relationships and learn how to communicate in a respectful and meaningful way.

1. Listen Carefully

Listening is the first and most important step in any good conversation (Taylor, 2020). Paying attention to what the other person is saying shows that you respect their thoughts and feelings. It is also important to avoid interrupting and instead show that you are listening by nodding or saying simple words like, "I understand."

Example 1: If your friend is explaining why they are upset, listen fully before responding.

Example 2: During a group project, wait until your classmate finishes speaking before adding your ideas.

2. Stay Calm and Respectful

Conversations work best when both people speak politely. If someone yells or uses rude words, the conversation can quickly become negative. Staying calm and using a polite voice helps keep the discussion respectful (Davis, 2019). If you feel upset, taking deep breaths can help calm you emotions before you respond.

Example 1: If someone disagrees with you, do not get angry. Instead, say, "I see your point, but I have a different opinion."

Example 2: If a classmate criticizes your work, take a deep breath before responding to avoid reacting emotionally.

3. Use "I" Statements

When sharing your feelings, it is better to use "I" statements instead of blaming the other person (Johnson, 2021). Saying "You always..." or "You never..." can make the other person feel attacked and defensive. Instead, focus on your own feelings by saying "I feel..."

Example 1: Instead of saying, "You never listen to me," say, "I feel ignored when I talk and do not get a response."

Example 2: Instead of "You are always late," say, "I feel frustrated when we start late because it affects our time."

4. Ask Questions

Asking questions is a great way to show interest and understand the other person's point of view (Taylor, 2020). Instead of assuming what they mean, politely ask for more details. This helps avoid misunderstandings and encourages better discussions.

Example 1: Ask, "Can you explain why you think that?" or "What do you mean by that?"

Example 2: If a friend has a different opinion on a school rule, ask, "Why do you feel that way about it?"

5. Find Common Ground

Finding something both people agree on makes solving problems easier (Davis, 2019). Even when people disagree, they often have shared goals. Looking for common ground helps keep the conversation positive and productive.

Example 1: "We both want to make our group project better. Let's find a way to do that."

Example 2: "We both agree that this game is fun. Maybe we can find a way to make the rules fair for everyone."

6. Know When to Take a Break

Sometimes, conversations get too emotional or heated. If this happens, taking a short break can help (Johnson, 2021). Stepping away for a little while allows both people to calm down and think before continuing the conversation. It is important to agree on when to return and finish the discussion.

Example 1: "Let's take a break and talk about this in an hour when we are both relaxed."

Example 2: If an argument with a friend gets intense, step away for a while and continue the conversation the next day.

Case Study: Using Appropriate Communication Strategies in a Cross-Cultural Friendship

One day, Emily asks Aisha if she wants to go out for coffee after class. Aisha wants to go but not right now because she has a big test in two weeks. If she does not pass, she will have to repeat the class, and she is not going to be able to finish on time. This is especially important to her since she is an international student with a set time to complete her studies. She needs time to study and focus.

Instead of saying, "No, I can't right now, but maybe after my test," Aisha responds, "Maybe later, Inshallah (God willing)." She says this because she does not want Emily to feel bad. Her real plan is to go after the test, but she does not explain this clearly.

Emily thinks Aisha is still interested in going soon, so she asks again the next day. Aisha, feeling nervous about disappointing her friend, says, "We'll see, maybe another time." She does not say exactly when she will be free.

Emily starts to feel confused and frustrated. She wonders if Aisha is avoiding her or does not really want to go out. Aisha, on the other hand, feels pressured but does not want to seem rude.

Respectful Dialogue Using "I" Statements

Instead of assuming the worst, Emily decides to express her feelings in a calm and respectful way using an "I" statement with a clarifying question:

- Emily (gently and calmly): "Aisha, I just wanted to check in with you about getting coffee. I feel like maybe my company isn't wanted, or maybe I'm missing something. Am I on to something?"
- Aisha (realizing the misunderstanding): "Oh no, Emily! I really do want to go! I just have a huge test in two weeks, and I must pass it, or I'll have to repeat the class. I didn't mean to make you feel unimportant. I should have told you clearly that I'd love to go after my test."

- Emily (understanding now): "That makes sense! I wish I had known earlier. I totally support you focusing on your studies. Let's plan for after your test!"
- Aisha (smiling): "Yes! That sounds great. Thanks for understanding."

Lesson Learned: Communication Differences Can be Solved

Good communication means expressing feelings calmly and asking questions instead of assuming the worst.

- Emily used an "I" statement to express how she felt without blaming Aisha.
- Aisha realized she needed to be clearer about her schedule so that Emily would not feel ignored.
- Both friends listened to each other and found a solution that worked for them.

By being patient and explaining their thoughts, they strengthened their friendship and avoided unnecessary frustration. This example shows how understanding cultural differences in communication can help people build stronger relationships.

Key Takeaways

- Listen carefully to understand others before you respond (Taylor, 2020).
- Stay calm and respectful, even if you disagree (Davis, 2019).
- Use "I" statements to express your feelings without blaming others (Johnson, 2021).
- Ask questions to show interest and to better understand the other person's point of view (Taylor, 2020).
- Look for common ground. Finding shared values or goals can help you work together to solve problems (Davis, 2019).
- Take a break if the conversation becomes too difficult or emotional (Johnson, 2021).

By following these steps, you can have better conversations, solve problems more effectively, and build stronger relationships.

Reflection Questions

1. Why is listening carefully an important part of having a constructive conversation? How can you show someone that you are truly listening to what they are saying?
2. Using "I" statements instead of blaming others helps keep conversations respectful. How would you rephrase the statement "You never listen to me" using an "I" statement? Why is this approach more effective in a discussion?

References

Davis, R. (2019). *Respectful Conversations in Everyday Life*. Boston: Etiquette Books.

Johnson, M. (2021). *Effective Communication for Everyone*. New York: Communication Press.

Taylor, C. (2020). *The Art of Listening*. Chicago: Social Studies Press.

SECTION 8: CITIZENSHIP AND LONG-TERM INTEGRATION

Chapter 32: Becoming a U.S. Citizen

Naturalization is the process of becoming a U.S. citizen. If you were not born in the U.S., you can apply for citizenship after meeting certain rules. Typically, green card holders can apply for naturalization after living in the U.S. for a certain number of years. Other immigration paths may have different requirements. Once you become a citizen, you have the same rights as someone born in the U.S., like voting in elections and getting a U.S. passport.

Important Note: This information is for learning purposes. Always check the U.S. Citizenship and Immigration Services (USCIS) website (www.uscis.gov) for the most recent updates.

Who Can Apply for U.S. Citizenship?

To apply for U.S. citizenship, you must meet these basic rules (U.S. Citizenship and Immigration Services [USCIS], 2024):

- You must be at least 18 years old.
- You need a Green Card (Permanent Resident Card) for 5 years (or 3 years if you are married to a U.S. citizen).
- You must live in the U.S. for the required time.
- You must have good moral character (no serious crimes).
- You must pass an English and U.S. Civics test.
- You must take the Oath of Allegiance to promise loyalty to the U.S.

Step-by-Step Guide to Becoming a U.S. Citizen

Step 1: Check If You Qualify

Before you apply, make sure you meet all the requirements. If you are not sure, check the USCIS website or talk to a lawyer (USCIS, 2024).

Step 2: Fill Out Form N-400

To apply for U.S. citizenship, you must fill out Form N-400, which is the official application for naturalization. You can submit the application either online or by mail. The total cost for applying is $640, plus an additional $85 fee for fingerprinting and a background check. It is important to keep a copy of all your documents for your records to ensure you have proof of your application and any required information for future reference.

Step 3: Biometrics Appointment

After submitting your application for U.S. citizenship, USCIS will schedule a biometrics appointment. At this appointment, they will take your fingerprints, photo, and signature to conduct a background check. This step is important to confirm your identity and check your records. The biometrics appointment usually takes place 1 to 2 months after applying.

Step 4: Interview with a USCIS Officer

About 6 to 12 months after applying, you will have an interview at a USCIS office. During the interview, an officer will ask you questions about your application, background, and reasons for wanting to become a U.S. citizen. You will also take the citizenship test, which includes questions about U.S. history, government, and English skills. This interview is an important step in the naturalization process.

Step 5: Take the Citizenship Test

The U.S. citizenship test has two parts: the English test and the Civics test.

1. English Test – This test checks your ability to read, write, and speak in English. You must:

   - Read one sentence in English.
   - Write one sentence in English.
   - Answer simple questions in English during your interview.

2. Civics Test – This test covers U.S. history and government.

- You will be asked 10 questions, and you must answer at least 6 correctly to pass.
- Study materials are available on the USCIS website (www.uscis.gov). These free resources can help you prepare! Practicing answering questions will help you feel confident and ready for the test.

Step 6: USCIS Decision

After your interview, USCIS will review your application and then either approve, deny, or request more information. If your application is approved, you will receive a notice for your naturalization ceremony. If USCIS needs more documents from you, they will ask you to send them before your application can continue. It is important to respond quickly to any requests to avoid delays in the process.

Step 7: Take the Oath of Allegiance

The final step in becoming a U.S. citizen is attending the naturalization ceremony and taking the Oath of Allegiance. After taking the oath, you will officially become a U.S. citizen! You will also receive a Certificate of Naturalization, which is an important document that proves your citizenship. Be sure to keep it safe. This marks the end of your naturalization process and the beginning of your new life as a U.S. citizen.

How Long Does It Take?

The process usually takes 12-18 months. However, it may take longer based on where you live and how many people are applying.

Estimated Timeline

Step	Time
File Form N-400	0-1 months

Biometrics Appointment	1-2 months
Interview & Test	6-12 months
USCIS Decision	12-16 months
Oath Ceremony	12-18 months

Start preparing early, especially for the citizenship test!

Do You Need a Lawyer?

You do not need a lawyer to apply for U.S. citizenship, but it can be helpful in certain situations. For example, if you have a complicated case such as problems with your Green Card or criminal history, if you are unsure how to fill out the application, or if you need legal advice about your immigration status, a lawyer can provide guidance. If you decide to get a lawyer, make sure they are licensed and trustworthy. Be cautious of scams that often target immigrants. To find a reliable lawyer, you can check the American Immigration Lawyers Association (AILA, 2024) at www.aila.org.

What Happens After You Become a Citizen?

Once you become a U.S. citizen, you gain several important rights and privileges. You can apply for a U.S. passport, allowing you to travel freely in and out of the country. As a citizen, you also have the right to vote in U.S. elections and participate in the democratic process. You can sponsor family members for Green Cards, helping them join you in the U.S. Additionally, U.S. citizens can apply for government jobs, which are often restricted to citizens. These new opportunities allow you to fully participate in U.S. society and contribute to the country.

Case Study: Overcoming Fear of Legal Paperwork

One common fear among many immigrants I have spoken with is making mistakes on legal paperwork. This fear often comes from feeling like a guest in the country, struggling with reading and writing in English, and going through a long process to become a naturalized citizen. Several factors contribute to this fear, including confusing legal terms, language barriers, differences in education systems, and limited English proficiency.

For many immigrants, this fear extends beyond just immigration paperwork. It can apply to any important legal document or deadline. I have experienced this fear firsthand. I have helped my parents with paperwork for years, yet even now, I feel uneasy when dealing with official documents. When I visit my mom's house, there is often a stack of mail waiting for me or my siblings to sort through. At first, my parents kept every letter because they were afraid of throwing away something important. I had to go through a lot mail, including scams that tried to trick people into thinking they had won money. Now, I help them sort the mail, keeping only what matters and throwing away the rest.

Fortunately, my mom always makes delicious food, so after finishing the paperwork, we sit down, eat, and talk. This makes the process feel less stressful and reminds us that we are not alone in facing these challenges.

Lesson Learned: Actions Help Lessen the Fear

These actions can make dealing with paperwork feel less scary:
- Get help when needed. Legal paperwork is important, so ask someone for help to avoid mistakes or delays.
- Sort mail regularly. Many letters are junk mail. Keeping only the important ones helps avoid stress and clutter.
- Use translation software. Instead of relying only on children to translate, try using Google Translate or other apps to understand letters in your language.
- Push through the fear. The only way to overcome discomfort is to face it. The more you practice reading and filling out forms, the more confident you will become.

- Remember this. You belong here. You are wanted here. You can do this.

No one should feel alone when dealing with paperwork. With support, practice, and patience, this fear can be overcome, allowing you to handle legal documents with more confidence.

Key Takeaways

- Naturalization is the process of becoming a U.S. citizen.
- To qualify for citizenship, you must meet several requirements. These include age, residency, and passing certain tests.
- The process includes filling out Form N-400, a biometrics check, an interview, a test, and an oath.
- The citizenship test covers English skills and U.S. history/government.
- The process takes 12 to 18 months, but some cases take longer.
- A lawyer is optional but can help with difficult cases.
- New citizens can get a passport, vote, and sponsor family members.
- Being prepared and patient will make the process easier.

Reflection Questions

1. What are two important benefits of becoming a U.S. citizen? How do these benefits help new citizens?
2. What are the two parts of the U.S. citizenship test? Why do you think these topics are important for new citizens to learn?

References

American Immigration Lawyers Association (AILA). (2024). *How to Find a Trustworthy Immigration Lawyer*. Retrieved from www.aila.org

U.S. Citizenship and Immigration Services (USCIS). (2024). *Naturalization Process*. Retrieved from www.uscis.gov

Chapter 33: Advice for Newcomers to America

Embrace the Journey of a New Life

Moving to a new country is an adventure filled with both opportunities and challenges. Adjusting to a new language, culture, and way of life takes time, but the United States offers many pathways to success for those who are willing to learn, grow, and adapt (Anderson, 2021). This book was created to help guide you through your journey, offering practical advice and encouragement as you navigate life in the U.S.

Connect with Others

One of the most powerful lessons I learned during my own journey was that you don't have to do it alone. Connecting with other immigrants who understand your struggles and share similar experiences can make a huge difference. When I volunteered with a nonprofit organization that supported immigrants, I found a community that embraced me. For a long time, I forgot what it felt like to connect with people who had resettlement experiences, accents, and the challenge of learning a new culture in common with me. Volunteering with these other women nourished my soul and empowered me. It reminded me that I belong to me, and I can choose to connect with people that help me be my best self.

Prior to this, I spent years learning to function like an American, adopting all the American ways, learning how to fit in, and fully integrate. I did not want to be seen differently. However, I did not realize that full acculturation came with a price. The price was dimming my own shine, my own unique bicultural identity as a Bosnian American. Seeing others go through the same process, trying to lessen their accents (accents that typically never fully go away if you resettle after the age of 7 or 8, no matter how hard you study English), and trying to just fit in, reminded me to embrace my own roots, culture, language, accent, and traditions. It gave me the confidence to speak without fear, make friends, embrace both of my cultures, and most importantly, realize how much this book was needed.

Surrounding yourself with people who understand your journey will help you feel less isolated and more empowered to embrace life in the U.S. Your English does not have to be perfect. You may feel like you will never quite fit in completely, but guess what? You are not meant to because you walk between two cultures, just like the rest of us. You already belong to you just the way you are, your authentic self. We can also serve as valuable cultural navigators because our insights into both cultures are beneficial since we see that there is more than one way to live. We can function in both cultures, yet still may feel like we are often walking somewhere in between, and that is perfectly okay. The key is to keep learning, keep practicing, and keep connecting.

Learn English: It is a Step-by-Step Process

One of the most valuable tools for success in the U.S. is improving your English skills. Being able to communicate confidently will help you at work, in school, and in daily interactions (Johnson, 2021). Here are simple ways to practice English every day:

- Start with daily conversations. Even if you only say a few words, speaking English every day builds confidence. Small efforts add up over time (Miller, 2017).
- Use free learning tools. Apps like Duolingo, BBC Learning English, and YouTube tutorials are great for practicing at home. Many public libraries and nonprofit organizations also offer free ESL classes where you can practice speaking English (Taylor, 2021).
- Watch and listen. Watching TV shows, movies, and listening to music helps improve vocabulary and pronunciation. Use subtitles to match words with sounds, which helps connect what you hear with what you read and strengthens both listening and reading skills (Johnson, 2021).
- Find a language buddy. Practice with a friend or join a local conversation group. Do not be afraid to make mistakes. They are part of learning (Williams, 2022).

- Write down new words. Keep a notebook and write down three new words and their meanings each day. Over time, your vocabulary will grow naturally.
- Be patient and kind to yourself. Learning a language takes time. Don't be discouraged if you make mistakes, as they help you know what to do better next time. Every mistake is a step toward progress (Taylor, 2021).

Navigate Emotional Process

When people move to the United States, they usually go through different emotional stages as they get used to their new home. This is an emotional journey that many immigrants experience when adapting to a new culture and can vary in length. These steps can take different amounts of time and can be easy for some or hard for others, but many people experience these four common stages (Oberg 1960):

- Honeymoon Phase: At first, everything is exciting and new. Immigrants often enjoy discovering their new surroundings and all the different things about their new country.
- Frustration Phase: After a while, the excitement can start to fade. Things like speaking a new language, understanding different ways of doing things, and missing home can make people feel upset and worried (Oberg 1960).
- Adjustment Phase: Slowly, immigrants learn how to deal with these challenges. They start to understand the culture better and find ways to make everyday life easier.
- Acceptance Phase: Finally, immigrants begin to feel more comfortable. They mix parts of their own culture with the new culture, and life starts to feel more stable and happier.

These stages help us understand how people adjust to living in a new country. Some things can make the stages easier, such as learning the culture, joining community activities, and taking part in the everyday life in the new country.

It's important to remember that everyone's experience is unique. Things like having supportive friends, staying strong during hard times, and the environment you live in can all affect how these stages feel. One helpful way to stay positive is to focus on the good things each day. Try to think of three things that went well today and reflect on these before going to bed. This simple habit can help you build a more hopeful and positive mindset.

Learn American Culture and Social Norms

The U.S. is a diverse country with many customs and traditions. Knowing basic social norms will help you feel more comfortable and build strong relationships (Anderson, 2021).

- Small talk is common. Americans often chat about weather, sports, or weekend plans. Asking simple questions like, "How was your weekend?" can start friendly conversations (Taylor, 2021).
- Punctuality matters. Being on time is seen as respectful in American culture. Arriving late to work, school, or events can be considered rude (Brown, 2019).
- Respect personal space. Americans generally stand an arm's length apart when talking. Avoid touching people unless they offer a handshake or hug (Hall, 2020).
- Diversity is everywhere. The U.S. is home to many cultures, religions, and languages. Being open-minded and respectful helps you make friends easily (Anderson, 2021).
- Every challenge is a chance to grow. Ask questions, be curious, and embrace cultural differences. Making friends from different backgrounds will give you a new perspective (Williams, 2022).

Take Advantage of Opportunities

The U.S. is full of opportunities, but you need to seek them out. Education, networking, and career growth are key to building a better future (Johnson, 2021). In today's world, we not only need to work harder due to not knowing the system well, but we also cannot ever stop learning. Education is crucial. Many schools, libraries, and community centers offer free classes for English, job training, and citizenship preparation (Taylor, 2021). Finding a mentor, such as a teacher, coworker, life coach, or community leader who offers guidance, is invaluable. Set regular times to meet and discuss goals.

Motivation doesn't always come easily, especially when starting over in a new place. That's why accountability is important for continuing to move forward, even when motivation is low or nonexistent. Taking steps automatically, even when you do not feel like it (which will be most of the time), is a great way to build confidence and discipline. Every small action adds up to more progress (Davis, 2018). If your degree or experience from home does not directly transfer, there are ways to start fresh. Look for training programs, apprenticeships, or internships (Williams, 2022). Getting involved in your community through volunteering or attending cultural events will help you meet people and feel connected to your new home (Anderson, 2021). Remember, opportunities come when you step forward. Stay positive, work hard, and never stop learning (Miller, 2017).

Welcome to Your New Adventure: You Belong Here

Adjusting to a new country takes time, and some days will feel difficult. Stay open to new experiences, keep learning, and support others on the same journey.

- Remember to be patient with yourself; progress comes with time and effort (Brown, 2019).
- Stay connected to your culture while learning new traditions; keep your own customs as they are part of who you are (Williams, 2022).
- Surround yourself with support by finding people who encourage you and help you grow (Taylor, 2021). You are part of America's story. Your skills, culture, and experiences make the country stronger (Hall, 2020).
- Believe in yourself; every success story starts with a first step. Keep moving forward, and each day brings you closer to your goals (Davis, 2018). The U.S. is a place where hard work and persistence create endless possibilities (Williams, 2022).

Welcome home. You are not alone. You belong here. Your future is bright!

Key Takeaways

- Connecting with other immigrants will help you feel less isolated and more confident in your journey.
- Speaking English daily, even in small ways, will help you improve over time (Miller, 2017).
- Understanding American culture will make social interactions easier (Brown, 2019).
- Taking advantage of education and job training will help you succeed professionally (Taylor, 2021).
- Building a strong community and finding support will help you feel at home in the U.S. (Williams, 2022).
- Stay patient, keep learning, and trust yourself (Davis, 2018). You belong here!

Reflection Questions

1. What steps can you take this week to practice your English in real-life situations?
2. What social norms in the U.S. feel different from your home country? How can learning about them help you adapt?

References

Anderson, J. (2021). *Cultural norms and social etiquette*. New York: Social Studies Press.

Brown, L. (2019). *Personal space in American culture*. New York: Culture Press.

Davis, R. (2018). *Politeness in everyday life*. Boston: Social Etiquette Books.

Hall, E. (2020). *Direct and indirect communication styles*. Chicago: Communication Press.

Johnson, M. (2021). *Speaking volumes: Understanding speech norms*. Los Angeles: Language House.

Miller, J. (2017). *The power of a smile: Social etiquette in America*. San Francisco: Friendly Press.

Oberg, K. (1960). *Cultural Shock: Adjustment to New Cultural Environments*. Practical Anthropology, 7, 177-182.

Taylor, C. (2021). *Small talk: The key to social success*. Miami: Conversational Press.

Williams, K. (2022). *Hospitality norms in America*. Dallas: Cultural Guidebooks.

References

Afterschool Alliance. (2020). *Benefits of afterschool programs.* Retrieved from www.afterschoolalliance.org

Amazon. (2023). *Career choice program.* Retrieved from www.amazon.com

American Academy of Dermatology (AAD). (2019). *Personal hygiene and skin care guidelines.* Retrieved from www.aad.org

American Academy of Pediatrics. (2021). *Reading with children: Benefits and strategies.* Retrieved from www.aap.org

American Bar Association. (2023). *Understanding leases and rental agreements.* Retrieved from https://www.americanbar.org

American Civil Liberties Union. (2022). *Religious freedom in public spaces.* Retrieved from www.aclu.org

American Dental Association (ADA). (2020). *Brushing and oral hygiene recommendations.* Retrieved from www.ada.org

American Economic Association. (2021). *The motherhood penalty: How career breaks affect earnings.* Retrieved from https://www.aeaweb.org

American Hospital Association. (2023). *Tuition reimbursement in healthcare.* Retrieved from www.aha.org

American Immigration Lawyers Association (AILA). (2024). *How to find a trustworthy immigration lawyer.* Retrieved from www.aila.org

American Medical Association. (2023). *Understanding medical roles.* Retrieved from www.ama-assn.org

American Psychological Association. (2023). *Stress and health: Understanding the connection.* Retrieved from www.apa.org

American Psychological Association (APA). (2023). *Understanding panic attacks and how to manage them.* Retrieved from https://www.apa.org

Andersen, P. A., Gannon, J. L., & Tan, J. (2002). *Nonverbal communication: Forms and functions.* Wadsworth.

Anderson, J. (2021). *Cultural norms and social etiquette.* New York: Social Studies Press.

Anderson, K., & Patel, S. (2021). *The American social guidebook: Understanding family and friendships.* Culture Press.

Anderson, K., & Patel, S. (2021). *The American social guidebook: Hosting and attending events*. Culture Press.

Anderson, P., & Patel, R. (2016). *The effects of physical activity on mental health*. Health & Wellness Journal, 12(3), 45-56.

Apple. (2023). *Using spoken content on iPhone and iPad*. Retrieved March 7th, 2025, from https://support.apple.com

Argyle, M., & Dean, J. (1965). Eye-contact, distance, and affiliation. *Sociometry*, 28(3), 289-304.

Arnett, J. J. (2016). *The importance of balancing protection and independence in adolescent development*. *Journal of Adolescent Research*, 31(1), 10-20.

Aronson, E. (2018). *The social animal*. Worth Publishers.

Ballotpedia (2023). "Republican and Democratic Party Platforms Explained." Retrieved from www.ballotpedia.org

Banaji, M. R., & Greenwald, A. G. (2013). *Blindspot: Hidden biases of good people*. New York, NY: Delacorte Press.

Baumeister, R. F., & Leary, M. R. (1995). The need to belong: Desire for interpersonal attachments as a fundamental human motivation. *Psychological Bulletin, 117*(3), 497-529.

Baumrind, D. (1991). *The influence of parenting style on adolescent competence and substance use*. *Journal of Early Adolescence*, 11(1), 56-95.

BBC Learning English. (n.d.). *Learn English online*. Retrieved from http://www.bbc.co.uk/learningenglish

Bertrand, M., & Mullainathan, S. (2004). Are Emily and Greg more employable than Lakisha and Jamal? *American Economic Review*, 94(4), 991-1013.

Big Interview. (n.d.). *Big Interview*. Retrieved April 8, 2025, from https://www.biginterview.com

Brach, T. (2019). *Radical compassion: Learning to love yourself and your world with the practice of RAIN*. HarperCollins.

Brown, L. (2021). *Managing chronic stress: A guide to long-term wellness*. Mindful Living Press.

Brown, L. (2019). *Personal space in American culture*. New York: Culture Press.

Brown, P., & Levinson, S. C. (1987). *Politeness: Some universals in language usage*. Cambridge University Press.

Bruno, M. (2018). *Cultural etiquette in the United States*. American Customs Society.

Burgoon, J. K., Buller, D. B., & Woodall, W. G. (1989). *Nonverbal communication: The unspoken dialogue*. Harper & Row.

Cambridge Dictionary. (2024). *Basic English phrases for communication.* Retrieved from https://dictionary.cambridge.org

Canva. (n.d.). *Resume templates.* Retrieved from https://www.canva.com/resumes/templates

CareerOneStop. (n.d.). *Job search tools.* https://www.careeronestop.org

CareerOneStop. (2024). *Job search help for new immigrants.* Retrieved from www.careeronestop.org

Casey, B. J., Jones, R. M., & Hare, T. A. (2008). *The adolescent brain. Annals of the New York Academy of Sciences,* 1124(1), 111-126.

Centers for Disease Control and Prevention (CDC). (2021). *Bullying prevention and school policies.* Retrieved from https://www.cdc. gov/violenceprevention/youthviolence/bullyingresearch

Centers for Disease Control and Prevention (CDC). (2021). *Handwashing and personal hygiene practices.* Retrieved from www.cdc.gov

Centers for Disease Control and Prevention (CDC). (2023). *Emergency room visits and when to seek care.* Retrieved from www.cdc.gov

ChatGPT. (n.d.). *ChatGPT.* OpenAI. Retrieved April 8, 2025, from https://chat.openai.com

Chick-fil-A. (2023). *Scholarships & education assistance.* Retrieved from www.chick-fil-a.com

Clark, J. (2019). *Party planning basics: Hosting with confidence.* Event Experts Publishing.

Clark, M. (2019). *Emotional resilience: Handling breakups and moving forward.* Mindful Living Press.

College Board. (n.d.). *BigFuture: Plan for college.* https://bigfuture.collegeboard.org

College Board. (n.d.). *How to calculate your GPA on a 4.0 scale.* BigFuture. Retrieved from https://bigfuture.collegeboard.org/plan-for-college/get-started/how-to-calculate-gpa-4.0-scale

College Board. (2023). *SAT and ACT testing policies.* Retrieved from www.collegeboard.org

Common Application. (2023). *How to write a personal statement.* Retrieved from www.commonapp.org

Consumer Financial Protection Bureau. (2022). *Understanding U.S. payment systems*. Retrieved from https://www. consumer finance.gov

Consumer Financial Protection Bureau. (2023). *Building credit and managing debt*. Retrieved from https://www. consumerfinance.gov

Consumer Financial Protection Bureau. (2023). *Understanding credit scores and rental applications*. Retrieved from https://www.consumerfinance.gov

Cornell Law School. (2023). *First Amendment and Fourteenth Amendment of the U.S. Constitution*.

Covey, S. (1989). *The 7 habits of highly effective people*. Simon & Schuster

Crenshaw, K. (1989). *Demarginalizing the intersection of race and sex: A Black feminist critique of antidiscrimination doctrine, feminist theory, and antiracist politics*. University of Chicago Legal Forum, 1989(1), 139-167.

Coursera. (n.d.). *Business English communication skills*. Retrieved from https://www.coursera.org/specializations/business-english

Davis, K. (2021). *Time management for a stress-free life. Productivity & Wellness Magazine*, 8(2), 22-30.

Davis, R. (2018). *Politeness in everyday life*. Boston: Social Etiquette Books.

Davis, R. (2019). *Respectful conversations in everyday life*. Boston: Etiquette Books.

Deseret News. (2021). *Are immigrant families more stable than native-born families?* Retrieved from https://www.deseret.com/ indepth/2021/3/3/22309240/are-immigrant-families-more-stable-married-native-born-institute-family-studies-india-asia

Devine, P. G., & Sharp, L. B. (2009). Automatic and controlled processes in prejudice. *Psychological Science*, 20(10), 1257-1262.

Dovidio, J. F., & Gaertner, S. L. (2010). *Reducing intergroup bias: The common ingroup identity model*. Psychology Press.

Duolingo. (n.d.). *Learn a language for free*. Retrieved from https://www.duolingo.com

Duncan, L. (2018). *Parenting and independence in the U.S.: A guide for newcomers*. Parenting Matters.

Duncan, L. (2018). *RSVP and social norms: Understanding invitations*. Etiquette Matters.

Equal Employment Opportunity Commission. (n.d.). *Employee rights*. Retrieved from https://www.eeoc.gov/employees

ESL Library. (2024). *Speaking English in daily life*. Retrieved from https://esllibrary.com

Fannie Mae. (2023). *Guide to home buying and mortgages*. https://www.fanniemae.com

Fastweb. (n.d.). *Find scholarships for college*. https://www.fastweb.com

Federal Deposit Insurance Corporation. (2024). *Your insured deposits*. https://www.fdic.gov/deposit-insurance/your-insured-deposits-brochure-english

Federal Communications Commission. (2022). *Setting up internet and phone services*. Retrieved from https://www.fcc.gov

Federal Reserve. (2023). *The U.S. economic system and capitalism*. Retrieved from https://www.federalreserve.gov

Federal Student Aid. (2023). *Types of financial aid*. Retrieved from www.studentaid.gov

Federal Trade Commission. (2022). *Consumer rights and shopping rules*. Retrieved from https://www.ftc.gov

Federal Trade Commission. (2023). *Avoiding rental and housing scams*. Retrieved from https://www.ftc.gov

Fiske, A. P. (1992). *The four elementary forms of sociality: Framework for a unified theory of social relations*. Psychological Review, 99(4), 689-723.

Gee, G. C., & Ponce, N. (2010). *Associations between perceived racial discrimination and health outcomes among Asian Americans*. American Journal of Public Health, 100(8), 1456-1464.

Givens, D. B. (2005). *Love signals: A practical field guide to the body language of courtship*. St. Martin's Press.

Glassdoor. (n.d.). *Job search and company reviews*. https://www.glassdoor.com

Glassdoor. (n.d.). *Companies & reviews*. Retrieved from https://www.glassdoor.com/Reviews/index.htm

Gonzalez, J. (2020). *Meditation and relaxation techniques for stress relief*. Calming Minds Press.

Gonzalez, R. (2019). *Cultural values and food habits*. Global Cultural Studies Journal, 12(3), 45-62.

Google. (n.d.). *Google Maps*. Retrieved April 8, 2025, from https://www.google.com/maps

Google. (2024). *Google Translate Help Center*. Retrieved March 7, 2025 from https://support.google.com/translate

Google. (2024). *Use Select to Speak on Android*. Retrieved March 7, 2025 from https://support.google.com

GPO – U.S. Government Publishing Office (2022). "The U.S. Government: How It Works." Retrieved from www.govinfo.gov

Greater Good Science Center. (2023). *The three parts of an effective apology*. Retrieved from https://greater good.berkeley.edu

Gross, J. J. (2023). *Emotional regulation and social adjustment*. Retrieved from www.psychologytoday.com

Gudykunst, W. B., & Ting-Toomey, S. (1988). *Culture and interpersonal communication*. SAGE Publications.

Hall, E. T. (1966). *The Hidden Dimension: Personal Space in Different Cultures*. New York: Doubleday.

Hall, J. A. (2018). How many hours does it take to make a friend? *Journal of Social and Personal Relationships*, 36(4), 1278–1296. https://doi.org/10.1177/0265407518761225

Hall, E. (2020). *Direct and indirect communication styles*. Chicago: Communication Press.

Harris, T. (2016). *Mental wellness strategies for a healthy life*. Brain Health Research, 4(1), 14-28.

Harvard Business Review. (n.d.). *What to ask the interviewer*. Retrieved from https://hbr.org/2016/05/what-to-ask-the-interviewer

Harvard Family Research Project. (2020). *Parent involvement in schools: Key findings*. Retrieved from www.hfrp.org

Harvard Family Research Project. (2021). *Parental support and extracurricular activities*. Retrieved from www.hfrp.org

Harvard Graduate School of Education. (2022). *Helping newcomer students adjust to U.S. schools*. Retrieved from https://www. gse.harvard.edu

Harvard University Pluralism Project. (2023). *Respect for diversity in the U.S.* Retrieved from https://pluralism.org/

Henley, N. M. (1977). *Body politics: Power, sex, and nonverbal communication*. Prentice Hall.

HelloTalk. (n.d.). *Learn languages by chatting with native speakers*. Retrieved from https://www.hellotalk.com

Hofstede, G. (2001). *Culture's consequences: Comparing values, behaviors, institutions, and organizations across nations*. Sage Publications.

Hofstede, G. (2023). *Cultural differences in emotional regulation.* Retrieved from www.hofstede-insights.com

Hofstede, G. (2023). *Workplace culture and behavior in the U.S.* Retrieved from https://www.hofstede-insights.com

Institute for Family Studies. (2019). *Immigrant families are more stable.* Retrieved from https://ifstudies.org/blog/immigrant-families-are-more-stable

Institute for Healthcare Advancement. (2020, October 22). Language, culture, and medical tragedy: The case of Willie Ramirez. *Health Affairs.* https://www.healthaffairs.org/content/forefront/langu age-culture-and-medical-tragedy-case-willie-ramirez

Insurance Information Institute. (2023). *What is renter's insurance and why do you need it?* Retrieved from https://www.iii.org

Internal Revenue Service (IRS). (2023). *Guide to U.S. taxes.* Retrieved from https://www.irs.gov

Indeed. (n.d.). *Job search.* https://www.indeed.com

Indeed. (n.d.). *How to prepare for an interview in 11 steps.* Retrieved from https://www.indeed.com/careeradvice/inter viewing/how-to-prepare-for-an-interview

Indeed. (n.d.). *How to write a thank-you email after an interview.* Retrieved from https://www.indeed.com/careeradvice/inter viewing/how-to-write-a-thank-you-email

Internal Revenue Service. (n.d.). *Form W-4, Employee's withholding certificate.* Retrieved from https://www.irs.gov/ forms-pubs/about-form-w-4

Job-Hunt. (n.d.). *Guide to successful interviews.* Retrieved from https://www.job-hunt.org/guide-to-successful-interviews/

Johnson, M. (2021). Building healthy relationships: Communication and respect in dating. *Relationship Studies Journal,* 14(2), 19-35.

Johnson, M. (2021). *Effective Communication for Everyone.* New York: Communication Press.

Johnson, M. (2021). *Speaking volumes: Understanding speech norms.* Los Angeles: Language House.

Jones, A., & Lee, S. (2019). Adjusting to a new culture: The stress of immigration and adaptation. *Social Psychology Review,* 15(2), 67-80.

Jones, B. (2020). *Food culture in the United States.* National Food and Society Research.

Kabat-Zinn, J. (2017). *Mindfulness for beginners: How to handle stress with RAIN*. Harvard Mindfulness Center.

Kagitcibasi, C. (2007). *Family, self, and human development across cultures*. Erlbaum Associates.

Kendon, A. (1967). Some functions of gaze-direction in social interaction. *Acta Psychologica*, 26, 22-63.

Khan Academy. (n.d.). *Soft skills*. Retrieved from https://www.khan academy.org/career-content/soft-skills

Knapp, M. L., & Hall, J. A. (2013). *Nonverbal Communication in Human Interaction*. Boston, MA: Wadsworth, Cengage Learning.

Kreuz, R. J., & Roberts, R. M. (2017). *Becoming fluent: How cognitive science can help adults learn a foreign language*. MIT Press.

LanguageLine Solutions. (2024). *Language interpretation services*. Retrieved from https://www.languageline.com

LaFrance, M., & Mayo, C. (1976). *The social and personality functions of nonverbal behavior*. Springer Science & Business Media.

Lev-Ari, S., & Keysar, B. (2010). Why don't we believe non-native speakers? *Journal of Experimental Social Psychology*, 46(6), 1093-1096.

Library of Congress (2022). "Political Parties in the United States." Retrieved from www.loc.gov

LinkedIn. (n.d.). *Find jobs*. https://www.linkedin.com/jobs

LinkedIn. (n.d.). *Career advice*. Retrieved from https://www.linkedin.com/advice

LinkedIn. (n.d.). *LinkedIn Jobs*. Retrieved from https://www.linkedin.com/jobs

Lopez, R. (2019). *Self-esteem and confidence building for young adults. Psychology Today*, 11(4), 33-41.

Lyft. (n.d.). *Lyft – Your ride, anytime*. Retrieved April 8th, 2025 from, https://www.lyft.com

Manhattan Mental Health Counseling. (n.d.). *5-4-3-2-1 grounding technique for anxiety*. Retrieved from https://manhattan mentalhealthcounseling.com

Martinez, C. (2018). *The importance of social connections for mental health. Community Wellness Studies*, 7(1), 12-19.

Martin, D., & Lee, C. (2022). *Hosting guests in American society. Cultural Practices Journal*, 18(2), 78-95.

Matsumoto, D. (2000). *Culture and psychology: People around the world*. Wadsworth.

Mayo Clinic. (2022). *Financial wellness and budgeting for rent.* Retrieved from https://www.mayoclinic.org

Mayo Clinic. (2022). *Healthy Hygiene Habits for Children and Teens.* Retrieved from www.mayoclinic.org

Mayo Clinic. (2022). *Stress management: How to reduce and relieve stress.* Retrieved from www.mayoclinic.org

McDonald's. (2023). *Archways to opportunity program.* Retrieved from www.mcdonalds.com

Microsoft. (2024). *Microsoft Translator Help Center.* Retrieved March 7th, 2025, from https://translator.microsoft.com

Microsoft. (2024). *Use Read Aloud on Windows.* Retrieved March 7th, 2025, from https://support.microsoft.com

Miller, J. (2017). *The power of a smile: Social etiquette in America.* San Francisco: Friendly Press.

MindTools. (n.d.). *Building confidence for interviews.* Retrieved from https://www.mindtools.com/pages/article/newCD V_96.htm

Nakamura, H. (2021). *Finding meaning and purpose through spiritual wellness. Japan Wellness Research*, 10(3), 55-70.

National Afterschool Association. (2021). *The impact of after-school programs on student development.* Retrieved from www.naa.org

National Archives. (2023). *Civil Rights Act of 1964.* Retrieved from www.archives.gov

National Association of Career Colleges. (2021). *Vocational and trade school education.* Retrieved from www.nacc.ca

National Association of Realtors. (2022). *Steps to renting and buying a home.* Retrieved from https://www.nar.realtor

National Center for Education Statistics (NCES). (2021). *Extracurricular participation and student achievement.* Retrieved from www.nces.ed.gov

National Center for Education Statistics (NCES). (2022). *Fast facts: Public school system structure.* Retrieved from https://nces. ed.gov

National Center for Education Statistics (NCES). (2022). *Post-high school outcomes: Trends and statistics.* Retrieved from www.nces.ed.gov

National Education Association (NEA). (2018). *Creating a clean and respectful.* Washington, D.C.: National Education Association.

National Education Association (NEA). (2021). *Parent and community engagement in schools.* Retrieved from www.nea.org

National Education Association (NEA). (2023). *School discipline and behavior expectations.* Retrieved from https://www.nea.org

National Institute of Mental Health. (2023). *Coping with stress and mental health.* Retrieved from www.nimh.nih.gov

National Institute of Mental Health. (2022). *Social and emotional well-being in relationships.* Retrieved from www.nimh.nih.gov

National Restaurant Association. (2022). *Tipping Guide for Restaurants.*

National Science Foundation. (2023). *Innovation and scientific progress in the U.S.* Retrieved from www.resturant.org

National Women's Law Center. (2023). *Wage transparency and closing the gender pay gap.* Retrieved from https://www.nwlc.org

Oberg, K. (1960). *Cultural Shock: Adjustment to New Cultural Environments.* Practical Anthropology, 7, 177-182.

OpenAI. (2024). *User Guide.* Retrieved March 7th, 2025, from https://openai.com/chatgpt

OpenAI. (2024). *ChatGPT response to a prompt about AI tools* (Mar 14 version) [Large language model]. https://chat.openai.com/

Oxford English Dictionary. (2023). *Definition of parenting and discipline norms.* Oxford University Press.

Oxford English Dictionary. (2023). *Definition of RSVP and social norms.* Oxford University Press.

Park, Y. (2018). *The impact of hobbies and recreation on stress reduction. Lifestyle & Health Journal,* 9(1), 29-38.

Patel, S., & Anderson, K. (2021). *The American Social Guidebook: Understanding family and friendships.* Culture Press.

Pew Research Center. (2022). *Gender gaps in employment and income.* Retrieved from https://www.pewresearch.org

Pew Research Center. (2022). *Religious diversity in America.* Retrieved from www.pewresearch.org

Pew Research Center (2021). "The Political Typology: Political Divisions in the U.S." Retrieved from www.pewresearch.org

Purdue Online Writing Lab. (n.d.). *Cover letters.* Purdue University. Retrieved from https://owl.purdue.edu/owl/

job_search_writing/job_search_letters/cover_letters/index.html

Putnam, R. (2000). *Bowling alone: The collapse and revival of American community*.

ResearchGate. (2021). *Immigrant region of origin, divorce, and remarriage in the United States*. Retrieved from https://www. researchgate.net/publication/356022756_Immigrant_region_of_origin_divorce_and_remarriage_in_the_United_States

Reynolds, D. (2020). *Boosting self-esteem through positive thinking. Self-Help Today*, 14(2), 19-35.

Scholarships.com. (n.d.). *College scholarships, grants & financial aid*. https://www.scholarships.com

Skiba, R. J., Michael, R. S., Nardo, A. C., & Peterson, R. L. (2011). *The color of discipline: Sources of racial and gender disproportionality in school punishment. The Urban Review*, 34(4), 317-342.

Smith, P. (2020). *Eye contact and trust in American society*. Washington, D.C.: Human Behavior Studies.

Society for Human Resource Management. (n.d.). *Workplace etiquette*. Retrieved from https://www.shrm.org/resources andtools/tools-and-samples/hr-qa/pages/workplace-etiquette.aspx

Starbucks. (2023). *College achievement plan*. Retrieved from www.starbucks.com

Steinberg, L. (2014). *Age of opportunity: Lessons from the new science of adolescence*. Houghton Mifflin Harcourt.

Steinberg, L. (2017). *Age of opportunity: Lessons from the new science of adolescence*. Mariner Books.

Sue, D. W., Capodilupo, C. M., Torino, G. C., Bucceri, J. M., Holder, A. M. B., Nadal, K. L., & Esquilin, M. (2007). *Racial microaggressions in everyday life. American Psychologist*, 62(4), 271-286.

Takaki, R. (1993). *A different mirror: A history of multicultural America*. Back Bay Books.

Taylor, R. (2021). *Friendship in a Fast-Paced World*. Social Trends Press.

Tatum, B. D. (2017). *Why are all the black kids sitting together in the cafeteria? And other conversations about race*. Basic Books.

Taylor, C. (2020). *The art of listening*. Chicago: Social Studies Press.

Taylor, C. (2021). *Small talk: The key to social success*. Miami: Conversational Press.

Taylor, J. B. (2008). *My stroke of insight: A brain scientist's personal journey*. Viking Press.

The Balance Careers. (n.d.). *What to wear to a job interview*. Retrieved from https://www.thebalancemoney.com/dress-for-a-jobinter view-2058432

The Muse. (n.d.). *How to handle job rejection & ask for feedback*. Retrieved from https://www.themuse.com/advice/how-to-ask-for-feedback-after-job-rejection

The White House (2023). "American Government 101." Retrieved from www.whitehouse.gov

Thompson, M. (2017). *Developing problem-solving skills for success. Educational Strategies Journal*, 6(2), 41-57.

Tidd, K. L., & Lockard, J. S. (1978). *Effects of smiling and body position on interpersonal attraction*. Journal of Personality and Social Psychology, 36(12), 1531-1539.

Ting-Toomey, S. (1999). *Communicating across cultures*. The Guilford Press.

Tocqueville, A. (1835). *Democracy in America*. University of Chicago Press.

Toastmasters International. (n.d.). *Public speaking tips*. Retrieved from https://www.toastmasters.org/resources/publicspeak ing-tips

Triandis, H. C. (1995). *Individualism and Collectivism: Cultural Communication Differences*. Boulder, CO: Westview Press.

Uber. (n.d.). *Ride with Uber*. Retrieved from https://www.uber.com

UPS. (2023). *Earn & Learn tuition assistance program*. Retrieved from www.ups.com

U.S. Bureau of Labor Statistics. (2022). *Employment and training outlook for young workers*. Retrieved from www.bls.gov

U.S. Bureau of Labor Statistics. (2023). *The gender wage gap*. Retrieved from https://www.bls.gov

U.S. Census Bureau. (2023). *Diversity in America report*.

U.S. Citizenship and Immigration Services. (n.d.). *Form I-9, Employment eligibility verification*. Retrieved from https://www.uscis.gov/i-9

U.S. Citizenship and Immigration Services (USCIS). (2024). *Naturalization process*. Retrieved from www.uscis.gov

U.S. Department of Agriculture. (2023). *Grocery store shopping and food budgeting tips.* Retrieved from https://www.usda.gov

U.S. Department of Commerce. (2023). *Weights and measures in the United States.* Retrieved from https://www.commerce.gov

U.S. Department of Defense. (2022). *Military career pathways.* Retrieved from www.defense.gov

U.S. Department of Education. (2021). *Education in the United States.* Retrieved from www.ed.gov

U.S. Department of Education. (2022). *Gender equality in schools.* Retrieved from https://www.ed.gov

U.S. Department of Education. (2022). *How Extracurricular Activities Support Student Success.* Retrieved from www.ed.gov

U.S. Department of Education. (2022). *How families can support student success.* Retrieved from www.ed.gov

U.S. Department of Education. (2022). *Higher education and career pathways.* Retrieved from www.ed.gov

U.S. Department of Education. (2024). *Language learning for newcomers.* Retrieved from https://www.ed.gov

United States Department of Health and Human Services. (2023). *Your right to an interpreter at the doctor's office.* Retrieved from www.hhs.gov

U.S. Department of Housing and Urban Development. (2023). *Guide to homeownership and mortgage loans.* Retrieved from https://www.hud.gov

U.S. Department of Labor. (2024). *Employment and Training Administration.* Retrieved from www.dol.gov

U.S. Department of Labor. (n.d.). *Employment & Training Administration (ETA).* Retrieved from https://www.dol.gov/agencies/eta

U.S. Department of Labor. (2023). *Minimum wage laws.* Retrieved from https://www.dol.gov

U.S. Department of Labor. (2022). *Understanding equal pay laws.* https://www.dol.gov

U.S. Department of Labor. (2023). *Understanding work ethic in America.* Retrieved from https://www.dol.gov

U.S. Department of the Treasury. (2023). *Sales tax in the United States.* Retrieved from https://home.treasury.gov

U.S. Department of the Treasury. (2023). *Understanding U.S. currency and banking rules*. Retrieved from https://home.treasury.gov

U.S. Equal Employment Opportunity Commission. (2022). *Workplace gender equality*. Retrieved from https://www.eeoc.gov

USAJobs. (n.d.). *Federal government jobs*. https://www.usajobs.gov

Verywell Mind. (2023). *Feeling anxious? Try the 5-4-3-2-1 grounding technique*. Retrieved from https://www.verywellmind.com

Walmart. (2023). *Live Better U tuition program*. Retrieved from www.walmart.com

Weber, M. (1905). *The Protestant ethic and the spirit of capitalism*. Routledge Classics.

Weil, A. (2018). *Breathing: The master key to self-healing*. Weil Integrative Medicine Library.

White, L., & Kim, B. (2020). *Healthy living: Nutrition, exercise, and self-care*. Wellness & Health Publishing.

Williams, D. R., & Mohammed, S. A. (2013). *Racism and health I: Pathways and scientific evidence*. American Behavioral Scientist, 57(8), 1152-1173.

Williams, K. (2022). *Hospitality norms in America*. Dallas: Cultural Guidebooks.

Williams, R. (2017). *Social life and networking in America*. Community Living Press.

Williams, S. (2019). *Nutrition and mental health: The link between diet and emotions*. Mind-Body Health Press.

World Health Organization. (2023). *Mental health: Strengthening our response*. Retrieved from www.who.int

Zety. (n.d.). *Resume builder*. Retrieved from https://zety.com/resume-builder

Note: The above references and resources were either cited in this chapter or recommended for additional support. Some were not directly quoted or paraphrased but are included for transparency and to provide easy access for further learning.

List of Tables

Table 1: Category | Collectivist Cultures (Group-Focused) | Individualistic Cultures (Self-Focused)

Table 2: Meal Culture | United States | Other Cultures

Table 3: Parenting Style | United States (Individualistic) | Collectivist Cultures (Asia, Africa, Latin America)

Table 4: Account Type | Interest Rate | Money Saved | Interest Earned (1 Year)

Table 5: Expense | Amount ($) | Category

Table 6: Maria's Expense | Budget | Category

Table 7: Task | Person Responsible | Day to Complete

Table 8: Place | When to Visit | Examples

Table 9: Topic | Conservatism | Liberalism

Table 10: Age| Common Dating Milestone U.S.

Table 11: Topic | Concern| Actual Risk| Comparison| Compromise

Table 12: Concern | Actual Risk | Day to Complete

Table 13: Step | Time

GLOSSARY

Glossary of Terms

- **Acculturation** – The process of adapting to a new culture while maintaining aspects of one's original culture.
- **Adaptation** – Adjusting to new cultural norms, behaviors, and expectations in a new environment.
- **Adjustment Phase** - A stage of cultural adaptation where individuals begin to understand and cope with the new culture, feeling more settled.
- **Adjustment Period** – The time it takes for an immigrant to adapt to a new culture, language, and lifestyle in the U.S.
- **American Customs** - The behaviors, practices, and norms that are typical in the social and cultural context of the United States.
- **American Dream** – The belief that anyone, regardless of background, can achieve success through hard work and determination.
- **American Time vs. Bosnian Time** – A humorous way of describing punctuality differences: "American time" means arriving exactly on time, while "Bosnian time" allows for a more flexible, later arrival.
- **Apartment Lease** – A legal agreement between a landlord and a tenant that outlines the terms of renting a home.
- **Behavioral Expectations** - Anticipated and socially accepted behaviors in various settings within a culture.
- **Bias** – A preference or prejudice that affects judgment and decision-making.
- **Body Language** – Non-verbal communication through gestures, facial expressions, and posture.
- **Budgeting** - The process of creating a plan to spend your money, outlining projected income against expected expenses.
- **Capitalism** – An economic system where businesses are privately owned, and competition determines prices and wages.
- **Citizenship** – The legal status of being a recognized member of a country with rights and responsibilities.
- **Civic Engagement** – Participation in activities that contribute to the community, such as voting or volunteering.

- **Communication Styles** - The ways in which people express themselves in various cultural and social contexts, including verbal and nonverbal communication.
- **Community Support** - Assistance and resources provided by local organizations and fellow community members to support individuals in a society.
- **Cultural Adaptation** – The process of adjusting to a new culture while maintaining aspects of one's own traditions.
- **Cultural Awareness** – Understanding and respecting different customs, beliefs, and traditions.
- **Cultural Differences** – The ways in which traditions, behaviors, and social norms vary between different cultures.
- **Cultural Expectations** – Beliefs and behaviors that are considered normal within a specific culture.
- **Culture Shock** – The feeling of confusion or anxiety when experiencing a new culture for the first time.
- **Daily Routines** - Regular, day-to-day activities that structure an individual's day.
- **Danger Level Framework** – A method to evaluate risks by comparing situations to everyday dangers, such as "walking in a new neighborhood" (low risk) or "swimming with sharks" (high risk).
- **Decision-Making Chart** – A tool that helps evaluate choices by weighing risks, benefits, and possible compromises.
- **Deportation** – The forced removal of a person from a country due to legal or immigration violations.
- **Dining Etiquette** - The set of rules governing socially acceptable behavior while eating, which can vary greatly by culture.
- **Discrimination** – Treating people unfairly based on characteristics such as race, gender, or nationality.
- **Diversity** – The inclusion of people from different backgrounds, cultures, and perspectives.
- **Education System** - The formal institutional framework that provides education and learning environments in a country.
- **Employment Practices** - Standards and norms governing the professional environment and relationships between employers and employees.
- **English as a Second Language (ESL)** – Programs designed to help non-native speakers learn English.

- **Eviction** – The legal removal of a tenant from a rental property due to nonpayment or lease violations.
- **Financial Literacy** - The ability to understand and effectively use various financial skills, including personal financial management, budgeting, and investing.
- **Friendships, Building** - The process of creating and maintaining relationships based on mutual affection, trust, and respect.
- **Gender Roles** – Societal expectations about how men and women should behave, often influenced by cultural traditions.
- **Green Card** – A document that allows a non-U.S. citizen to live and work permanently in the United States.
- **Greeting Customs** - Conventional ways of acknowledging another person's presence in a social setting, varying widely across cultures
- **Harassment** – Unwanted behavior that creates a hostile environment, often in workplaces or public spaces.
- **Health Care, Accessing** - The methods and means by which individuals obtain health services and medical care.
- **Host Family** – A family that provides temporary housing and support for newcomers, helping them adjust to a new country.
- **Household Responsibilities** – Tasks related to maintaining a home, such as cooking, cleaning, and childcare, which can be divided differently across cultures.
- **Housing, Securing** - The process of obtaining a stable place to live, including renting or purchasing property.
- **Immigrant** – A person who moves to another country to live permanently.
- **Immigration Processes** - The legal and administrative procedures involved in moving and settling in a country that is not one's native country.
- **Implicit Bias** – Unconscious attitudes or stereotypes that affect understanding and behavior.
- **Intercultural Communication** - The verbal and nonverbal interaction between people from different cultural backgrounds.
- **Interview** – A formal meeting where a job applicant answers questions from an employer.

- **Job Interviews** - A formal meeting in which a potential employer evaluates a potential employee for prospective employment.
- **Job Market, Navigating** - The process of exploring and engaging with the employment sector to find job opportunities.
- **Language Learning** - The process of acquiring the ability to communicate in a language other than one's native language.
- **Logical Decision-Making** – Using reason and facts instead of emotions to make choices.
- **Mentorship** –Guidance and support from experienced individuals to help someone grow personally or professionally.
- **Microaggression** – Small, often unintentional comments or actions that discriminate against marginalized groups.
- **Money Management** - The process of budgeting, saving, investing, spending or otherwise overseeing the capital usage of an individual or group.
- **Multicultural Parenting** – Raising children in a household with parents from different cultural backgrounds, which may lead to differences in expectations and discipline.
- **Naturalization** – The legal process through which a non-citizen becomes a U.S. citizen.
- **Networking** – Building professional and social connections to gain job opportunities and support.
- **Nonprofit Organization** – A group that provides services for social good without making a profit.
- **Nonverbal Communication** - The transmission of messages or signals through a non-verbal platform such as body language, gestures, facial expressions, and tone of voice.
- **Personal Space** – The physical distance people prefer to keep between themselves and others during interactions.
- **Prejudice** – An unfair opinion about a group of people based on stereotypes.
- **Professional Boundaries** –The limits between work and personal life, such as setting time for family without checking emails.
- **Public Benefits** – Government programs that provide financial or healthcare assistance to eligible individuals.

- **Public Transportation, Using** - The act of utilizing publicly available transportation services such as buses, trains, subways, and other forms of transit.
- **Refugee** – A person who flees their home country due to war, persecution, or natural disaster.
- **Religious Diversity** - The existence of numerous religious beliefs, practices, and denominations within a given community or region.
- **Respect in Communication** –The way people show politeness in conversation, which varies across cultures (e.g., direct eye contact in the U.S. vs. avoiding it in other cultures).
- **Resume** – A document that outlines a person's work experience, skills, and education for job applications.
- **School Life** - The experiences and activities associated with attending school, including learning, participation in extracurricular activities, and social interaction.
- **Social Expectations** - Anticipated and prescribed behaviors that are culturally normative and expected in social interactions.
- **Social Norms** – The expected behaviors and customs in a society.
- **Social Security Number (SSN)** – A unique number given to people in the U.S. for work and identification.
- **Sports Culture** - The customs, practices, and organizations surrounding the participation in and fandom of sports.
- **Stereotype** – A generalized belief about a group of people that may not be accurate.
- **Tipping** – The practice of giving extra money to service workers, such as waiters and taxi drivers, for good service.
- **Traditional vs. Modern Roles** – The contrast between older cultural expectations (e.g., women staying home) and newer ones (e.g., women working and sharing household duties).
- **Translation Services** - Services that convert communication from one language into another, facilitating understanding between different language speakers.
- **U.S. Citizenship, Obtaining** - The legal process by which a non-U.S. citizen can become a United States citizen.
- **U.S. Civics Test** – A test on American history and government that immigrants must pass to become citizens.

- **Volunteering, Benefits of** - The advantages gained from engaging in volunteer work, such as skill development, social connections, and personal satisfaction.
- **Visa** – A document that allows a person to enter, stay, or work in the U.S. for a specific period.
- **Work Culture** - The environment and prevailing attitudes, behaviors, and practices within a workplace.
- **Workplace Etiquette** - The customary code of polite behavior in society or among members of a particular profession or group in the workplace.
- **Work-Life Balance** – Managing time between work and personal life to avoid burnout.
- **Work Ethic** – The belief that hard work, punctuality, and dedication lead to success.

APPENDICES

Appendix A: Newcomer Skills Checklist

After reading this book, you should feel more confident in the following areas:

Section 1: Understanding American Culture and Values
[ ] Learn key American values such as freedom, independence, and responsibility.
[ ] Understand how culture affects daily life, communication, and traditions.
[ ] Recognize the importance of diversity and respect for different backgrounds.
[ ] Adjust to common social norms, such as greetings, politeness, and small talk.

Section 2: Rights, Laws, and Responsibilities
[ ] Understand basic U.S. laws that affect daily life (e.g., tenant rights).
[ ] Learn about workplace rights, such as fair wages and protection from discrimination.
[ ] Recognize the importance of civic duties, including obeying laws and paying taxes.
[ ] Know what to do if you experience discrimination or unfair treatment.

Section 3: Financial Literacy and Work Culture
[ ] Understand how to manage money, including budgeting and saving.
[ ] Learn how to open a bank account, use credit cards, and avoid debt.
[ ] Know how to rent or buy a home, understand leases, and avoid scams.
[ ] Prepare for job interviews, including common questions and professional behavior.
[ ] Understand workplace expectations, communication, and rights.

Section 4: School Life and Youth Culture
[ ] Understand how the American school system works (grades, schedules, and expectations).

[ ] Learn how parents can support their children in school, including parent-teacher meetings.
[ ] Know the benefits of extracurricular activities, clubs, and sports.
[ ] Explore career planning options for students and adults.

Section 5: Daily Life and Practical Skills
[ ] Develop daily routines for managing time and responsibilities.
[ ] Learn how to shop for groceries, household items, and essentials.
[ ] Know how to schedule and visit a doctor, including health insurance basics.
[ ] Understand mental and physical wellness and where to seek help when needed.

Section 6: Social Expectations and Cultural Adaptation
[ ] Learn about religious diversity and respect for different beliefs.
[ ] Understand personal space and social norms in the U.S.
[ ] Recognize common social mistakes and how to avoid them.

Section 7: Advanced Social Understanding
[ ] Gain basic knowledge of the U.S. political system and how it affects daily life.
[ ] Understand stereotypes and how they impact people.
[ ] Recognize emotions in conversations and respond appropriately.
[ ] Learn how to have constructive and respectful discussions, even with different opinions.

Section 8: Citizenship and Long-Term Integration
[ ] Understand the steps to becoming a U.S. citizen, including naturalization.
[ ] Learn about civic responsibilities, such as voting and community involvement.
[ ] Find ways to build long-term success, including education and career growth.

By checking off these skills, you can see how much you have learned and what areas you may still want to practice. You are on your way to becoming more confident and independent in your new home!

Appendix B: Resources for Newcomers to the United States

This section provides a list of useful resources for immigrants, refugees, and newcomers to the U.S. These websites, organizations, and tools can help with learning English, finding jobs, understanding legal rights, and adjusting to American culture.

1. Learning English
Improving English skills is key to adjusting to life in the U.S. Here are some free and affordable resources:

- BBC Learning English – English lessons and pronunciation help: www.bbc.co.uk/learningenglish
- ChatGPT – Practice writing, grammar, speaking, and learning topics in English and other languages: https://chat.openai.com
- Duolingo – Free English language learning app: www.duolingo.com
- ESL Library – Online resources for English learners: www.esllibrary.com
- Khan Academy English Language Arts – Free courses: www.khanacademy.org
- Local Public Libraries – Many libraries offer free ESL classes and conversation groups. Check your city's library website.
- USA Learns – Free website for learning English and life skills: www.usalearns.org

2. Finding Jobs and Career Development
Looking for a job? These websites provide job listings and career advice:

- CareerOneStop – U.S. Department of Labor job search and training: www.careeronestop.org
- Glassdoor – Job reviews and salary information: www.glassdoor.com
- Indeed – Job search engine: www.indeed.com

- LinkedIn Jobs – Professional networking and job listings: www.linkedin.com/jobs
- Upwardly Global – Career support for skilled immigrants: www.upwardlyglobal.org
- USAJobs – Federal government job listings: www.usajobs.gov

3. Understanding Immigration, Citizenship, and Legal Rights
These organizations provide information on immigration processes, visas, and legal rights:

- U.S. Citizenship and Immigration Services (USCIS) – Official immigration and citizenship information: www.uscis.gov *(Listed first as the official resource)*
- American Immigration Council – Legal services and advocacy for immigrants: americanimmigrationcouncil.org
- American Immigration Lawyers Association (AILA) – Find trustworthy immigration lawyers: www.aila.org
- Families For Freedom – Support for noncitizens facing deportation: http://www.hias.org
- Immigrant Legal Resource Center (ILRC) – Legal help for immigrants: www.ilrc.org
- National Immigration Law Center (NILC) – Immigration policy and legal advocacy: www.nilc.org
- Refugee Council USA – Resources and advocacy for refugees: http://rcusa.org
- USA.gov Citizenship Guide – Overview of U.S. citizenship process: https://www.usa.gov/immigration-and-citizenship
- US Committee For Refugees And Immigrants – Services for refugees and immigrants: http://www.refugees.org

4. Finding a safe and affordable place to live is important for newcomers:

- Apartments.com – Search for rental apartments: www.apartments.com
- Federal Trade Commission (FTC) Rental Scams Guide – Avoid rental fraud: www.ftc.gov
- U.S. Department of Housing and Urban Development (HUD) – Affordable housing and renter's rights: www.hud.gov

- Zillow – Online housing search for renting and buying: www.zillow.com

5. Financial Literacy and Banking in the U.S.
Understanding how to manage money and build credit is essential:

- AnnualCreditReport.com – Get a free credit report once a year: www.annualcreditreport.com
- Bank of America Financial Education – Budgeting and saving resources: https://www.bettermoneyhabits.com
- Consumer Financial Protection Bureau (CFPB) – Information on credit, banking, and loans: www.consumerfinance.gov
- Federal Deposit Insurance Corporation (FDIC) Money Smart Program – Free financial education: www.fdic.gov/moneysmart

6. Healthcare and Medical Assistance
Finding affordable healthcare can be challenging. These resources can help:

- Find a Free Clinic (NAFC) – Search for free medical clinics: https://www.nafcclinics.org
- HealthCare.gov – Find health insurance options: www.healthcare.gov
- Mental Health First Aid USA – Mental health resources and crisis support: www.mentalhealthfirstaid.org
- Planned Parenthood – Low-cost medical services: www.plannedparenthood.org

7. School and Education for Children and Adults
Education is key to success. These resources support students and parents:

- FAFSA (Federal Student Aid) – Apply for college financial aid: www.fafsa.gov
- GED.com – Information on earning a GED (high school equivalency diploma): www.ged.com
- GreatSchools – Find and compare schools in the U.S.: www.greatschools.org
- Khan Academy – Free educational courses for all ages: www.khanacademy.org

- National PTA – Parent resources for school success: www.pta.org

8. Finding Safety, Food, and Shelter
Feeling safe and having the basic resources to live, like food, housing, and support, is essential. The following organizations can help you:

- Catholic Charities USA – Offers housing support, shelters, food pantries, and counseling. Services are available regardless of religion: www.catholiccharitiesusa.org
- Church World Service (CWS) – Provides refugee resettlement, legal immigration services, housing support, food assistance, and disaster relief to help individuals and families rebuild their lives: https://cwsglobal.org
- Feeding America – Operates the largest network of food banks and pantries in the U.S. Use their website to find food near you: https://www.feedingamerica.org
- Lutheran Services in America – Provides affordable housing, senior care, disability services, family support, and community health programs: https://lutheranservices.org
- The National Resource Center on Domestic Violence (NRCDV) – A national resource that supports individuals, organizations, and communities working to end domestic violence: https://www.nrcdv.org If you need immediate help, call the National Domestic Violence Hotline at 1-800-799-7233 (SAFE).
- Poison Control Center (1-800-222-1222) – Assistance with the ingestion of poisonous substances. They will connect you to a local line that is familiar with local chemicals and treatment.
- The Salvation Army – Provides emergency shelter, food, support services, job assistance, rehabilitation, and disaster relief nationwide: https://www.salvationarmyusa.org
- YWCA – Offers legal aid, English classes, advocacy, and safety resources to help immigrants and families build stable, empowered lives: https://www.ywca.org

- 211 (United Way's Help Line) – Call 211 any time (available 24/7 in most areas) to connect with local shelters, food, housing, and support services: https://www.211.org
- 911 (Emergency Services) – Call 911 for immediate assistance for police, fire, and medical emergencies.
- 988 (Suicide and Crisis Prevention Line) – Call or text 988, or Chat http://www.988lifeline.org (available 24/7). This is free and confidential help with many issues and is available to family, friends, or anyone concerned about a loved one. It is also helpful for individuals seeking mental health treatment. Callers are connected to nearby professionals: http://www.988lifeline.org

9. Connecting with Other Immigrants and Community Support
Building a support network is essential for adjusting to life in the U.S.:

- Aspire USA Coaching – Programs and resources to help immigrants integrate and achieve goals: http://www.aspireUSAcoaching.com
- Catholic Charities USA – Assistance for immigrants and refugees: www.catholiccharitiesusa.org
- Global Refuge – Support to refugees including resettlement services: www.globalrefuge.org
- HIAS Refugee Assistance – Refugee resettlement programs: www.hias.org
- International Rescue Committee (IRC) – Refugee and immigrant support services: www.rescue.org
- Meetup – Find groups and events to connect with others: www.meetup.com
- PAIRWN (Pennsylvania Immigrant and Refugee Women's Network) – Support to immigrant and refugee women: www.pairwn.org
- United We Dream – Advocacy and support for young immigrants: http://www.unitedwedream.org
- Welcoming America – Helping immigrants integrate into local communities: www.welcomingamerica.org
- YMCA Newcomer Support Services – Programs for immigrants: www.ymca.net

Adjusting to a new country is a process, but you don't have to do it alone. These resources can help make your transition easier, whether you need help finding a job, learning English, managing finances, or connecting with others who share your experience. If you need further assistance, don't hesitate to reach out to local organizations or support groups in your community. You are not alone on this journey!

Appendix C: Important Documents Checklist for Life in the U.S.

It is important to organize and keep your important documents safe. The checklist below can help you stay organized and prepared.

Personal Identification
[ ] Passport
[ ] Birth Certificate
[ ] U.S. Visa or Green Card
[ ] State ID or Driver's License

Work and Income
[ ] Social Security Card
[ ] Employment Authorization Document (EAD), if needed

Housing and Living
[ ] Lease or Rental Agreement
[ ] Utility Bills (to prove address)

Health and Insurance
[ ] Health Insurance Card
[ ] Immunization Records
[ ] Medical Records

Education
[ ] School Transcripts and Diplomas
[ ] Children's School Records

Financial
[ ] Bank Account Information
[ ] Tax Documents (W-2, 1099, etc.)

Legal
[ ] Legal Documents (marriage certificate, divorce papers, custody orders)

Other Helpful Legal Documents

These documents are not required, but they are good to have. They can make things easier in an emergency or help you plan for the future.

[ ] Financial Power or Attorney – allows someone you trust to handle your money and financial matters if you are unable to do it yourself.

[ ] Health Care Power of Attorney (also called a *Health Care Proxy*) – This allows someone to make medical decisions for you if you become seriously ill or unconscious.

[ ] Will – A legal document that explains how your property, money, and minor children should be cared for after you pass away.

Helpful Tips

- Store original documents in a safe place (like a locked box or folder).
- Make photocopies or digital scans as backups.
- Organize documents into folders (Immigration, ID, Health, Finances, etc.).
- Only carry essential documents with you when needed.

Appendix D: Legal and Privacy Disclaimer

The information provided in this book is for general informational and educational purposes only. It is based on my personal experiences, insights, and research, and is not intended to serve as legal, medical, financial, mental health, or other professional advice. While I strive to present accurate and current information, I make no warranties or representations regarding the completeness, accuracy, or reliability of the content. Any reliance you place on the material is strictly at your own risk.

This book is written solely by me, Selma Toporan, and published by my business, Aspire USA Coaching, LLC. It is not affiliated with, endorsed by, or representative of any other organization, employer, or entity with which I am or have been associated.

Names and identifying details have been changed to protect privacy, and certain events have been adjusted or partially fictionalized for clarity and illustrative purposes. In some cases, composite characters or events have been created. Any resemblance to actual persons, living or deceased, is entirely coincidental.

By reading this book, you acknowledge and agree that neither I, nor Aspire USA Coaching, LLC, shall be held liable or responsible for any loss, damage, or negative outcomes that may result from the use or misuse of the information presented. Readers are strongly encouraged to consult with appropriate licensed professionals before making any personal, financial, educational, or legal decisions based on the content of this book.

Detailed Index

A
About the Author – 308
Acknowledgments – xxiii
Adaptation, Cultural – 205
American Customs – 29, 163
American Values, Understanding – 214
Appendices – 291

B
Budgeting– 65-68
Building Personal Relationships – 29
Building Romantic Relationships – 45-49

C
Casual Dating vs. Serious Dating – 45
Citizenship, Becoming a U.S. Citizen –258-261
Communication Styles – 20
Communication, Everyday – 18, 36, 54, 245, 259
Conflicts, Handling – 54
Community Support – 51
Cultural Adaptation Without Losing Your Identity – 205
Cultural Differences –22-24, 32-33, 205

D
Daily Life and Practical Skills – 158, 244
Daily Routines – 112
Doctor's Office Visits – 273-175

E
Education for Children and Adults – 111-123
Education System – 111
Emotions, Regulating – 238-249
Employment – 90

F
Financial Rules – 61-71
Friendships, Building – 33

Final Thoughts – 218
Finding Jobs – 79

G
Gender Roles at School and Work – 152-155
Greeting – 203

H
Handling Conflicts and Disagreements – 54-58
Health Care, Accessing– 175
Healthcare and Medical Insurance – 178
Hosting Guests and RSVP – 39-42
Housing, Renting, Owning – 73-75

I
Immigration, Understanding Legal Rights – 226, 258-261
Interviews, Job – 83-86

J
Job Market, Navigating – 79
Job Interview Procedure and Skills for Newcomers – 79-90

K
Keeping Clean – 159-162
Kids, Parenting in the U.S. – 30-32

L
Language Learning – 13

M
Managing Stress and Wellness – 184-191
Money Management –61-71

N
Nonverbal Communication– 16-18

O
Onboarding and Starting Your New Job – 79-90

P
Parent Participation – 124-127
Personal Space, Understanding– 29, 100, 202

Political Systems, Understanding – 222-226
Public Transportation, Using – 11

R
References – 270-283
Religion– 196
Religious Practices, Understanding – 196-200
Renting and Buying a Home – 73-75

S
School Life and Structure – 111-116
Shopping Guide for Newcomers – 10, 166-169
Social Expectations – 43, 48, 95
Social Mistakes, Avoiding – 208-212
Social Norms, Everyday Communication – 16, 18, 90
Strategies for Career Advancement - 90

T
Translation Services and Helpful Tools – 1-5

U
Understanding American Values – 214
Understanding Cultural Differences – 22-24
Understanding Money and Financial Rules – 61-71
Understanding Non-Verbal Communication – 16-18
Understanding Political Systems – 222-226
Understanding Work Behavior – 95-98
Understanding Work Ethic – 103-104
U.S. Citizenship, Obtaining – 258-261

V
Volunteering, Benefits of – 129, 136, 138, 143

W
Work Culture – 95-96
Workplace Etiquette – 90

About the Author

Selma Toporan is an educator, researcher, and advocate dedicated to supporting diverse learners and immigrant communities. She holds a Bachelor of Science in Education in Social Sciences from Millersville University, with academic options in Sociology and Anthropology and a minor in African American Studies, and a Master of Arts in Community Psychology and Social Change from Penn State University. She has spent her career helping individuals navigate new environments, overcome challenges, and find opportunities for growth.

With a strong academic foundation, Ms. Toporan has contributed to educational research and was published in *Current Issues in Education* (2010). She has taught social studies at the middle school level and spent nearly a decade as an adjunct faculty member at the Pennsylvania College of Health Sciences, where she taught psychology, sociology, and cultural diversity.

Beyond academia, she has made meaningful contributions to immigrant and refugee advocacy through her leadership at a nonprofit organization. She played a key role in securing major funding to expand community services. As Program Director, she led culturally responsive programs and strengthened outreach to support immigrant families. She also developed coaching initiatives to help individuals build confidence, set personal goals, and access essential resources. Her bilingual and bicultural background allows her to connect deeply with families and students as they adjust to life in the United States.

Her personal journey as an immigrant has profoundly shaped her work. At just 14 years old, she became an interpreter for her family, helping them navigate education, healthcare, and legal systems. She understands firsthand the frustrations, barriers, and triumphs of starting over in a new country. These early experiences inspired her to create this comprehensive guide, giving newcomers the knowledge and confidence they need to thrive in the U.S.

One of the most meaningful parts of her journey has been volunteering, and later working, with an organization that supports immigrants. Through this work, she discovered the power of connection, and how finding a community that understands your struggles can make all the difference. It was in these moments, surrounded by newcomers sharing their dreams and challenges, that she truly realized how much this book was needed. Helping others nurtures her soul and fuels her lifelong passion for education and advocacy.

Ms. Toporan is also a proud mother of two children, a certified life coach, and a trained medical interpreter. She brings specialized expertise in mental health first aid, peer mediation, social and emotional learning, and instructional strategies tailored for English language learners. Throughout her 15-year career, she has worked in a middle school, a high school, a university, and a college, empowering students, families, and communities through education, mentorship, and advocacy.

She believes that every immigrant's journey is unique, but no one has to go through it alone. Through her work, she continues to create resources, foster understanding, and open doors for those building a new life in the USA.

Connect With Me

Thank you for taking the time to read this book. I hope it has provided valuable guidance, encouragement, and practical tools to help you navigate your journey in the United States.

Throughout my experience as an immigrant, educator, and advocate, I have had the privilege of helping others adjust to life in the U.S., whether through mentorship, coaching, or public speaking engagements. My passion is to empower newcomers with the confidence, knowledge, and community support they need to thrive in their new home.

How I Can Help

One-on-One Coaching – Personalized coaching sessions to help with:
- Adjusting to American culture
- Professional development
- Confidence building
- Communication skills

Speaking Engagements – Presentations at schools, community organizations, nonprofits, and corporate events on:
- Immigrant experiences
- Cultural adaptation
- Diversity and inclusion

Workshops & Training – Engaging workshops covering:
- Workplace culture
- Networking for immigrants
- Language confidence
- Building a supportive community

Why This Work Matters to Me

I know firsthand the struggles of moving to a new country, including language barriers, cultural adjustments, and moments of self-doubt. But I also know the power of having the right support system and the tools to build a successful and fulfilling life in a new place.

One of the most impactful moments in my journey was volunteering with a nonprofit that supported immigrants. This experience empowered me and reinforced my belief that no one should have to face these challenges alone. Through that work, I saw firsthand how community, education, and encouragement could transform lives.

That experience, along with my own frustration of figuring it out on my own, inspired me to write this book so that others wouldn't feel lost or alone.

If you believe that you or your organization could benefit from a conversation, coaching session, or event, I would love to connect!

Free Downloadable – Workbook

A free downloadable workbook is available to help you reflect on, practice, and apply what you have learned in each chapter. It includes activities, journaling pages, and goal setting tools. You can download it at www.aspireUSAcoaching.com. If you would like free ESL lessons that match each chapter, please email me at aspireusacoaching@gmail.com with proof of book purchase. These resources are intended to support English language learners in both group and individual settings; however, they may be updated or discontinued in the future.

Get in Touch

Email: selmatoporan503@gmail.com
aspireUSAcoaching@gmail.com
Website: AspireUSAcoaching.com
Social Media: @AspireUSAcoaching

I look forward to connecting, sharing, and supporting you in your journey. Remember, you are not alone, and you belong here.

www.ingramcontent.com/pod-product-compliance
Lightning Source LLC
Chambersburg PA
CBHW021703120626
46545CB00004B/1372